Benjamin Franklin in American Thought and Culture 1790–1990

Benjamin Franklin in American Thought and Culture 1790–1990

NIAN-SHENG HUANG
Assistant Professor of History
Bentley College
Waltham, Massachusetts

American Philosophical Society
Independence Square • Philadelphia
1994

Memoirs of the
AMERICAN PHILOSOPHICAL SOCIETY
Held at Philadelphia
For Promoting Useful Knowledge
Volume 211

Library of Congress Catalog Card Number 94-71935
International Standard Book Number 0-87169-211-2
US ISSN 0065-9738

To

Michael Kammen

Contents

List of Illustrations

Acknowledgments

This book originated from a Ph.D. dissertation that I began to prepare at Cornell University in 1986. I express my deep gratitude to my advisory committee, Professors Michael Kammen, Daniel Baugh, and Nick Salvatore, whose guidance and encouragement were indispensable to the completion of the project. I would particularly like to thank the chair of the committee, Professor Kammen, who first suggested this research topic and whose insight and criticism were pivotal in helping me to organize a great amount of material into a coherent work. Furthermore, his vast knowledge of American history and culture, high standard of scholarship, unfailing devotion to his students, and strong faith in the discipline have always been an inspiration to me. This book is dedicated to him.

I am also pleased to take this opportunity to acknowledge the intellectual debt that I have accumulated from numerous individuals and institutions during the past several years. Many advisers at Tufts University, especially Professors Martin Sherwin and Lynda Shaffer, introduced me to the varied approaches to historical inquiries in the United States. Their counsel and kindness are most appreciated and always treasured. The History Department and the Graduate School of Cornell University fully sponsored my program from 1984 to 1990, for which I am exceedingly grateful. The Library Company of Philadelphia and the Historical Society of Pennsylvania awarded me a Summer Research Fellowship in 1988, which enabled me to explore the admirable Franklin collections at the two institutions. The Philadelphia Center for Early American Studies and its director Professor Richard S. Dunn kindly appointed me Visiting Research Fellow in the summer of 1989 and in the spring of 1992, which provided me further opportunities to utilize materials in the Philadelphia area. The final revisions of this book were made possible by a generous and timely Postdoctoral Research Grant from the American Philosophical Society.

The excellent collections and courteous and efficient service provided by Cornell University Libraries, especially by the John M. Olin Research Library, not only ensured a fruitful study but also made my frequent visits a real pleasure. In addition, I would like to thank the following libraries and institutions that have kindly granted me access to their invaluable collections concerning Franklin and other related sources: the Library of Congress; the National Archives; Widener and Houghton Libraries, Harvard University; Sterling Memorial and Beinecke Libraries, Yale University; the American Philosophical Society; the American Antiquarian Society; Van Pelt Library, University of Pennsylvania; the Free Library of Philadelphia; the Franklin Institute and the Benjamin Franklin National Memorial in Philadelphia; the Rosenbach Museum and Library, Philadelphia; New York Public Library; Boston Public Library; Boston Athenaeum; the Massachusetts Historical Society; Green Library, Stanford University; the Main and Bancroft Libraries, University of California at Berkeley; the Huntington Library, San Marino, California; Honnold and Mudd Libraries, the Claremont Colleges; the Lion Feuchtwanger Memorial Library, University of Southern California; Franklin Public Library, Franklin, Massachusetts; Cayuga County Historian's Office and Seymour Library at Auburn, New York; the Ontario County Historical Society, and Ontario County Record, Archives and Information Services, Canandaigua, New York; and the university libraries at Potsdam College of the State University of New York, at the California State University in San Bernardino, at the California State Polytechnic University in Pomona, and at the California State University in Los Angeles.

My deep appreciation and heartiest thanks go to the following individuals for their cordial advice and patient assistance at various stages of my investigation: Caroline T. Spicer of Olin Library; Barbara Oberg, Claude-Anne Lopez, and Ellen Cohn, editors of *The Papers of Benjamin Franklin*, Yale University; Dr. Whitfield J. Bell, Jr. and Roy Goodman of the American Philosophical Society Library; Dr. Larry Tise of the Franklin National Memorial; James Green of the Library Company of Philadelphia; Peter Parker of the Historical Society of Pennsylvania; Professor Emeritus I. Bernard Cohen of Harvard University; Professor J. A. Leo Lemay of the University of Delaware; Professor David Brion Davis, Professor Harry S. Stout, and Mr. Kenneth P. Minkema of Yale University; Professors Michael Zuckerman and Michael Bodle of the University of Pennsylvania; Professor Robert Dawidoff of the Graduate School of the Claremont Colleges; Professor Barry Schwartz of the University of Georgia; Benedict K. Zobrist of the Harry S. Truman Library; Nancy Sahli of the National Historical Publications and Records Commission; Professor Jeffery A. Smith at the

School of Journalism and Mass Communication, University of Iowa; Dennis W. Creedon, Henrietta S. Gay, and Ralph Archbold of Philadelphia; Carrie Rebora and Hikmet Dogu of the Metropolitan Museum of Art; Thomas Mackie and Linda M. McIlveen of the Ontario County Historical Society; Mary Mahoney and Mary L. Chute of the Franklin Public Library; Robert N. Anderson of the Rensselaer County Historical Society; and Nancy Evans of Book-of-the-Month-Club in New York City.

Since the time when I first arrived in the United States I have been very fortunate to make a number of friends and live with several host families: Robert Smith and Alice Moore of Ithaca, New York, Virginia Newman and her late husband George Newman of Sarasota, Florida, Xiao Ping Shi and Alan Saltzman, Geraldine Seyler of Philadelphia, and Harvey M. and Lee Ann Grossman of Los Angeles. For the past ten years these friends have helped me in more ways than I can recount. Their wonderful hospitalities and genuine friendship are most amiable, and their diverse experiences and knowledge have taught me a great deal about American culture. I am particularly grateful to the Grossmans and their daughter Randy G. Lu, who generously took time to read and comment on part of the manuscript.

I would like to thank the two anonymous reviewers whose comments are most pertinent and whose suggestions are very valuable to my revisions. My editors Carole N. Le Faivre and Susan M. Babbitt at the American Philosophical Society handled the entire review, editing, and publication processes with great care, skill, and professionalism. It has been a wonderful experience and true pleasure to know and work with them.

Careful acknowledgment is made to the following for permission to incorporate my published articles into this book: "The Literary Legacy of William Temple Franklin: Controversy over the Publication of Franklin's Autobiography," *The Pennsylvania Magazine of History and Biography*, vol. 116 (April 1992): 213–24; and "Benjamin Franklin," in Richard Fox and James Kloppenberg, eds., *A Companion to American Thought* (Cambridge, Mass., Blackwell Publishers).

The past literature of Franklin has been so enormous that no student can claim that he is working alone in Franklin studies. Numerous authors, scholars, and Franklinists have paved the way for the present investigation. I sincerely hope that their contributions have been adequately documented in the footnotes and bibliography of this volume. Needless to say, I am solely responsible for any errors and shortcomings that remain.

Introduction

Benjamin Franklin (1706–1790) was one of the most accomplished men of his time as well as one of the most fascinating figures in American history. While many acknowledge the important role that he played in his lifetime, few have studied the scope and degree of his influence in American thought and culture since his death. This book attempts to fill the void: It is not another biography of Franklin, but an exploration of his diverse legacies in American life from 1790 until 1990. This book also focuses on the intricate relations between the functions of images and perceptions in society on the one hand and the changing social and cultural conditions that have constantly affected the alterations of those images and perceptions on the other. The investigation of the vicissitudes of Franklin's reputation, therefore, is a case study that sheds light on American culture.

People have long attempted to assess Franklin; their assessments ranged from extraordinary adulation to ambivalence and overt contempt. The Scottish empiricist David Hume proclaimed that he was the first philosopher from the New World. The French statesman and economist Turgot praised that "he snatched the lightning from heaven, and the scepter from tyrants." Even his caustic colleague John Adams acknowledged that Franklin's reputation in Europe was more universal than that of Leibnitz, Newton, Frederick, or Voltaire, and that his character was more beloved and esteemed than any or all of them. Adams quickly added, of course, that had Franklin been blessed with formal education, he might have become a great philosopher. The nineteenth-century writer Herman Melville believed him to be jack-of-all-trades, but master of none. Early this century English novelist D. H. Lawrence ridiculed Franklin as "the first dummy American."

Dummy or sublime, an enormous amount of Franklin material has appeared for the last two hundred years, as the bibliographies compiled by Paul Leicester Ford (*Franklin Bibliography*, 1889) and Melvin H. Buxbaum (*Benjamin Franklin, 1721–1983*, 1983–88) have indicated. For example, from 1790 to the 1950s, complete or selected works by Franklin were printed at least 145 times, *The Way to Wealth* 114 times, and his *Autobiography* 336 times. During the same period more than 1,400 indexed articles relating to him were published in American periodicals.

It is surprising that few have thoroughly explored these rich sources. It is also a pity that even less attention has been given to scrutinizing the ways Americans memorialized him.* Several specialized studies do exist, such as John Clyde Oswald's *Benjamin Franklin in Oil and Bronze* (1926), I. Bernard Cohen's *Franklin and Newton* (1956), Antonio Pace's *Benjamin Franklin and Italy* (1958), Charles Coleman Sellers's *Benjamin Franklin in Portraiture* (1962), and John Platt's *Franklin's House* (1969). Overall assessments, however, are conspicuously lacking, except for Richard D. Miles's brief review article, "The American Image of Benjamin Franklin," in *American Quarterly* 9 (Summer 1957). A collection of essays entitled *Benjamin Franklin and the American Character* (1955), edited by Charles L. Sanford, is a useful introduction to Franklin historiography, especially for the first half of the twentieth century, although the volume presents a series of controversial points of view rather than a systematic analysis.

A number of doctoral candidates have tried to address the issue of Franklin's legacy; their efforts can be found in such unpublished dissertations as Leo L. Van Scyoc's "Benjamin Franklin's Reputation among the Literati, 1790–1860" (University of Kansas, 1958), and Eugene Saul Bodzin's "American Popular Image of Benjamin Franklin, 1790–1868" (University of Wisconsin, 1969). Yet these studies do not reflect the rapid development of American cultural history in recent years, which stimulates today's student to investigate more fully the rich popular materials concerning Franklin, such as those in almanacs, newspapers, journals, and magazines; in plays and fiction; in public lectures and speeches; and in records of festivals, ceremonies, and celebrations.

Based on information from these sources, I will demonstrate that unlike the images of George Washington and Thomas Jefferson, Franklin's image has, on the whole, symbolized neither the solemnity of the state nor the profoundness of a political principle. On the one hand, his image is a combination of truths and myths pertaining to a legendary individual whose characteristics epitomize the nation's char-

---

*As a foreign-born student, I have used in this book the simple and direct term *Americans*, with no implication of its inclusiveness.

acter. On the other, it suggests a genius whose career was so complex and whose versatility was so extraordinary as to make his own identity kaleidoscopic. Because of his distinctive character and individuality, ironically, he used to be regarded as the most typical American. His philosophy exemplified American attitudes toward life, wealth, and happiness; his fruitful career demonstrated as well as inspired peoples' dreams of success; and he was long portrayed as an illustrious model for young Americans.

His critics, however, attributed Franklin's popularity to his influence on the nation's materialistic tendency. Many correctly pointed out that his model was a crucial link between the Protestant heritage in the seventeenth and eighteenth centuries and the emergence of a modern business mentality in the nineteenth century. But few attempted to examine how his mode was promoted historically. Some observers overlooked the diverse social forces and concrete cultural elements that contributed to his popularity, and failed to reveal the gradual rise of his reputation, especially during the first several decades of the nineteenth century.[1]

Franklin's fame did not remain static; the public perception of him changed significantly before and after the Civil War. This change coincided with one transformation that historian Warren I. Susman has suggested in 1984: namely, that through roughly the same period, America underwent a profound shift from a culture concerned about character to one preoccupied with personality.[2] Accordingly, I have divided the book into three parts. In part one (from Franklin's death

---

1. See Alfred Whitney Griswold, "The American Gospel of Success" (Ph.D. dissertation, Yale University, 1934), 1–55; Louis B. Wright, "Franklin's Legacy to the Gilded Age," *The Virginia Quarterly Review* 22 (1946): 268–79; Irvin G. Wyllie, *The Self-Made in America: The Myth of Rags to Riches* (New Brunswick, N.J., 1954), 5–25; John G. Cawelti, *Apostle of the Self-Made Man* (Chicago, 1965), 9–24; Moses Rischin, ed., *The American Gospel of Success: Individualism and Beyond* (Chicago, 1965), 23–38; Richard Weiss, *The American Myth of Success: From Horatio Alger to Norman Vincent Peale* (New York, 1969), 28–44; and Richard M. Huber, *The American Idea of Success* (New York, 1971), 15–22. Most of these discussions have a gap between Franklin's death in 1790 and the Gilded Age of the 1870s. A more comprehensive review is Peter Baida's *Poor Richard's Legacy: American Business Values from Benjamin Franklin to Michael Milken* (New York, 1990).

2. Susman, *Culture as History: The Transformation of American Society in the Twentieth Century* (New York, 1984), xix–xxx, 271–85. Susman added that "these are assertions, not proofs; these are not established propositions" (ibid., 274). I hope that the present study continues the search for clues to his provocative propositions.

in 1790 to the eve of the Civil War), I analyze how and why Franklin could enjoy a high esteem at a time when most Americans deeply appreciated his character. After that, in part two (from 1870 to 1938), I discuss the question of how and why people became less interested in Franklin's character, but began to concentrate on his intriguing personal qualities. Finally, in part three (from the end of World War II to the bicentennial of his death), I deal with the fragmented stage of Franklin's reputation, one torn between character and personality.

I emphasize that any attempt to investigate Franklin's legacy calls for a serious awareness of the discrepancy between his own life on the one hand and his posthumous reputation on the other, because the former is complicated and the latter has often been associated with a simplified stereotype of him. No matter how popular his own writings are, they should not be construed as an exact depiction of his whole life. Thus, although I do not minimize the importance of Franklin's own works, particularly his *Autobiography* and *The Way to Wealth*, in shaping the public's opinions of him, I do not think that the history of his changing image should be limited to a study of his self-portrait. Above all, I am convinced that Franklin's varied images have evolved over the years not in a vacuum or a writer's study. Rather, they have evolved along with changing social sentiments. My conclusion is that Benjamin Franklin's legacy has a distinctive place in American history, not only because he is an exceedingly complex individual, or because his popular writings have obscured his real characteristics, but also because Americans' changing emphasis, first on character, and then on personality, has continuously shaped and reshaped their perceptions of him.

Part I:
Character
1790–1860

Chapter 1

"Returned to the Bosom of the Divinity"

Keywords in society embrace the kind of social values and cultural conditions that historians cannot afford to ignore.[1] In the present chapter and throughout this study Franklin's legacy is chiefly viewed from two perspectives: his character and his personality.

Today, the words *character* and *personality* are nearly interchangeable, for both refer to a person's marked individual traits. It is important to note, however, that historically the two terms meant different things.[2] Although John Wycliffe used the word *personality* in the English language as early as the 1380s, it was not until the late nineteenth century that the concept of achieved popularity.[3] Since the issue of personality will be treated at length in Part II, for the moment one only needs to keep in mind that it is morally neutral and pertains to those individual qualities that differentiate one person from other people.

Character, on the other hand, has been used in a different vein. From the eighteenth through the first half of the nineteenth centuries, people frequently emphasized the importance of character. For most of them a person's character meant the propriety of his public and private conduct, which was judged primarily by those moral stan-

---

1. Raymond Williams, *Culture and Society, 1780–1959* (New York, 1960) and *Keywords: A Vocabulary of Culture and Society* (New York, 1976).
2. In linguistics the two terms have many meanings, but at least two things differentiate them: 1) Personality carries no moral implications as character does, and 2) character can designate the quality of an entity that is other than a person or a type of persons, such as a quality of a substance or of a nation. According to the *Oxford English Dictionary*, character is "the sum of the moral and mental qualities which distinguish an individual or a race, viewed as a homogeneous whole." Personality is "that quality or assemblage of qualities which makes a person what he is, as distinct from other persons."
3. A. A. Roback, *Personality* (Cambridge, Mass., 1950), 42–43.

dards generally accepted in the society. In some instances, one's character meant his reputation, referring first to his moral strength and second to the fame that he might have achieved through specific accomplishments. A cultural environment that stressed character, therefore, reflected a prevailing concern with moral values as well.

I

Character is a Greek word, χαραχŋ́ρ (from χαράόόειν, χαράττειν, "to engrave"). It referred originally to a mold for stamping coins and the device stamped upon them. From the meanings of engraving, impressing, or being stamped, it was later expanded to suggest a distinctive mark or quality.

Aristotle used that word in his discourse, *The Nicomachean Ethics.* He defined moral virtue as "a state of character," and suggested that different types of human actions could be prompted by different degrees of feelings, passions, and temperament. Take the last case, for example: ranging from insensibility, sensitivity, temperance, self-indulgence, to irascibility, these different categories of human temperament formed a scale of different characteristics. Aristotle concluded that virtue corresponded to the intermediate range of the scale and lay in habitually avoiding extremes. "Virtue, then," he wrote, "is a state of character concerned with choice, lying in a mean . . . between two vices."[4]

For the English-speaking people *character* was a translation from an alien word, which for a long time remained obscure in their vocabulary. Apparently, the word did not become popular in England until the seventeenth century when many publications were devoted exclusively to the portrayal of different human types. In 1608 Joseph Hall published *Characters of Vertues and Vices,* which heralded a significant revitalization of treatises on character modeled after Theophrastus.[5] For the next fifty years dozens of authors, including Sir Thomas Overbury, John Stephens, John Earle, John Cleveland, Sam-

---

4. Sir David Ross, trans., *The Nicomachean Ethics of Aristotle* (London, 1925), 35–36, 39.

5. Some scholars suspect that Theophrastus wrote his moral characters to illustrate his teacher Aristotle's doctrines of ethics. They also point out that Aristotle outlined in his *Nicomachean Ethics* the moral characteristics of several human types, such as the magnificent man, the proud man, the boastful man, and others. Benjamin Boyce, *The Theophrastan Character in England to 1642* (Cambridge, Mass., 1947), 11–16.

uel Butler, and Thomas Fuller, were so involved in such endeavors that expositions on character became a distinctive genre in the English literature of the time. By the end of the century as many as 1,430 treatises on "character" had been published in more than three hundred editions.[6]

Writers often categorized people according to their moral qualities, such as a wise politician, a faithful Christian, or an avaricious merchant. Moreover, character writers persistently used biting language to expose human weaknesses and foibles of all sorts, such as vanity, hypocrisy, egotism, greed, jealousy, and meanness. In particular, some writers on character ridiculed devout Christians and professed moralists by satirizing their fanatic piety, pretentious conduct, and obsession with self-righteousness.[7]

Although English writers were concerned with religious and ethical issues, the word *character* itself did not necessarily carry a positive meaning or suggest moral goodness. On the whole, character treatises in seventeenth-century England represented a vogue that was best known for its sharp criticisms and poignant caricatures. Nevertheless, because of the proliferation of such literature, the word *character* also became increasingly popular in the English vocabulary. When the nation was in continuous turmoil from the 1640s to the 1660s, the word was frequently adopted in various sorts of polemics, such as *A Character of the Enemies of the Church* (1657), *A Character of Richard Baxters Abilities* (1659), *Character or Ear-Mark of Mr.*

---

6. Gwendolen Murphy, comp., *A Bibliography of English Character-Books, 1608–1700* (Oxford, 1925). In France the satirical moralist Jean de La Bruyère published *The Characters, or Manners of the Age, with the Characters of Theophrastus* in 1688. It had gone through eight editions by the time the author died in 1696, and was considered as a very important and influential book after Theophrastus's *Characters*.

7. Two quotations illustrate the essence of what character might suggest during that period. Samuel Butler wrote: A Catholic "says his Prayers often, but never prays, and worships the Cross more than *Christ*. He prefers his Church merely for the Antiquity of it . . . as some do to old Cheese, only for the blue Rottenness of it." A hypocritical nonconformist, he also wrote, "is an Embassador Extraordinary of his own making. . . . He preaches the Gospel in despite of it self, . . . makes what Agreements he pleases; and gives himself such Conditions as are conducible to the Advantage of his own Affairs. . . . He is an implacable Enemy to Superstition and Profaneness . . . but is very tender of meddling with Hypocrisy" (Charles W. Daves, ed., *Samuel Butler (1612–1680): Characters* [Cleveland, 1970], 103, 45, 46, 55). For a selection of character writings see Gwendolen Murphy, ed., *A Cabinet of Characters* (London, 1925).

William Prinne (1659), and *The Character of a Town-Mistress* (1675).

While in these treatises *character* meant no more than personal traits and reputation, the increasing application of the word was sometimes intended to designate other qualities as well. Thus, one could find titles like *An Essay towards a Real Character and a Philosophical Language* (1688) and *The Character of the Beaux* (1696). Starting from the mid-1600s the use of the word was further extended to describing the nature and characteristics of a nation, as in works like *Brief Character of the Low-Countries* (1652), *A Character of England* (1659), *A Character of France* (1659), *The Character of Italy* (1660), and *The Character of Spain* (1660).[8]

II

Despite the diverse applications of the word in England, there seemed to be a generally accepted understanding that above all, character would suggest "the aggregate (not a description of the aggregate) of a person's individual qualities."[9] This basic meaning remained intact when *character* was used in the English colonies in North America.

Underneath the continuity, however, there was an important though subtle difference in usage between the mother country and her colonies. English writers did not necessarily use the word *character* to relate reputable qualities and sometimes their portrayal of a character could be quite sarcastic. In the colonies, by contrast, those who utilized the word were inclined less to satirize than to express approbation of conduct. Such a peculiar adaptation had a great deal to do with the different social and cultural conditions of the colonies in general and with the strong religious influence throughout New England in particular.

In many parts of the southern colonies, attention to character was based on an aristocratic belief that appropriate manners were manifestations of good breeding and gentility. Gentlemen or gentlewomen must carefully cultivate their character, that is, observe rigorous decorums that stressed dignity, piety, honor, temperance, and courtesy. Two manuals about proper etiquette were particularly popular in the

---

8. Benjamin Boyce, *The Polemic Character, 1640–1661* (New York, 1969), 42–46.

9. Ibid., 46. An example is [Thomas Gordon], *The Character of an Independent Whig* (3rd ed.: London, 1720).

South: *The Whole Duty of Man* (1658) and *The Gentleman's Calling* (1660). Both were written by the English author Richard Allstree, whose book *The Ladies Calling* (1673) became one of the most influential guides for genteel women during the seventeenth century. Because of the highly moralistic contents of Allstree's works, Louis B. Wright pointed out that the gentry must have been concerned with "the externals of behavior" as much as with those inner determinants that would shape their image and reputation.[10]

Convinced that they were the chosen people of God, many leading Puritans in New England believed that each person's good behavior was imperative for the maintenance of their holy community. The impieties of a few might easily jeopardize the spiritual welfare of the commonwealth and lead God to withdraw His favor and revoke the national covenant.

Cotton Mather, one of the most prominent Puritan divines in Boston, strongly emphasized the importance of exemplary behavior on the part of the Puritan leaders themselves. He published *Magnalia Christi Americana* in 1702 and took pains to delineate the model lives of such early colonial governors as William Bradford, John Winthrop, Edward Winslow, and William Phips.[11] Because these leading figures had been chosen for their expected high morals, their manifested virtues like piety, wisdom, and justice could inspire imitation, which might in turn enhance the godliness of the community. Thus, when Mather recounted the life of Edward Hopkins, governor of Connecticut colony, he praised him this way: "Most Exemplary was his piety and his Charity; and while he governed others by the Laws of God, he did himself yield a profound Subjection to those Laws. He was exemplarily watchful over his own Behaviour. . . . [which was] the Character of his Life."[12] The historian Sacvan Bercovitch discovered an evident linkage between Mather and the English character writers. Commenting on Mather's approach to biography in the *Magnalia Christi Americana*, Bercovitch wrote:

---

10. Wright, *The First Gentlemen of Virginia* (Charlottesville, Va., 1940), 1–17, 133; Angeline Goreau, ed., *The Whole Duty of a Woman* (Garden City, New York, 1985), 43.

11. For a modern study on colonial rulers see T. H. Breen, *The Character of the Good Ruler: A Study of Puritan Political Ideas in New England, 1630–1730* (New Haven, 1970).

12. Mather, *Magnalia Christi Americana* (John Harvard Library ed.: Cambridge, Mass., 1977), 248. Mather's extensive discussions on virtuous and exemplary conduct can be found throughout book two of this work.

Its aim is to teach by use of examples. . . . This transitional mode—we might call it exemplary biography—suggests Mather's place in the main currents of English biography of his time. His concept of Winthrop as individual and as *exemplum* follows from his belief that the discrete fact and the moral generality could complement one another. . . . In fact, the proper comparison here is with the Character, the abstract rendering of a certain social or psychological type, which (as it became popular in Restoration England) reinforced the didactic trends in biography. Mather's brief Lives share many traits with those leading Character-writers, especially Thomas Fuller and Joseph Hall. So do a number of his longer biographies, some of whose titles seem to designate Virtuous Characters: "*Scholasticus*," "A Man of God," "Early Piety Exemplified," even "Nehemias Americanus."[13]

III

When Benjamin Franklin was alive, apparently, it was character, not personality, that preoccupied most people's attention. It was no accident that in his famous *Autobiography* he did not use the word *personality*, but *character* repeatedly.[14] Yet Franklin was never a simple person and his legacy was far from one-sided. Franklin's complex experiences reflected a deep concern with the image of his character as well as an earnest desire to fulfill his individuality. To understand this complexity, one should see how he dealt with character and personality, particularly by analyzing his attitudes toward life, toward the Protestant ethic, and toward religion.

At a time when society emphasized character, moral values were readily adopted as a set of rules to discipline individual behavior. People's actions could be categorized into two distinct groups based on propriety or impropriety. Moral imperatives were such that people were highly conscious of their moral obligations and were often induced to conform.

Franklin was born and raised in Boston, the tenth and youngest son in a family with seventeen children. His pious parents, Josiah and Abiah Franklin, considered sending him to the ministry, but were unable to provide him with more than two years of elementary education. As an independent-minded lad, Franklin's distaste for the family trade of soap and candle-making and his strong inclination for the sea intrigued his father. He took his son to visit various shops in Boston and allowed him to choose a craft as he pleased. Exceedingly

---

13. Bercovitch, *The Puritan Origins of the American Self* (New Haven, 1975), 4.
14. Most evident is that Franklin used *character* nine times in the outline of his autobiography.

fond of reading, the boy was finally apprenticed to his older brother James, a printer. A few years later, at the age of seventeen, Franklin broke with his brother, ran away from Boston, and arrived in Philadelphia, where he had no relatives or acquaintances.

It was during this critical period of the late 1720s and early 1730s that Franklin formed his fundamental outlook on life and ethics. Having made a series of mistakes, he gradually realized the need to change his behavior and the importance of obtaining a reputable name. At the age of twenty, he felt that he was entering a new stage of life, and determined to "live in all respects like a rational creature." He formulated a plan of conduct and resolved to be industrious, frugal, and truthful.[15]

When Franklin and his friends, most of whom were young merchants and artisans, organized the Junto in 1727, two questions that they often discussed were: "What unhappy effects of intemperance have you lately observed or heard? of imprudence? of passion? or of any other vice or folly?" and "What happy effects of temperance? of prudence? of moderation? or of any other virtue?"[16] After they set up a circulating library in 1731, many of the first books they ordered from England concerned history and morality. Franklin believed that if history is primarily viewed as the acts of amiable characters, it also becomes an important way to learn virtue.[17] *A Catalog of Books belonging to the Library Company of Philadelphia*, compiled in 1741, indicated that on the topic of ethics and moral conduct, the friends of the library were provided with such volumes as La Bruyère's *Works*, including *The Characters*, Shaftesbury's *Characteristics*, Hutcheson's *Inquiry into the Original of Our Ideas of Beauty and Virtue* and *An Essay on the Conduct of the Passions*, Lord Halifax's *Miscellanies*, Pierre Nicole's *Essays on Morality*, and such popular works as *The Ladies Library* (1732), *The Manners of the Age* (1733), and *The Gentleman's Library* (1734). Consequently, when Edwin Wolf 2nd reviewed the early years of the library, he made this point: "Perhaps it was symptomatic of the members' position in society—not yet in the

---

15. Leonard W. Labaree et al., eds., *The Papers of Benjamin Franklin* (New Haven, 1959–), 1: 99–100 (hereafter cited as *Papers*).

16. J. A. Leo Lemay, ed., *Benjamin Franklin: Writings* (Library of America ed.: New York, 1987), 206 (hereafter cited as *Writings*).

17. "Proposals Relating to the Education of Youth in Pensilvania" (*Writings*, 335–36).

higher ranks, but determined to rise—that they chose a comparatively large number of books on behavior and manners."[18]

Franklin also contemplated what he called "The Art of Virtue." He listed a series of virtues that he hoped to achieve, including temperance, silence, order, resolution, sincerity, justice, moderation, and chastity. Then he began to adjust his behavior, using a simple but practical method which he described as follows:

> I made a little Book in which I allotted a Page for each of the Virtues. I rul'd each Page with red ink, so as to have seven Columns, one for each Day of the Week, marking each Column with a Letter for the Day. I cross'd these Columns with thirteen red Lines, marking the Beginning of each Line with the first Letter of one of the Virtues, on which Line and in its proper Column I might mark by a little black Spot every Fault I found upon Examination to have been committed respecting that Virtue upon that Day.[19]

Franklin became particularly sensitive about how people would comment on his behavior. One of his Quaker friends once told him that he appeared to be vain, and that his manner in conversations with others was "overbearing and rather insolent." Franklin decided to cure this folly, and added humility to his list.[20] After much effort, Franklin still could not boast of a complete success with the virtue of humility. But he was at least satisfied that he had achieved "a good deal with regard to the *Appearance* of it."[21]

Indeed, Franklin well understood that the public image of his conduct could be critical to both his business and his community status. He acutely observed the close relationship between (his social rep-

---

18. *A Catalogue of Books Belonging to the Library Company of Philadelphia* (Philadelphia, 1741); Edwin Wolf 2nd, "Franklin and His Friends Choose Their Books," *Pennsylvania Magazine of History and Biography* 80 (January 1956), 31. For related titles in Franklin's own library see Edwin Wolf 2nd, "Franklin's Library," J. A. Leo Lemay, ed., *Reappraising Benjamin Franklin: A Bicentennial Perspective* (Newark, Del., 1993), 319–31, and James N. Green, ed., *Poor Richard's Books* (Philadelphia, 1992).

19. Leonard W. Labaree et al., eds., *The Autobiography of Benjamin Franklin* (New Haven, 1964), 151 (hereafter cited as *Autobiography*).

20. It is interesting to note the supplemental nature of humility on Franklin's list. According to the Bible, humility is principally a Christian virtue, Luke 14: 6, 7; Philippians 2: 8; Colossians 3: 12; and 1 Peter 5: 5. For an extensive discussion of religious influences on Franklin's views of virtue see Norman S. Fiering, "Benjamin Franklin and the Way to Virtue," *American Quarterly* 30 (Summer 1978): 199–223.

21. *Autobiography*, 158–59.

utation) character and (his business reputation) credit. He realized not only the importance of being virtuous in private conduct but also the importance of appearing virtuous in public: "In order to secure my Credit and Character as a Tradesman, I took care not only to be in *Reality* Industrious and frugal, but to avoid all *Appearances* of the Contrary." Therefore, he dressed plainly and avoided being seen at "Places of idle Diversion," like fishing pools and shooting grounds.[22]

On another occasion he patiently recommended the same tactics to a young tradesman. After stating that "Time is Money" and "Credit is Money," he added:

> The most trifling Actions that affect a Man's Credit, are to be regarded. The Sound of your Hammer at Five in the Morning or Nine at Night, heard by a Creditor, makes him easy six Months longer. But if he sees you at a Billiard Table, or hears your Voice at a Tavern, when you should be at Work, he sends for his Money the next Day. . . . It shews, besides, that you are mindful of what you owe; it makes you appear a careful as well as an honest Man; and that still encreases your Credit.[23]

In 1749, after he was retired from active business, he reviewed his career and had the leisure to share with the public several golden rules based on his successful experience. He concluded that it was vital for an enterprising businessman to "strive to maintain a *fair character* in the world: That will be the best means for advancing your credit, gaining you the most flourishing trade, and enlarging your fortune."[24]

IV

Through most of Franklin's life Protestantism was a predominant force in British America. Protestants believed in callings, and "a calling always meant work."[25] Protestants insisted that human activities were not callings unless they could produce some good for society.

---

22. Ibid., 125–26.
23. "Advice to a Young Tradesman," *Papers* 3: 307.
24. "Rules Proper to be Observed in Trade," *Writings*, 346.
25. Edmund S. Morgan, ed., *Puritan Political Ideas, 1558–1794* (Indianapolis, 1965), xvi. My account of the interpretations of *calling* is based upon the following discourses: William Perkins on callings, ibid., 35–59; "A Model of Christian Charity" by John Winthrop, ibid., 75–93; John Cotton on Christian calling, in Perry Miller, ed., *The Puritans* (New York, 1938), 319–27; and

The Protestant work ethic, therefore, involved a set of beliefs and values that were particularly beneficial to producers like tradesmen and artisans. Specifically, that work ethic emphasized such merits as skill, labor, and craft, and such virtues as industry, diligence, frugality, prudence, and economy. A successful printer and publisher, Franklin deeply appreciated these values and became a champion to promote them.

In his adopted city of Philadelphia the founder of the colony, William Penn (1644–1718), was an advocate of Quakerism and morality. Some of his major works dealt with spirituality and moral conduct, and his pamphlets, like *Some Fruits of Solitude* (1693), *More Fruits of Solitude* (1702), and *Fruits of a Father's Love* (1726), enjoyed wide readership in the New World. *Some Fruits of Solitude* contained more than four hundred moral maxims; it went through ten editions within the author's lifetime. Its expanded version, *More Fruits of Solitude*, had more than eight hundred maxims and was reprinted at least twenty times in London and Philadelphia. In his tracts Penn explicitly preached virtues like industry and frugality, which Franklin would continue to emphasize decades later in *Poor Richard's Almanacs*.[26]

Strongly influenced by the Puritans in Boston and the Quakers in Philadelphia, the young Franklin embraced the Protestant work ethic enthusiastically. Like many Protestants in the colonies Franklin valued industry, frugality, prudence, and economy because they were the opposite of such vices as idleness, sloth, unscrupulousness, and waste. Franklin subscribed to the work ethic because he believed this could avoid the worst evil, economic dependence. More importantly, however, his strong support for those particular Protestant virtues not only showed his distaste for moral degradation, but also revealed his mental and philosophical inclinations.

According to Aristotle, the ultimate morality lay in "the habit of mediocrity," which avoided extremes. For instance, industry opposed both idleness and drudgery. By the same token, frugality lay between

---

Cotton Mather, *Bonifacius: An Essay upon the Good* (1710), ed. David Levin (Cambridge, Mass., 1966).

26. Mary Maples Dunn and Richard S. Dunn, eds., *The Papers of William Penn* (Philadelphia, 1981–87), 3: 364–74; 4: 20; 5: 514–16. See also Frederick B. Tolles, chapter 3, "The Way to Wealth," *Meeting House and Counting House: The Quaker Merchants of Colonial Philadelphia, 1682–1763* (Chapel Hill, N. C., 1948). The Quaker influence on Franklin was such that not a few later took him to be a Friend, including Max Weber, *The Protestant Ethic and the Spirit of Capitalism* (Charles Scribner's Sons ed.: New York, 1958), 36.

avarice and extravagance, and prudence was the way to eliminate exorbitant pleasure and pain.[27] Franklin's adherence to those doctrines affected his attitudes toward business and his conduct in other areas. During his many years of public service, he was known for his tolerance and inclination toward compromise. He was certainly not without strong commitments and principles, but he was very careful about the means of achieving his goals. His tactic was to adopt a middle-of-the-road manner; he rarely became too conservative or too radical in public affairs.

Important as it was, the necessity of engaging in a calling did not imply complete individual freedom. "Calling" in the Protestant, especially the Puritan terminology, had a crucial social implication. It meant that people of all callings, whether master or servant, husband or wife, father or son, should regard each of their roles as being indispensable to the good of society. Like a human body whose healthy function relies on the total coordination of every part, true believers, according to many Puritan divines and magistrates, should faithfully fulfill their callings in order to maintain social order and stability, which often appeared in the phrase *commonweal* or *common good.*

While Franklin was doubtless concerned with his personal success and happiness, he was also known for his determination to do good for the public. This idea, he acknowledged, was greatly influenced by Cotton Mather. Late in his life, in 1784, Franklin wrote to Samuel Mather and recalled:

When I was a boy, I met with a book, entitled '*Essays to do Good*,' which I think was written by your father. It had been so little regarded by a former possessor, that several leaves of it were torn out; but the remainder gave me such a turn of thinking, as to have an influence on my conduct through life; for I have always set a greater value on the character of a *doer of good*, than on any other kind of reputation; and if I have been, as you seem to think, a useful citizen, the public owes the advantage of it to that book.[28]

---

27. See also Adam Smith, "The Theory of Moral Sentiments," in Herbert W. Schneider, ed., *Adam Smith's Moral and Political Philosophy* (New York, 1948), 8–34.

28. Albert H. Smyth, ed., *The Writings of Benjamin Franklin* (New York, 1905–07), 9: 208. What Franklin did not remind the addressee, however, was that when he first adopted the pen name of "Silence Dogood" and wrote a series of articles in his brother's newspaper, *New England Courant*, he satirized such Boston institutions as the magistracy, the ministry (including Cotton Mather), and Harvard College.

Franklin's idea of doing good was not exactly the same as that implied in Mather's essay, though both seemed to utilize similar language. Conventional Puritans held that an avowed Christian should be content with his status in order to maintain social order. Most of them did not believe that the doctrine of "calling" included an idea of releasing individual initiatives. Nor did they think that the doctrine was concerned more with the quality of civic life than with the *status quo* of their church.

Franklin, on the other hand, redefined his relationship with the community. He concluded that a useful citizen should actively improve his surroundings. Over the years he initiated or helped to establish a number of new institutions in Philadelphia, such as the Junto, the Library Company, the American Philosophical Society, the Philadelphia Academy (now the University of Pennsylvania), and the Pennsylvania Hospital. His actions suggested that for the good and the future of a community, individual creativity should always be encouraged.

Interestingly enough, the book that inspired Franklin so much was written when Mather became somewhat disillusioned with his circumstances. According to Mather's most recent biographer, Kenneth Silverman, "*Bonifacius* [the formal title of *Essay upon the Good*] is a revealing biographical document. It records a period in Mather's life when he diverted his attention from the supernatural to the civic, from New England to the world, from regeneration to progress."[29] If *Essay upon the Good* contained any such clue, Silverman's assessment also indirectly suggests that Franklin was willing to adapt Mather's ideas, not because he suddenly wished to embrace orthodoxy, but because the "civic" and "progressive" tendencies in that work satisfied him.

V

Franklin lived in an age when religion and morality were hardly separable. Notwithstanding the ancient heritage from Greek philos-

---

29. Silverman, *The Life and Times of Cotton Mather* (New York, 1985), 234. About the fundamental difference between Mather and Franklin, Silverman writes: "Franklin emulated Mather's ingenuity in contriving projects for Doing Good, but he lacked Mather's fervor for private mystical conversion and worldwide evangelical reformation, and he conceived goodness as making life more comfortable. When Mather begins sounding like Franklin in *Bonifacius*, it is not because he has abandoned inward piety but because he has moved away in thought from New England, as Franklin later did in person." Ibid., 235.

ophers or the strong influence from contemporary English literature, the concept of character in colonial America carried an unequivocal religious overtone. From the time of St. Augustine *character* was applied as a theological term to express the spiritual signs that were indelibly impressed upon the soul after baptism, confirmation, and ordination.[30]

Using that expression to illuminate moral perfection, Protestant ministers became one of the most articulate promoters of character. They maintained that ethics was an intrinsic part of piety, and that nothing could substitute for religion in providing a sound basis for morality. Religious virtues should be the paramount criteria for judging a person's character, and no one's behavior could be considered moral unless he was a devout Christian.

Therefore, topics like the character of a ruler, or that of a minister or public servant, and that a woman occasioned some of the most publicized sermons throughout the eighteenth century.[31] Many clergymen insisted that although it was a single word, *character* was

---

30. "The Son of God is the Character of the Father's substance" (*Hebrews* 1: 3). In Catholic theology character is a supernatural and ineffaceable mark obtained after three sacraments. Sacramental character, therefore, is "the mark of Christ as Priest. It is a participation in His priesthood and an assimilation to it." Such a tenet was strongly defended by St. Augustine in 400, and was sanctioned by the Council of Florence and the Council of Trent in the fifteenth and sixteenth centuries. "If anyone says that in three sacraments, namely, baptism, confirmation and order, there is not imprinted on the soul a character, that is a certain spiritual and indelible mark, by reason of which they cannot be repeated, let him be anathema." M[ichael] J[ames] Ryan, "Character," in Charles G. Herbermann et al., eds., *The Catholic Encyclopedia* (New York, 1907–14), 3: 586–88; H. J. Schroader, *Canons and Decrees of the Council of Trent* (St. Louis, Mo., 1941), 52, 330; Rudolf Eucken, "Character," in James Hastings, ed., *Encyclopaedia of Religion and Ethics* (New York, 1960), 3: 364.

31. See, for example, Samuel Willard, *The Character of a Good Ruler* (Boston, 1694); Joseph Sewall, *The Character and Blessedness of the Upright* (Boston, 1717); Samuel Fisk[e], *The Character of the Candidates for Civil Government, Especially for Council* (Boston, 1731); Archibald Cummings, *The Character of a Righteous Ruler* (Philadelphia, 1736); Elnathan Whitman, *The Character and Qualifications of Good Rulers, and the Happiness of Their Administration* (New London, [Conn.], 1745); Ebenezer Gay, *The Character and Work of a Good Ruler, and the Duty of an Obliged People* (Boston, 1745); Nathaniel Walter, *The Character of a True Patriot* (Boston, 1745); James Fordyce, *The Character and Conduct of the Female Sex, and the Advantages to be Driven by Young Men from the Society of Virtuous Women* (3rd ed.: Boston, 1781); Clark Brown, *The Character of Our Lord and Saviour Jesus Christ* (Stonington-Port, Conn., 1799); and Joseph Barker, *The Character and Blessedness of the Upright Man* (Boston, 1800).

comprehensive. Under the overarching emphasis on the fear of God, character represented virtue and suggested a series of spiritual and moral qualities, such as faith, truth, charity, humility, obedience, peace, sincerity, and integrity. Because the Protestant clergymen viewed character primarily from a religious perspective, it is not surprising that their ideal models of character were biblical figures, like King David, King Solomon, and Jesus Christ.

It is true that some classical works on morality were adopted and studied in colonial institutions like Harvard and Yale Colleges. But they were used mainly as texts to learn rhetoric, grammar, and logic, as well as the Latin and Greek languages. Orthodox clergy, particularly some strong-minded Puritan ministers, took great care to ensure that classical moral philosophy should not "pose an alternative system of values." Deeply aware of the pagan origin of moral philosophy, Cotton Mather warned that ethics was a sham. "It presents you with a Mock-Happiness," he said, "It prescribes to you Mock Vertues for the coming of it: And it pretends to give you a Religion without a *CHRIST*, and a Life of *PIETY* without a Living Principle; a Good Life with no other Dead Works filling of it. . . . Study no other Ethics, but what is in the Bible."[32]

Jonathan Edwards, the leading theologian of the colonial period, believed that virtues like honesty, courage, and prudence were based on the principle of self-love. These qualities became necessary only insofar as the preservation of human welfare was concerned. Such morality was not "true virtue." "True happiness," according to Edwards, "consists in the worship and the service of God, in seeking the glory of God, which is the proper exercise of true virtue."[33]

For Mather, Edwards, and like-minded divines, if pagan moral thoughts had to be taught, careful distinctions should be made, so that divinity was always above classical philosophy, theology above ethics, piety above virtue, grace above conscience, spiritual purity above sensuous pleasure and happiness, and the Holy Scriptures above the classics.

Franklin, however, made a distinction between Protestant values and religion. His acceptance of the Protestant work ethic indicated his willingness to conform to certain moral creeds if they proved to be

---

32. See Norman Fiering's illuminating *Moral Philosophy at Seventeenth-Century Harvard* (Chapel Hill, N.C., 1981), 40.
33. Edwards, *Nature of True Virtue* (Ann Arbor, Mich., 1960), 73–75; Joseph Haroutunian, *Piety versus Moralism: The Passing of the New England Theology* (New York, 1932), 72–76.

useful to his advancement. At the same time, his emphasis on morality suggests his evasive attitude toward religion. Franklin maintained that he was not an atheist because he believed in "one Supreme most perfect Being." God was *"the infinite father"* and "the Author and Owner of our System." Above all, "our Saviour was a Teacher of Morality or Virtue" and "what is Christ's Sermon on the Mount but an excellent moral Discourse." Franklin insisted that we "ought first to *believe* in him as an able and faithful Teacher. Thus Faith would be a Means of producing Morality, and Morality of Salvation." "Morality or Virtue is the End," he emphasized, "Faith only a Means to obtain that End: And if the End be obtained, it is no matter by what Means."[34]

Traditionally, the society's guardians of public morals had been the clergy, and the cardinal moral values that they promoted in the eighteenth century were not economic virtues like industry and frugality, but Christian qualities such as faith, hope, and charity. Some people deeply resented those who actively promoted civic morality, and charged them with an attempt at "reducing infidelity to a system."[35]

Not only did Franklin insist on the importance of ethics, but his career suggested that, with defined goals and methods, he ensured his own morality. Moreover, once he adopted moral values as a guideline in his life, he could be much less concerned about faith. Franklin acknowledged that very early in his youth his "indiscrete Disputations about Religion" led good people to consider him "as an Infidel or Atheist."[36] Although he considerably modified his attitudes as he grew older, it is doubtful whether he was ever converted to any sect or dogma. Instead, he wrote his own prayer book and articles of faith, and remained throughout his life no more than a pew-holder in Christ Church at Philadelphia.[37]

---

34. "Articles of Belief and Acts of Religion," *Writings,* 83, 84, 88; "Dialogue between Two Presbyterians," ibid., 256, 257; To Ezra Stiles, 9 March 1790, ibid., 1179.

35. John Witherspoon, *Lectures on Moral Philosophy* (1800: Princeton, 1912), 1. The earliest record of his lectures at Princeton College was made in 1772.

36. *Autobiography,* 71.

37. It is characteristic that when his parents were concerned about his faith, Franklin responded: "I think vital Religion has always suffer'd, when Orthodoxy is more regarded than Virtue. And the Scripture assures me that at the last Day, we shall not be examin'd by what we *thought,* but what we *did;* and our Recommendation will not be that we said, *Lord, Lord,* but that we did GOOD to our Fellow Creatures." To Josiah and Abiah Franklin, 13 April 1738 *(Papers* 2: 204, 204n). On another occasion, Franklin went so far as to assert: "The *SCIENCE OF*

Religious people in the eighteenth century generally believed that character was a gift from God, which man could do little to amend. Franklin's career suggested that he was able to shape his character however he saw fit. His thought echoed a profound new principle that character "does not depend on what Nature makes of man, but what man makes of himself."[38] Thus he praised Cato, the character of virtue, and asserted: "Virtue alone is sufficient to make a Man Great, Glorious, and Happy"; and "There was never yet a truly Great man that was not at the same Time truly Virtuous."[39]

Franklin confessed in his memoirs that he had made a number of mistakes in his youth. They included his misuse of a friend's money, his contact with some "low women," his mistreatment of Miss Read, and more. According to eighteenth-century tradition, those mistakes were doubtless sins. Franklin, the printer, called them "errata," a secular term he derived from his trade. He corrected those mistakes without a clergyman or a church. No God, no rituals, no revelation had to be present. Strongly committed to virtue and moral goodness, he managed his own life, served as his own church, redeemed his own failings, and achieved his own salvation.

Rarely was Franklin obsessed with the status of his spiritual health, or with whether his soul would be saved. Ideologically speaking, his ideas closely resembled those of a deist. He insisted that "the most acceptable Service to God is doing Good to Man," and that "God helps them that help themselves." Yet he was never too serious not to make fun of his pious contemporaries: "Serving God is Doing Good to Man, but Praying is thought an easier Service, and therefore more generally chosen."[40]

Deeply concerned with his material well-being and happiness, Franklin often put men before God and this life before the next. Although he embraced the Protestant work ethic, he was quite proud that he could achieve success mainly through self-endeavor. He seldom used the term *calling*, but spoke of *business* instead. When he talked about his business, he never hesitated to discuss profit, but rarely treated his

---

VIRTUE is of more worth, and of more consequence to his Happiness than all the rest put together" ("A Man of Sense," *Writings*, 248).

38. Immanuel Kant, *Anthropology from a Pragmatic Point of View*, trans. Victor Lyle Dowdell (Carbondale, [Ill.], 1978), 203.

39. *Writings*, 96, 98.

40. *Autobiography*, 45, 162; *Papers* 7: 341; "Poor Richard Improved," 1753 (*Papers* 4: 406).

vocation as a way to glorify the church of God.[41] He insisted that as the benevolent Father, God would be delighted and pleased when He realized that His children were virtuous and happy.[42]

Franklin never entirely abandoned his faith. Especially toward the last years of his life, he became readier to say that "we are spirits." When his brother John died, he wrote to his niece: "It is the will of God and Nature that these mortal bodies be laid aside, when the soul is to enter into real life; 'tis rather an embrio state, a preparation for living; a man is not completely born until he be dead."[43]

Studies of eighteenth-century history have shown that Franklin was not the only one who had non-orthodox experiences in religious life. His younger colleagues George Washington and Thomas Jefferson were not enthusiastic churchgoers. Compared with Thomas Paine's publicized agitations, Franklin's cynical words and private deeds, unholy as they were, appeared all the more modest.[44] What seems remarkable, therefore, is not as much his secular tendencies as his ability to maintain a good reputation in a very religious society. John Adams once observed:

> While he had the singular felicity to enjoy the entire esteem and affection of all the philosophers of every denomination, he was not less regarded by all the sects and denominations of Christians. The Catholics thought him almost a Catholic. The Church of England claimed him as one of them. The Presbyterians thought him half a Presbyterian, and the Friends believed him a wet Quaker. The dissenting clergymen in England and America were among the most distinguished asserters and propagators of his renown. Indeed, all sects considered him, and I believe justly, a friend to unlimited toleration in matters of religion.[45]

As a devout Puritan from New England, Adams's depiction of Franklin's spiritual affiliations was by no means complimentary, but his

---

41. *Autobiography*, 46, 53, 80, 106, 113, 124, 127, 164, 171, 180, 181, 191, 208.

42. "I believe he is pleased and delighted in the Happiness of those he created; and since without Virtue Man can have no Happiness in this World, I firmly believe he delights to see me Virtuous, because he is pleas'd when he sees me Happy" ("Articles of Belief and Acts of Religion," *Writings*, 84).

43. To Elizabeth Hubbart, 22 February 1756, *Papers*, 6: 406–07.

44. See Herbert M. Morais, *Deism in Eighteenth[-]Century America* (New York, 1960) and G[ustav] Adolf Koch, *Republican Religion: The American Revolution and the Cult of Reason* (New York, 1933).

45. Charles Francis Adams, ed., *The Works of John Adams* (Boston, 1856), 1: 661.

observation did testify that Franklin had managed to keep a subtle relationship with numerous religious institutions around him. In addition to what Adams called "unlimited toleration," Franklin also used several other tactics to protect his reputation. In the first place, although he was firm about his commitment, he was not officious about what others ought to believe, seldom attempting to impose his beliefs on others and being mindful about how others might judge his. At the age of nineteen, he wrote *A Dissertation on Liberty and Necessity, Pleasure and Pain,* in which he questioned some of the most fundamental principles of Christianity, such as the omnipotence of Almighty God, His unfailing wisdom and judgment, the doctrine of the elect and non-elect, the immortality of the soul, and the existence of the afterlife. Shortly after the tract was printed, he was cautious enough to destroy most copies, for he realized that his militant language and blatant attacks would certainly offend his religious contemporaries and arouse their dissent against him.

Second, while Franklin did not think that organized religion had much to do with his personal life, he did not deny the usefulness of religion in society at large. "If men are so wicked as we now see them *with religion,*" he once said, their conduct would become unthinkable should the churches disintegrate. For this reason, he urged Thomas Paine not to publish his manuscript, "The Age of Reason." "Burn it," he suggested. Because the author attacked "the Foundation of all Religion," the publication of such an outspoken work would not benefit society.[46]

Franklin did not alienate himself from clerics because he was not interested in their tenets. He understood that it was essential for him to maintain a good relationship with the clergy, who were among the most informed and influential people in society. Among his numerous friends many were religious figures from various denominations, including Jonathan Shipley, John Carroll, George Whitefield, and Ezra Stiles. He also had cordial relationships with a number of English Unitarians and rationalists who had been trained as clergymen, such as Joseph Priestley and Richard Price.

Finally, Franklin's serious concern with his reputation led him to contemplate how to minimize the damage done by his frequent absence from church services. Not least did he begin to think of the behavior of his family members and relatives. In order to avoid further criticisms from opponents, he carefully advised his daughter:

---

46. [To Thomas Paine], 3 July 1786 (Smyth, ed., *Writings of Franklin* 9: 520–22).

You know I have many Enemies . . . and very bitter ones, and you must expect their Enmity will extend in some degree to you, so your slightest Indiscretions will be magnified into crimes, in order the more sensibly to wound and afflict me. It is therefore the more necessary for you to be extreamly circumspect in all your Behaviour that no Advantage may be given to their Malevolence. Go constantly to church whoever preaches.[47]

Franklin's exhortation was revealing, not only because he was the one who seldom went to church and was far from indifferent about who was preaching,[48] but also because what really concerned him was not his daughter's faith but his reputation.

VI

Despite Franklin's serious concern with his public image, he did not entirely erase his deeply rooted individualistic tendencies, which can be seen in his writings.

Franklin was not a character writer, but one of his most remarkable literary legacies lay in the distinctive personalities he depicted. Among his voluminous writings, his lively characterizations of Silence Dogood, the Busy-Body, Poor Richard, Miss Polly Baker, and Father Abraham stand out, and these figures are as vivid and fascinating today as they were originally created. Above all, the portrayal in his autobiography of a homely, hard-working, and highly spirited young Benjamin Franklin has remained one of the most familiar and influential images in American consciousness. Didactic as he was on moral issues, the author's relaxed manner and spontaneous wit in his animated presentations clearly indicate an unfailing attempt to entertain his readers.[49] If the achievement of virtue was one of his favorite topics, humor was his trademark. This striking combination of serious commitment on the one hand and light-hearted detachment on the other reflected Franklin's basic approach to morality from his days as an energetic apprentice printer and an indefatigable newspaper writer in the 1720s.

Although Franklin liked to comment on moral issues from time to time, he remained a practical moralist and seldom attempted to the-

---

47. To Sarah Franklin, 8 November 1764 (*Papers* 11: 449).
48. Once he was persuaded to go to church, "he went five successive weeks but, finding no morality in the minister's sermons, was 'disgusted, and attended his Preaching no more'" (*Papers* 1: 101).
49. "Silence Dogood, No. 1, No. 2" (*Writings*, 5, 7).

orize his beliefs. It is true that he was a son of the Age of Reason, whose achievements in science and public affairs were representative of the Enlightenment.[50] It is also true that he lived at a time when many prominent middle-class thinkers seriously contemplated new meanings of and empirical approaches to morality. As mentioned earlier, around the turn of the eighteenth century a growing number of people were asserting their own standards of morality, such as work, industry, frugality, and honesty.[51] Discussions of ethical issues began to attract wider public attention in England. Lord Shaftesbury's *Characteristics* appeared in 1694, Bernard de Mandeville's *The Fable of the Bees; or, Private Vices, Public Benefits* in 1714, Francis Hutcheson's *Inquiry into the Original of Our Ideas of Beauty and Virtue* in 1725, and Archibald Campbell's *Enquiry into the Original of Moral Virtue . . . Against the Author of the Fable of the Bees* in 1733. Two decades later David Hume's *Enquiry Concerning the Principles of Morals* was published in 1751, and Adam Smith's *Theory of Moral Sentiments* in 1759.

Franklin was familiar with these treatises and he was a personal friend to Hume and Smith.[52] Yet his instinctive interest in morality did not lead him to become a theorist. Franklin's moral education was essentially self-taught and his convictions were based on many sources. The young Franklin was a professed admirer of Richard Steele and Joseph Addison. Their publications, such as *Tatler*, *Guardian*, and most of all, *Spectator*, were full of humorous essays that bitterly satirized the old and privileged classes' idleness, extravagance, and hypocrisy.[53] Franklin admitted that he used to learn the style of prose by imitating Steele's essays. Later in his life he pur-

---

50. See Frank Luther Mott and Chester E. Jorgenson, eds., introduction to *Benjamin Franklin: Representative Selections* (New York, 1936), and Alfred Owen Aldridge, *Benjamin Franklin: Philosopher and Man* (Philadelphia, 1965).

51. Joseph Haroutunian, *Piety versus Moralism*, xvi.

52. "Proposals Relating to the Education of Youth in Pensilvania" (*Writings*, 323).

53. "The general purpose of this paper," Steele declared from start, "is to expose the false arts of life, to pull off the disguise of cunning, vanity, and affection, and to recommend a general simplicity in our dress, our discourse, and our behaviour." "The general Purpose of the whole has been to recommend Truth, Innocence, Honour, and Virtue, as the chief Ornaments of life." "As for my labours . . . if they can but wear one impertinence out of human life, destroy a single Vice, or give a Morning's Chearfulness to an honest Mind: in short, if the World can be but one Virtue the better, or in any Degree less vicious, or receive from them the smallest Addition to their innocent Diversions, I shall not think my Pains, or indeed my Life, to have been spent in vain." *The Tatler*, ed. Donald F. Bond (New York, 1987), no. 89 (2: 60); no. 271 (3: 363).

chased a complete set of three collections by his most admired English essayists.

Journalistic experience aside, many sayings in Franklin's almanacs were often used as printer's fillers. They were chosen from works as diverse as James Howell's *Lexicon Tetraglotton* (1659), Thomas Fuller's *Introductio ad Prudentiam* (1727) and *Gnomologia* (1732), and Lord Halifax's *Thoughts and Reflections* (1750).[54] Selecting more than a hundred of the most useful maxims and proverbs from his almanacs, Franklin composed *Father Abraham's Speech*, better known as *The Way to Wealth*. He asserted that those maxims and proverbs contained "the Wisdom of many Ages and Nations," and that they were used as vehicles to demonstrate "the Means of procuring Wealth and thereby securing Virtue."[55]

It is clear that despite Franklin's interest in ethical issues, he remained a casual observer and was apt to use his journalistic talents to promote virtue as well as to ridicule human follies. His homespun sayings indicated that he did not attempt to treat morality in a dogmatic manner, and the highly colloquial expressions in his publications often emphasized the practicality of virtue.

Franklin tried to discover realistic means to achieve morals, as in the daily journal he mentioned in his memoirs. His example suggested that conduct is habit, which can be modified. To become a reputable citizen, one needs not erudition but common sense. The way to virtue lies in his willingness to control the natural instinct that may lead to a bad habit. Franklin not only demonstrated his path to virtue, but also indicated: it was for "every one's Interest to be virtuous, who wish'd to be happy even in this World." "Vicious Actions," he added, "are not hurtful because they are forbidden, but forbidden because they are hurtful."[56]

Franklin's concern with morality, his intimate knowledge of human nature, his practical advice, his indefatigable exhortation on morals, and his own illuminating example, all led a French commentator to

---

54. In this regard, the most extensive study is Robert Howard Newcomb, "The Sources of Benjamin Franklin's Sayings of Poor Richard" (Ph.D. dissertation, University of Maryland, 1957). See also his articles: "Poor Richard's Debt to Lord Halifax," *Publications of the Modern Language Association* 70 (June 1957), 535–39; "Franklin and Richardson," *Journal of English and German Philology* 57 (January 1958), 27–35; and "Poor Richard and the English Epigram," *Philological Quarterly* 40 (April 1961), 270–80.

55. *Autobiography*, 164. Kant also remarked: "Character requires maxims, which proceed from reason and from ethicopractical principles" (*Anthropology*, 205).

56. *Autobiography*, 158.

believe that "Franklin is a born moralist."[57] At the same time, Franklin understood the limits of morality and repudiated the idea of moral perfection. He once suggested that maybe an appearance of virtue might satisfy his rigid contemporaries. After he found it too tedious to achieve high morals in all aspects of life, he concluded that moral perfection was as impossible as unnecessary. Insisting that *"a speck-led Ax was best,"* he excused himself and became cynical enough to say: "A perfect Character might be attended with the Inconvenience of being envied and hated; and that benevolent Man should allow a few Faults in himself, to keep his Friends in Countenance."[58]

Franklin was the architect of his life. His willingness to be (or appear to be) righteous was a way to protect himself in society. At a time when most people were accustomed to religious and moral rigidity, Franklin did not suppress his personal characteristics. His conformity to the moral values of the time did not overshadow but protected his individuality, and paved the way to a very fruitful life. Always conscious about who he was and what he wanted, Franklin was equally mindful of what kind of legacy he might leave behind. When he was twenty-two years old, he composed a humorous epitaph, which revealed both his customary concern with righteousness of conduct and his firm belief in shaping his personal destiny. It read:

The Body of
B. Franklin
Printer;
Like the Cover of an old Book,
Its Contents torn out,
And stript of its Lettering and Gilding,
Lies here, Food for Worms.
But the Work shall not be wholly lost,
For it will, as he believ'd, appear once more,
In a new & more perfect Edition,
Corrected and amended
By the Author.[59]

---

57. Édouard Laboulaye, *Memoirs de Benjamin Franklin.* Quoted from John Bigelow, *The Life of Benjamin Franklin* (Philadelphia, 1874), 1: 73.

58. *Autobiography*, 156.

59. *Papers* 1: 111. More than forty years later when Franklin began to write his memoirs, he expressed a similar idea by saying: "I should have no Objection to a Repetition of the same Life from its Beginning, only asking the Advantage Authors have in a second Edition to correct some faults of the first" (*Autobiography*, 43).

1. Benjamin and Deborah Franklin's grave in Christ Church Cemetery at Arch and Fifth Streets, Philadelphia. Visitors customarily toss
coins on the tombstone—perhaps
as a rejoinder to Poor Richard's saying "a penny saved is a penny
earned."

VII

Famous as he was, Franklin's legacy was not fully recognized at
once. Although he was generally regarded as a distinguished citizen,
scientist, and statesman, immediately after his death there was a period when few Americans seemed compelled to eulogize him.

Four days after Benjamin Franklin's death, his funeral took place on
the afternoon of Wednesday, April 21, 1790. Along with the clergy
and dignitaries, twenty thousand people in Philadelphia participated
in the funeral procession and witnessed the interment in the yard of
Christ Church, a few blocks away from his house[60] (Fig. 1). It was a
rare occasion for the public to gather in such a huge crowd, and a
touching moment to see the city submerged beneath a pervasive
sadness.

The same sort of feeling was shared by other Americans as news of
his death gradually spread.[61] In Connecticut alone, newspapers in big

---

60. *American Intelligence* 7 (1790), 35; George W. Corner, ed., *The Autobiography
of Benjamin Rush* (Princeton, 1948), 182, 183, 184; W. J. Bruce, "The Death
and Funeral of Franklin," *The American Historical Record* 3 (1874): 13–16; and
Horace Wemyss Smith, ed., *Life and Correspondence of the Rev. William Smith*
(Philadelphia, 1880), 2: 324–47.

61. For examples of people's tribute to Franklin, including articles, monodies,

and small towns alike, such as New Haven, New London, Norwich, Middletown, Hartford, and Litchfield, reported Franklin's funeral.[62] Before long a monody by an anonymous author appeared in the *Brunswick Gazette* of New Jersey. Its pathetic lines, like many monodies of that time, mourned the painful loss of a beloved friend and venerable patriot. It began,

> 'Tis done—death triumphs
> —Franklin yields his breath,
> Columbia mourns—of father, friend, bereft,
> Oppress'd with sickness and fatigued with age
> He view'd us free, then left this mortal stage;
> Who can recount what he for us has done,
> No tender parent for an only son—
> But stop, my Muse—such similes are faint;
> His worth consummate, man can never paint;
> But O! 'tis hard in silence thus to part
> With him who reign'd deep in each patriot's heart![63]

Beneath his professed sorrow the poet also revealed a trace of uncertainty. He seemed to fear that the patriarch's contributions to the new nation might not be adequately appreciated, and that some of his countrymen, if not the whole nation, might remain indifferent to his departure. But was it not a purely poetic imagination? For who could anticipate that Franklin, a genius embraced by the two worlds, would be unfairly treated in his own country?

Convinced that the nation should not remain silent, many sympathizers began to take action. In Congress James Madison praised the

---

verse, elegies, eulogies, and ceremonies, see *Gazette of the United States*, 28 April 1790; *The Christian's, Scholar's, and Farmer's Magazine* 2 (April and May 1790): 109–10; *The Massachusetts Magazine* 2 (May 1790), 259–62, 309; *The American Museum* 7 (June 1790), appendix 1, 35–38; and William Temple Franklin, ed., *Memoirs of the Life and Writings of Benjamin Franklin* (London, 1817–18), 1: 439–42; 2: 238–42.

62. *The Connecticut Journal* (New Haven), 28 April 1790, p. 2; 5 May, p. 2; *The Connecticut Gazette* (New London), 30 April, p. 3; 14 May, p. 4; *The Norwich-Packet & Country Journal* (Norwich), 7 May, p. 2; *Middlesex Gazette, or Foedeal Adviser* (Middletown), 8 May, p. 4; 15 May, p. 3; *The American Mercury* (Hartford), 3 May, pp. 1, 3; *The Connecticut Courant, and Weekly Intelligence* (Hartford), 3 May, pp. 1, 3; *Weekly Monitor* (Litchfield), 8 May, pp. 2–3; 23 May, p. 4.

63. "A Monody for the *Brunswick Gazette*," in Bruce, "The Death and Funeral," 15.

deceased, saying that Franklin was "an illustrious character, whose native genius has rendered distinguished services to the cause of science and mankind in general; and whose patriotic exertions have contributed in a high degree to the independence and prosperity of this country in particular." He then moved that members of the House of Representatives wear the customary badge of mourning for one month. The House adopted his proposal without debate.[64]

Yet the Senate refused. Never an admirer of Franklin, Senator William Maclay of Pennsylvania said in his diary that the rude manner in which the Senate rejected the ceremony was "insulting." Later he further lamented that the institution demonstrated "a coldness and apathy that astonished me."[65] Thomas Jefferson proposed to President George Washington that the executive branch should wear mourning. Washington declined. He held that since Franklin was the first eminent revolutionary who died as a civilian, he did not know where to "draw a line" to stop that kind of ceremony once it started. According to Jefferson's recollection, he continued to argue: "I told him the world had drawn so broad a line between himself & Dr. Franklin, on the one side, and the residue of mankind, on the other, that we might wear mourning for them, and the question still remains new & undecided as to all others. He thought it best, however, to avoid it."[66]

Ultimately, the federal government's inaction became a national embarrassment when Americans learned of the tributes paid by foreign countries to Franklin.[67] No sooner had the news of his death arrived than the French National Assembly decided to wear mourning for three days, believing that the United States Congress had done the same.[68] "Franklin is dead! The genius, that freed America and poured

---

64. Joseph Gales, Sr., comp., *The Debates and Proceedings in the Congress of the United States* (Washington, 1834), 2: col. 1586.

65. Charles A. Beard, ed., *The Journal of William Maclay* (New York, 1927), 232, 240–41, 339–40.

66. Paul Leicester Ford, ed., *The Writings of Thomas Jefferson* (New York, 1892–99), 8: 265.

67. The only official action was taken by the Supreme Executive Council of Pennsylvania, which decided on 22 April 1790, the day after Franklin's funeral, to wear mourning for one month (*The Pennsylvania Mercury, and Universal Advertiser* [Philadelphia], 24 April 1790, p. 4).

68. Almost a year later Jefferson had the delicate task, requested by Washington, to thank the French National Assembly for the honor and respect that they paid to Franklin. He wrote: "That the Loss of such a Citizen should be lamented by us, among whom he lived, whom he so long and eminently served, and who feel

a flood of light over Europe, has returned to the bosom of the Divinity." Like a thunderbolt, Mirabeau's powerful words in his masterfully prepared discourse shocked the Assembly and rolled across his country. That piece of splendid eloquence, published in numerous newspapers on both continents, instantly became a classic.[69] Within less than ten months, six additional eulogies were delivered in Paris[70] and a street at Passy was renamed for Franklin.[71]

In the United States, however, it was not until almost a year later, in March 1791, that a semi-official eulogy was presented by a vice president of the American Philosophical Society, the Reverend William Smith, who had been Franklin's political enemy for several decades[72] (Fig. 2). A commentator objected that Smith was

---

their Country advanced and honoured by his Birth, Life, and Labors, was to be expected. But it remained for the National Assembly of France to set the first Example of the Representative of one Nation, doing Homage by a public Act to the private Citizen of another, and, by withdrawing arbitrary Lines of Separation, to reduce into one Fraternity the Good and the Great, wherever they have lived or died." The secretary of state to the president of the National Assembly, 8 March 1791, Julian P. Boyd et al., eds., *The Papers of Thomas Jefferson* (Princeton, 1974), 19: 114–15.

69. Comte de Mirabeau, speech before the French National Assembly on 11 June 1790. Quoted from the translation in Jared Sparks, ed., *The Works of Benjamin Franklin* (Boston, 1836–40), 1: 592.

70. Those eulogies were 1) 13 June, Louis Alexandre, duc de La Rochefoucauld d'Enville, before the Society of 1789; 2) 21 July, Abbé Claude Fauchet, a civic eulogy on behalf of the Commune of Paris; 3) and 4) 10 August, Loustalot (a lawyer and publicist), in the name of "M. L." as an apprentice printer, and Belot (another lawyer), in the name of a soldier of the Battalion of Veterans, both before the journeymen printers of Paris; 5) 13 November, Marie Jean A. N. Caritat, marquis de Condorcet, before the Academy of Sciences; and 6) 14 March 1791, Felix Vicq d'Azyr, before the Royal Society of Medicine. Sources: Gilbert Chinard, "The Apotheosis of Benjamin Franklin, Paris, 1790–1791," *Proceedings of the American Philosophical Society* 99 (December 1955): 440–73; Alfred Owen Aldridge, *Franklin and His French Contemporaries* ([New York], 1957), 212–34.

    In November 1790 Mexican scientist José Antonio Alzate y Ramirez delivered a eulogy on Franklin. Alma M. Reed, "José Antonio Alzate y Ramirez: Mexico's Ben Franklin," *Mexican Life* 32 (February 1956), 16.

71. See John Bigelow, *The Life of Benjamin Franklin* (Philadelphia, 1874), 3: 468–69.

72. For a description of how Smith was chosen see Thomas Firth Jones, *A Pair of Lawn Sleeves: A Biography of William Smith (1727–1803)* (Philadelphia, 1972), 165–66. When a eulogy was considered at a special meeting of the American Philosophical Society, a ballot was cast and William Smith and David Rittenhouse got an equal vote. It was then left to them to decide who should

```
┌─────────────────────────────────────────┐
│                                           │
│          E U L O G I U M                  │
│                                           │
│                  O N                      │
│                                           │
│                                           │
│      Benjamin Franklin, LL. D.            │
│                                           │
│   PRESIDENT OF THE AMERICAN PHILOSOPHICAL SOCIETY, │
│                &c. &c.                    │
│                                           │
│                                           │
│            D E L I V E R E D              │
│                                           │
│   March 1, 1791, in PHILADELPHIA, before both HOUSES of │
│   CONGRESS, and the AMERICAN PHILOSOPHICAL SOCIETY, &c. │
│                                           │
│                                           │
│         By WILLIAM SMITH, D. D.           │
│                                           │
│   One of the Vice-Presidents of the said Society, and Provost of the College │
│              and Academy of Philadelphia. │
│                                           │
│                                           │
│                                           │
│             L O N D O N:                  │
│    PRINTED FOR T. CADELL IN THE STRAND.   │
│               MDCCXCII.                    │
│                                           │
└─────────────────────────────────────────┘
```

2. Title page of William Smith's eulogy delivered on March 1, 1791. This only semi-official eulogy on Franklin was not published until 1792, when a Philadelphia edition was also printed by Benjamin Franklin Bache. (Courtesy of The Papers of Benjamin Franklin, Yale University Library)

never "accurately" acquainted with the character he was to portray. He seemed to have assumed the role of a poor biographer, but not that of a talented eulogist. His eulogy exhibited no ingenuity, was stuffed with "a minute detail of events," and sounded like a piece of "fulsome and unmerited panegyric."[73] The eulogist, on the other hand, complained during his delivery that perhaps he should not have assumed such a responsibility in the first place. After the event, when his daughter asked whether or not the father

---

prepare and deliver the eulogy. [Henry Phillips, Jr., comp.], *Early Proceedings of the American Philosophical Society, 1744 to 1838* (Philadelphia, 1844), 187–92.

73. *The Universal Asylum and Columbia Magazine* 8 (May 1792), 323. William Maclay thought the eulogy "trite and trifling" (Beard, ed., *Journal*, 396).

believed one-tenth of what he said, he did not answer but laughed heartily.[74]

Indeed, it took some time before Americans realized the lasting implications of Franklin's legacy. But when memories of him did revive, there would be a new image under very different circumstances.

---

74. Smith, *Eulogium on Dr. Franklin* (London, 1792), 2, 3, 4; H. W. Smith, ed., *Life and Correspondence* 2: 344.

Chapter 2

"Incarnation of the True American Character"

Unlike most Founding Fathers, Franklin, who died in 1790, was spared an entanglement with the growing partisan struggles that characterized the early republic. Except in a few cases, his posthumous reputation was not affected by those intense political disputes that younger public figures were unable to avoid. For example, compared with the controversies over Thomas Jefferson's reputation,[1] Franklin's life did not represent a particular party and the defense of his name did not need to invoke the action of a political apparatus. Franklin was one of the few Revolutionary leaders whose varied genius transcended politics, and whose image ultimately evolved from a personal inspiration to a cultural symbol. Thus, the federal government's inaction in 1790 was not atypical. After all, official efforts to preserve Franklin's legacy have been scarce throughout the past two centuries.

What is remarkable, however, is that Franklin's popularity has been sustained over those years through the admiration and voluntary action of thousands of average citizens. His continued influence lies in his long-lasting personal attraction to his fellow countrymen. Within such a context, a reporter wrote to the *New York Times* in 1856 and claimed that Franklin "was the incarnation of the true American character. . . . Franklin was the true type of the pure, noble, republican feeling of America." Apparently the anonymous reporter knew that representation of the nation's character is a relative matter for he continued by making this distinction: "George Washington was but a noble British officer, made a Republican by circumstances. Franklin was a Republican by birth, by labor, by instinct, and by thought."[2]

---

1. Merrill D. Peterson, *The Jefferson Image in the American Mind* (New York, 1962), chaps. 1–3. Peterson further reveals that not until the 1940s did Jefferson begin to appear as a national symbol, rather than as a partisan one.
2. *New York Times*, 19 September 1856, p. 1.

Using Franklin as an American symbol, the reporter's statement marked the end of ambiguity since the 1790s. Although his assertion of the true American character was not the sophisticated notion it would become in the next century, the praise did indicate a popular enthusiasm that might well be called a cult of Franklin. At the same time, his report raised two basic questions. First, if Franklin's legacy was not fully appreciated when he died, why did his reputation rise so high, more than half a century later, to rival Washington's fame? And second, what were the circumstances that transformed his image, making people believe that Franklin's personal qualities represented the nation's republican values and sentiments? This chapter will study and answer these questions.

I

The eighteenth century ended with no tendency to see Franklin as a saint; from the day he died some individuals attempted to slander his name. As Benjamin Rush recorded, a man of some importance in Philadelphia said: "It would have been happy for America if he and Lord North had died twenty years ago." About the same time, having heard that Franklin was said to be a good man, a loyalist woman in New Jersey contested that belief: "How can he be a good man? Did he not help to bring on Independence?"[3] Expressions of that sort were commonplace among his enemies—many of them Tories who had opposed the American Revolution.[4]

The 1790s was also a time when the debate between Federalists and Republicans intensified. This partisan struggle generated violent vilification and vicious personal abuse in those newspapers that supported different camps. It was in such a political atmosphere that Franklin's integrity was attacked. When one of his grandsons, Benjamin Franklin Bache, published a newspaper called the *Philadelphia General Advertiser* (later known as the *Aurora*) and used it to support the Republican party, his opponent, William Cobbett, the editor of *Porcupine's Gazette*, soon discovered a tactic to discredit him.

Cobbett, born in England and self-educated, was a journalist capa-

---

3. George W. Corner, ed., *The Autobiography of Benjamin Rush* (Princeton, 1948), 184.

4. While referring to the incident of Hutchinson letters, Peter Oliver, a loyalist in Massachusetts, called Franklin a "base Theft" and "a Traitor to his Friends as well as to his Country." Quoted from J. A. Leo Lemay and P. M. Zall, eds., *Benjamin Franklin's Autobiography* (New York, 1986), 240.

ble of undisguised personal attacks of all kinds. After he came to America in the early 1790s and aligned himself with Federalist politics, he soon found out that an easy way to ridicule Bache was to satirize both the grandfather and his grandson indiscriminately. At one point he charged that Bache was "a scoundrel, a hireling of France, an atheist educated in immorality by a grandfather who was master of the art." At another he wrote:

> Every one will, I hope, have the goodness to believe that my grandfather was no philosopher. Indeed he was not. He never made a lightning-rod nor bottled up a single quart of sun-shine in the whole course of his life. He was no almanach-maker [*sic*], nor quack, nor chimney-doctor, nor soap-boiler, nor ambassador; nor printer's devil; neither was he a deist, and all his children were born in wedlock. The legacies he left were his scythe, his reap-hook, and his flail; He bequeathed no old and irrecoverable debts to an hospital; he never *cheated the poor during his life or mocked them in his death*. He has, it is true, been suffered to sleep quietly beneath the green sward; but . . . his descendants . . . have not the mortification to hear him accused daily of having been a whoremaster, an hypocrite and an infidel.[5]

Another staunch supporter of the Federalists, Joseph Dennie, published a magazine called the *Port Folio*. While one's stand toward the French Revolution was important in American politics,[6] he portrayed Franklin as a menace to the country who embraced all the French vices, and charged that Franklin "was one of our first jacobins, the first to lay his head in the lap of French harlotry; and prostrate the Christianity and honour of his country to the deism and democracies of Paris."[7]

In addition to his antagonism against the French, Dennie's hatred was deeply rooted in his desire to vindicate old traditions. An advocate of the English heritage, he "sincerely admired English literature,

---

5. Bernard Faÿ, *The Two Franklins: Fathers of American Democracy* (Boston, 1933), 284, 288. The most recent study of the relationship between Franklin and Bache and of the political climate of the 1790s is James Tagg, *Benjamin Franklin Bache and the Philadelphia Aurora* (Philadelphia, 1991) and Jeffery A. Smith, *Franklin and Bache: Envisioning the Enlightened Republic* (New York, 1990).

6. For further details see "Death of Franklin: The Politics of Mourning in France and the United States," Julian P. Boyd et al., eds., *The Papers of Thomas Jefferson* (Princeton, 1974), 19: 78–115.

7. *Port Folio*, 1st ser., 1 (14 February 1801), 54. See also Lewis Leary, "Joseph Dennie on Benjamin Franklin," *Pennsylvania Magazine of History and Biography* 72 (July 1948): 240–46.

English politics, and English culture."[8] Wishing he had been born in the mother country,[9] he deliberately adopted the pen name, "Oliver Oldschool," to demonstrate his commitment. Meanwhile, he disdained Americans, especially the lower strata of society, whom he considered to be ignorant and untrustworthy. "He will not strive to please the populace," Dennie said, "the lower classes of our motley vulgar [were] too often composed of the scoundrels of all nations, and perpetually restless and rebellious."[10]

With these convictions, Dennie found Franklin's character particularly intolerable. He believed that Franklin's deism was a clear sign of his discontent with church authority, which only revealed his inner desire to break with all traditions. On the other hand, he viewed the populace's enthusiasm for Franklin's fame as a destitute mentality. Sounding like a foreign observer, he lamented:

Americans are so little in the habit of literary research, and so arrogantly confident [that] ours "is the first and most enlightened country in the world," that, without examination, they eulogize extravagantly every thing that is their own; and as Dr. Benjamin had the double honour to be born in Boston, and print in Philadelphia, therefore he must be an Addison in stile, and a Bacon in philosophy.[11]

This view, Dennie thought, was vain and absurd. Compared with the great English heritage in literature and science, Dennie insisted, Franklin invented little but stole much. He said that Franklin's idea of an "air bath" was but a copy of two Englishmen's innovations, and that his essay on how to procure pleasant dreams was in fact a paraphrase of what John Aubrey had recorded in *Miscellanies* (1696) about one of Dr. William Harvey's discoveries.[12]

Nevertheless, many pronounced Franklin an innovator. "Such a strange opinion as the last," Dennie asserted, "never could have been

---

8. Frank Luther Mott, *A History of American Magazines* (Cambridge, Mass., 1957–68), 1: 229.

9. Laura Green Pedder, ed., "The Letters of Joseph Dennie, 1768–1812," *University of Maine Studies*, 2nd ser., no. 36 (January 1936), 182.

10. [Joseph Dennie], *Prospectus of a New Weekly Paper, Submitted to Men of Affluence, Men of Liberality, and Men of Letters* [Philadelphia, 1800], 2, 2n.

11. *Port Folio*, 1st ser., 1 (14 February 1801), 53.

12. Ibid. As a severe critic, John Adams did not believe that charges of plagiarism against Franklin had any foundation. Charles Francis Adams, ed., *Works of John Adams* (Boston, 1850–56), 1: 659.

entertained, except in a country, from its newness, paucity of literary information, and the imperfection of its systems of education, puzzled to distinguish an original from a copy."[13] That many Americans were willing to use Franklin to represent the new nation horrified Dennie to no small degree. He warned that Franklin's example provided no future for the country, but "to lose history by being severed from the traditions of England." It was clear that Dennie disliked Franklin because this indigenous hero was viewed as a symbol of an emerging culture, with which the former was unable to come to terms. What Dennie found more lamentable than Franklin's defects was the populace's ignorance, which led them to portray him as the champion of a fantasized "new culture."

Dennie's career as an editor was a short one. Eleven years after the first publication of the *Port Folio* he died in 1812 at the age of forty-four. Soon his view of Franklin became rare, even in his own magazine. Subsequent editors continued to use the pseudonym "Oliver Oldschool," but their commentaries on Franklin seldom resembled those of Dennie. When William Temple Franklin's edition of his grandfather's works was published late in the 1810s, the magazine quickly responded that thus far "this is the best arrangement" of Franklin's writings. A few years later, in 1823, when a reviewer again commented on Franklin's memoirs for the *Port Folio*, he praised Franklin's "high character" and declared that he was "a philosopher and statesman of great celebrity."[14] These remarks suggested that overt political attacks on Franklin had largely subsided.

II

If Franklin's reputation suffered during the first decade or so immediately after his death, in the long run, his enemies failed to alter the public's image of Franklin because personal attacks, prejudices, and distortions hurt their own credibility rather than his.

Interestingly enough, scurrilous and political as Cobbett's and Dennie's rhetoric was, their criticisms never discussed the economic dimension of Franklin's thought, which was a major factor in his popularity. Though a cynical critic, before he returned to England in 1800, Cobbett said little about Franklin's economics. As an outspoken

---

13. *Port Folio*, 1st ser., 1 (14 February 1801), 53.
14. *Port Folio*, 4th ser., 8 (October 1819), 313; 4th ser., 16 (December 1823), 453, 441.

Franklin hater, Dennie declared his intention in 1801 to write a comprehensive analysis of his economic system, "the adoption of which has degraded our national character." But nothing came of this.[15] Because Franklin's economic views were rarely discussed in depth, even his most hostile detractors failed to challenge this crucial aspect of his life that would attract the public's interest for decades.

On the other hand, after the American Revolution, especially around the turn of the nineteenth century, a new emphasis on republicanism began to emerge. To be sure, Protestantism continued to play an important role in American life. At the same time, because of both the increasing influence of republicanism and the willingness of most clerics to associate themselves with the new republican state,[16] the foremost criteria for judging a person's character included evidence of being a staunch republican as well as a pious Christian.

Many Americans believed that their fight for independence was "a moral struggle." After the victory of the Revolutionary War, a new man also emerged because in that struggle "individual characters were exhibited, strongly operated upon, and brought into powerful action." Republicanism to Americans, therefore, meant more than a form of government; it was a way of life as well. The independence of the United States not only separated the thirteen colonies from the mother country and established a constitutional government, "it added a moral dimension, a utopian depth . . . a depth that involved the very character of their society."[17]

Nevertheless, "a republic was such a delicate polity precisely because it demanded an extraordinary moral character in the people." Americans believed that, as ancient Greek and Roman traditions had shown, the livelihood of a republic lay not in the force of its arms, but in the character and spirit of its people. On the one hand, the soundness of public morals was the basis of good government. On the other hand, public morality was the ultimate safeguard against social evils, such as luxury, idleness, indulgence, and corruption. In short, so long as every citizen adhered to republican principles, there could be little

---

15. *Port Folio*, 1st ser., 1 (14 February 1801), 54; 1st ser., 1 (4 April 1801), 110.
16. John Higham has pointed out the convergence of republican and Protestant ideologies in America. He says: "By giving the millennium a temporal and secular character, the Protestant clergy began to identify the Kingdom of God with the American Republic; and the Protestant ideology thereupon attached itself to American nationalism" ("Hanging Together: Divergent Unities in American History," *Journal of American History* 61 [June 1974], 14).
17. *The North American Review* 7 (1818): 311. Gordon S. Wood, *The Creation of the American Republic, 1776–1787* (New York, 1969), 47.

fear of despotism, because the virtue of the people was "the greatest determinant of whether a republic lived or died."[18]

The principal republican values were twofold: public and private virtue. The first related to a citizen's willingness to participate in civic affairs and to do good for the public, the second to the style and propriety of that citizen's personal life. Only those who could embrace both sorts of virtue were true republicans. Only those few consummate individuals whose conduct embodied the highest morals could be regarded as exemplary Americans.

For the first several decades of the nineteenth century, such public men as George Washington, Thomas Jefferson, and Andrew Jackson, were praised most for their honesty, fortitude, perseverance, courage, and will.[19] As a member of the venerable Revolutionary generation, Franklin's long public service was well known. He was the only leading American who signed all four of the major documents that laid the foundation of the republic: the Declaration of Independence (1776), the Treaties of Alliance and of Amity and Commerce with France (1778), the Peace Treaty between Great Britain and the United States (1783), and the Constitution of the United States (1787). Although most of his activities during the war took place abroad and although the details of his diplomatic missions in France caused some controversy among his colleagues, in the public eye he was a great patriot who contributed significantly to the making of the new nation.

Few instances could be more illustrative of the public's admiration for Franklin than the following case. William Strahan, one of Franklin's close friends in England, considered Americans' taking arms against the mother country to be an act of rebellion, and therefore voted in Parliament with the British ministry. His stand prompted Franklin to write a letter on July 5, 1775. It read:

---

18. Wood, *Creation*, 47, 68; Robert E. Shalhope, "Republicanism and Early American Historiography," *William and Mary Quarterly*, 3rd ser., 39 (April 1982): 335.

19. On Washington's character see Daniel Webster, "The Character of Washington," *The Works of Daniel Webster* (4th ed.: Boston, 1853), 1: 217–33; Robert C. Winthrop, "National Monument to Washington," *Addresses and Speeches on Various Occasions* (Boston, 1852–86), 1: 70–89; Edward Everett, "The Character of Washington," *Orations and Speeches on Various Occasions* (Boston, 1879), 4: 3–51; and Marcus Cunliffe, *George Washington: Man and Monument* (Boston, 1958), 8–12. On the controversy over Jefferson's character see Peterson, *The Jefferson Image*, 115–49. On Jackson's character see John William Ward, *Andrew Jackson: Symbol for an Age* (New York, 1955), 166–80, 258n.

Mr. Strahan,

You are a Member of Parliament, and one of the Majority which has doomed my Country to Destruction. You have begun to burn our Towns and murder our People. Look upon your Hands! They are stained with the Blood of your Relations! You and I were long Friends: You are now my Enemy, and I am, Yours,

B Franklin[20]

This brief note became one of Franklin's most famous writings, because it was quoted in almost every major selection of his works and in numerous editions of his biographies. The intention beneath those frequent reprints was clearly to highlight Franklin's deep commitment to independence. Americans seemed to be captivated by the thought that, when his countrymen were fighting for freedom, Franklin's patriotic passions ran so high that he broke with one of his long-time friends. Indeed, his commitments to the American cause were unmistakably articulated in the letter, and so was his outrage at both the friend's compromise and the British army's brutality.

Yet the letter was never sent. Two days later, Franklin changed his mind and wrote a friendly letter to Strahan, who also responded courteously.[21] Franklin seldom lost his temper, and when he did, he usually recovered it quickly.[22] Interestingly throughout this period little effort was made to investigate the real consequence of the first letter. It seemed that if the letter documented Franklin's patriotic sentiment, that was all people wanted. No early editors of his works, including his grandson, William Temple Franklin, and the indefatigable scholar Jared Sparks, bothered to reveal whether or not Strahan had actually received the letter.

Less need be said about Franklin's private life, which exemplified industry, frugality, prudence, and simplicity. Many were impressed by his numerous achievements, in printing and publishing, in scientific observation (especially in the field of electricity), and in public service. Moreover, they appreciated the ways in which he accomplished those achievements. They praised his remarkable disinterestedness,

---

20. *Papers* 22: 85.

21. Ibid.; Carl Van Doren, *Benjamin Franklin* (New York, 1938), 539–40. The second letter by Franklin was lost. Paul Leicester Ford first pointed out that the often quoted note was never sent, *The Many-Sided Franklin* (New York, 1899), 216.

22. *Papers* 21: 526–29. Franklin said to the same friend a few months later: "I make it a Rule not to mix personal Resentment with Public Business." To William Strahan, 3 October 1775, *Papers* 22: 219.

tranquil mind, plain common sense, sound judgment, benign manner, and benevolent and humanistic feelings. These amiable qualities, some insisted, belonged to a man who was more than a genius: he was a sage. In short, what Franklin's admirers really wanted to stress was not only his distinctive characteristics, but also the sublimity of his wisdom. Calling him "this illustrious defender of American freedom," Noah Webster stated: "I revere a character equally known and respected in this and foreign countries."[23] Sparks made this point:

> [Franklin] possessed a perfect mastery over the faculties of his understanding and over his passions. Having this power always at command, and never being turned aside either by vanity or selfishness, he was enabled to pursue his objects with a directness and constancy, that rarely failed to insure success.[24]

George Bancroft also believed that "with placid tranquillity, Benjamin Franklin looked quietly and deeply into the secrets of nature." His clear understanding was never perverted by passion, or corrupted by the pride of theory. Skeptical of tradition as the basis of faith, he respected reason rather than authority. Loving truth, without prejudice or bias, he intuitively explored the laws of nature. His mind was so pure that he could discover natural laws without distortion as if the universe were reflecting itself in a mirror.[25]

Americans were particularly delighted when they learned that foreign commentators were making similar observations. Henry Brougham, Scottish lawyer and politician, believed Franklin to be "one of the most remarkable men." "In this truly great man," he said, "everything seemed to concur that goes towards the constitution of exalted merit."[26] The British philosopher and historian James Mackintosh appreciated Franklin's independent thought and his capacity for striking illustrations from homely objects. He called Franklin "the American Socrates."[27] The English historian John Foster observed that

---

23. Webster, *Dissertations on the English Language* (1789; Gainesville, Fla., 1951), vi.
24. Sparks, ed., *The Works of Benjamin Franklin* (Boston, 1836–40), 1: 534.
25. Bancroft, *History of the United States* (Boston, 1834–74), 3: 378.
26. Quoted from *Memoirs of Benjamin Franklin* (Harper's School District Library ed.: New York, 1840), 2: 285.
27. Quoted from James Parton, *Life and Times of Benjamin Franklin* (New York, 1864), 1: 664.

Franklin reasoned in a manner that was marvelously simple, direct, and decisive. He could reduce a subject to its plainest principles. Never afraid of opposition, he was apt to use common sense to resolve the most uncommon difficulties.[28]

Finally, it was a French painter, Joseph-Siffred Duplessis, whose artistic characterization of Franklin gained the widest popularity. In 1778 he painted a portrait of Franklin which was exhibited in the gallery of the Louvre the following year. An American visitor, Elkanah Watson, later proudly reported that, "as a mark of distinguished respect," the portrait was presented at a place close to those of the king and queen.[29]

One of the most talented portrait painters of his time, Duplessis depicted a Franklin of dignity and intelligence, dressed in a fur collar coat. Subsequently known as the "fur collar" portrait, it was repeatedly engraved and copied by both the original and many other artists, and thus became the most widely recognizable picture of Franklin.[30] When a French observer saw the portrait, he commented: "His large forehead suggests strength of mind and his robust neck the firmness of his character. Evenness of temper is in his eyes and on his lips the smile of an unshakable serenity. . . . They have put under his portrait that laconic inscription: *Vir*. There is not one trait in him nor in his life to belie it." The French admirer was convinced that Franklin's good moral character and his benevolence toward humanity best qualified him as what the word *vir* ultimately meant—virtue and man.[31]

---

28. Ibid.

29. Watson, *Men and Times of the Revolution*, ed. Winslow C. Watson (New York, 1856), 89.

30. Charles Henry Hart, ed., "Life Portraits of Great Americans: Benjamin Franklin," *McClure's Magazine* 8 (January 1897): 269; *Papers* 1: xix; Charles Coleman Sellers, *Benjamin Franklin in Portraiture* (New Haven, 1962), 138.

31. Sellers, *Portraiture*, 127; J. G. A. Pocock, *The Machiavellian Moment* (Princeton, 1975), 37. This is not to imply that the French were one-sided. Franklin "was, if you will, the shrewdest and most prudent of honest men, but also the least hypocritical," the French critic Charles Augustin Sainte-Beuve wrote. "An ideal is lacking" in this upright, reasonable, and utilitarian American. He added: "Even though we, of the hasty and vivacious French race, would like him to have a little of ourselves in him,...there is a flower, a bloom, of religion, of honour, of chivalry, which we must not ask of Franklin." Originally written in 1852, the quotes are from his "Benjamin Franklin," *Portraits of the Eighteenth Century, Historic and Literary* (New York, 1964), 1: 322–27.

III

Implausible as it may have seemed at the time, republican virtue had an inherent difficulty: what if the public and private interests came into conflict? A traditional solution was the theory of "sacrificing private interest to the public good." From Franklin's example, however, many Americans discovered a different answer, because his successful personal career combined with a distinguished record of public service suggested that there might be no intrinsic conflict at all. Franklin's experience indicated that the more each individual gained in his own life, the more he was able to contribute to the improvement of society. Therefore, realization of self-interest was what the public needed for continuous progress. By the same token, the lovely dream of each individual's success would prove the goodness of a society, which should provide unlimited opportunities for its members.

Here American republicanism began to differ from traditional republican theories. Republicanism in America meant not only public and private virtues; republicanism itself was now judged by how much economic opportunity and individual freedom the new nation could offer. The American republic was far better than the Old World, not only because traditional morals were high, but also because this New World provided the kind of opportunity, freedom, and success that peoples in other lands never dared to dream of. The French observer Alexis de Tocqueville discovered that one important element distinguishing the New World from the Old was American individualism, which he described as "self-interest properly understood." Noticing that Americans rarely talked about the beauties of virtue, but studied its utility, he wrote:

American moralists do not pretend that one must sacrifice himself for his fellows because it is a fine thing to do so. But they boldly assert that such sacrifice is as necessary for the man who makes it as for the beneficiaries. . . . They therefore do not raise objections to men pursuing their interests, but they do all they can to prove that it is each man's interest to be good.[32]

It is clear that in addition to political principles and moralistic theories, republicanism in America had to do with economic progress as

---

32. Alexis de Tocqueville, *Democracy in America*, ed. J. P. Mayer (Anchor Books ed.: Garden City, N.Y., 1969), 525–26.

well. Americans believed that a sustained economic progress was a sign of moral good, whereas economic stagnation was that of moral decay.[33] While the goodness of society was judged by economic terms, so was a person's morality. This blend of moral sanction over economic success was an American invention. Highlighting an individual's obligation and ability to control his own destiny, such sanction was phrased in a typical expression—"self-made man."[34]

For most of the first half of the nineteenth century, many insisted that an ultimate test of a person's character was whether he could raise himself to a higher social status. Franklin's mode was so attractive because he had raised himself from obscurity to eminence. As long as other people paid adequate attention to the simple virtues he stressed, many could succeed. It seems clear that if the self-made man ethos reflected Americans' optimistic belief in the New World, staunch commitment to individualism, and earnest dreams of success, Franklin's classic example symbolized them all.

IV

While Franklin was widely viewed as an inspiration for individual advancement, his *Autobiography* and *The Way to Wealth* were simple and straightforward texts that illuminated the virtuous path to personal success.

By 1850 *The Way to Wealth* had been printed more than eighty times, a figure suggesting that during the first and second decades of the nineteenth century this tract was more readily available than any other work written by Franklin, including his autobiography. Widely

---

33. Eric Foner, *Free Soil, Free Labor, Free Man* (New York, 1970), 11–72. Defenders of slavery portrayed the bustling, competitive, and reckless free labor system that Franklin represented as the opposite of the peaceful, benevolent, and paternalistic system in the South. George Fitzhugh wrote: "Free society has continued long enough to justify the attempt to generalize its phenomena, and calculate its moral and intellectual influences. It is obvious that, in whatever is purely utilitarian and material, it incites invention and stimulates industry. Benjamin Franklin, as a man and a philosopher, is the best exponent of the working of the system. His sentiments and his philosophy are low, selfish, atheistic and material. They tend directly to make man a mere 'featherless biped,' well-fed, well-clothed and comfortable, but regardless of his soul as the 'beasts that perish'" (*Sociology for the South, or The Failure of Free Society* [1854; New York, 1965?], 90).

34. See Irvin G. Wyllie's excellent study, *The Self-Made Man in America: The Myth of Rags to Riches* (New Brunswick, N.J., 1954).

regarded to be the antidote to poverty and the most suitable textbook for enterprising youth,[35] that little piece was published as a separate pamphlet, chapbook, or broadside, and appeared in many journals, newspapers, magazines, anthologies, and other almanacs as well. Apparently aimed at less educated readers, simplified and even distorted versions also emerged, for example those heavily illustrated broadsides such as *Bowle's Moral Pictures* and *The Art of Making Money Plenty in Everyman's Pocket*[36] (Figs. 3 and 4).

In the meantime, the *Autobiography* was reprinted nearly one hundred and twenty times till the end of the 1850s. Publishers included not only those in big cities like New York, Philadelphia, and Boston, but also those in Auburn and Buffalo, New York; Cincinnati, Cleveland, and Hudson, Ohio; Milwaukee, and San Francisco. Evidence further suggests that Franklin had his most serious impact on the minds of many young people not from formal textbooks, but from individual readings after school.[37] Silas Felton of Marlborough, Mas-

---

35. Weems, comp., *The Immortal Mentor, or, Man's Unerring Guide to a Healthy, Wealthy, and Happy Life* (1793; Carlisle, Penn., 1815), 75, 78, 85; Simeon Ide, ed., *The Way to Wealth by DR. FRANKLIN* (New Ipswich, [N.H.] 1816), 36, 37.

36. *Bowle's Moral Pictures; or Poor Richard Illustrated. Being Lessons for the Young and the Old* (London, n.d.). Paul L. Ford believed that it was first printed in Manchester in 1796. The American version of the piece was sometimes entitled *Poor Richard Illustrated: Lessons for the Young and Old, on Industry, Temperance, Frugality & c. by Benjamin Franklin* (New York, n.d.), which remained popular until the end of the 1850s. See Dixon Wecter, *The Hero in America* (New York, 1941), 60–61. Numerous copies of *The Art of Making Money Plenty in Everyman's Pocket* survived, which can be found in the American Philosophical Society, the Library Company of Philadelphia, the Free Library of Philadelphia, Beinecke Library of Yale University, and the Library of Congress.

37. Beyond Franklin's role in the Revolution, school histories of the eighteenth century in the Northeast said very little about his other activities. This observation is based on the following material: Charles A. Goodrich, *A History of the United States of America* (Hartford, [Conn.] 1823) (Bellows Falls, Vt., 1825); Salma Hale, *History of the United States* (Cooperstown, N.Y., 1837) (New York, 1825, 1840) (Buffalo, 1851); Marcius Willson, *History of the United States* (New York, 1847); and Emma Willard, *History of the United States* (New York, 1830); *Universal History in Perspective* (New York, 1852), and *Abridged History of the United States* (New York, 1856). One exception was the Harper Brothers' ambitious scheme of school district libraries for New York State, which included, in its second series, two volumes of the life and works of Franklin (1840). Exceedingly popular in the West and the South, the *McGuffey Readers*, except for quoting maxims from Franklin's almanacs, contained little information about his life. See Richard D. Miles, "The American Image of Benjamin Franklin," *American Quarterly* 9 (Summer 1957): 123–26; and Karl Lyman Smart, "A Man for All Ages: The Changing Image of Benjamin Franklin in the

3. Broadside: *Poor Richard Illustrated: Lessons for the Young and Old, on Industry, Temperance, Frugality & c. by Benjamin Franklin*, New York, n. d. (Courtesy of the American Philosophical Society)

sachusetts obtained a copy of Franklin's life as early as 1796 when he was eighteen years old. "I perused them attentively, and found many very valuable precepts, which I endeavoured to treasure up and follow. . . . From that time I determined to *adhere strictly to Reason, Industry, and good Economy*," the young villager declared. He actively participated in community affairs, became interested in the diffusion of knowledge to the countryside through libraries and newspapers, and even began writing an autobiography at the age of twenty-five.[38]

Some well-known bankers and businessmen, such as Thomas Mellon and James Harper, readily admitted that the *Autobiography* and *The Way to Wealth* were crucial to their careers.[39] It was after reading Franklin's life at sixteen that Harper decided not to stay on his father's

Nineteenth-Century American Popular Culture" (Ph.D. dissertation, University of Florida, 1989), 91–92.

38. Rena L. Vassar, ed., *The Life or Biography of Silas Felton Written by Himself*, reprint from *The Proceedings of the American Antiquarian Society* for October 1959 (Worcester, Mass., 1960), 119, 125, 126, 129–30.

39. Irvin G. Wyllie, *The Self-Made Man in America*, 15–16.

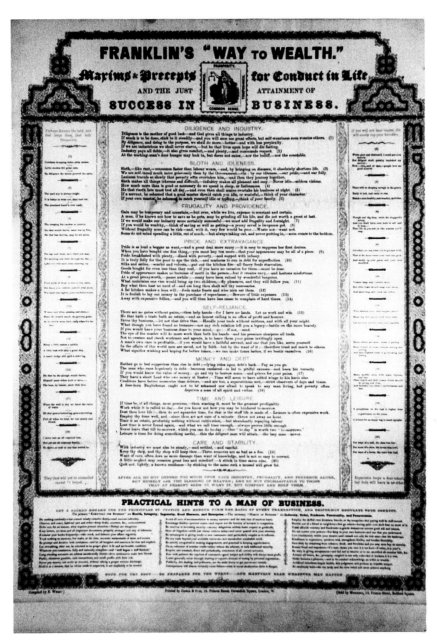

4. Broadside: a simplified version of *Franklin's "Way to Wealth": Maxims & Precepts for Conduct in Life and the Just Attainment of Success in Business*, England, n. d. (Benjamin Franklin Collection, Beinecke Rare Book & Manuscript Library, Yale University)

farm near Newtown, Long Island. On a cold December day in 1810 he entered New York City with one shilling in his pocket. Thirty-four years later he was elected mayor of the city and owned one of the most successful publishing companies in the nation. One of his grandnephews declared that James Harper's "entire capital was a sound mind in a strong body." A biographer quoted what the publisher once told a friend: "Yes, sir, the basis on which we commenced was *character*, and not *capital*." The entrepreneur's admiration for Franklin was such that he instructed an artist to paint a profile of Franklin in his own portrait, which later hung in the City Hall of New York.[40]

Born on a farm of twenty-three acres in Tyrone county, Ireland, Thomas Mellon emigrated with his family to America in 1818 when he was only five. He recalled:

> It was about my fourteenth year, at a neighbor's house, . . . that I happened upon a dilapidated copy of the autobiography of Dr. Franklin. It delighted me with a wider view of life and inspired me with new ambition— turned my thoughts into new channels. I had not before imagined any other course of life superior to farming, but the reading of Franklin's life led me to question his view. For so poor and friendless a boy to be able to become a merchant or a professional man had before seemed an impossibility; but here was Franklin, poorer than myself, who by industry, thrift and frugality had become learned and wise, and elevated to wealth and fame. The maxims of "poor Richard" exactly suited my sentiments. I read the book again and again, and wondered if I might not do something in the same line by similar means. I had will and energy equal to the occasion, and could exercise the same degree of industry and perseverance, and felt no misgiving except on the score of talent. . . . After that I was more industrious when at school, and more constant than ever in reading and study at leisure hours. I regard the reading of Franklin's Autobiography as the turning point of my life.[41]

But Franklin's influence was not limited to farm boys or to the business community. Sparks read Franklin's *Autobiography* in his

---

40. Eugene Exman, *The Brothers Harper: A Unique Publishing Partnership and Its Impact upon the Cultural Life of America from 1817 to 1853* (New York, 1965), 1–2; *The House of Harper: One Hundred and Fifty Years of Publishing* (New York, 1967), 9, 31. J. Henry Harper, *The House of Harper: A Century of Publishing in Franklin Square* (New York, 1912), 15.

41. Mellon, *Thomas Mellon and His Time* (1885; New York, 1969), 139, 169–70. Franklin's influence on Mellon was such that he set up a life-size statue of Franklin in the doorway of his office building (D. Koskoff, *The Mellons* [New York, 1978], 31).

teens; many years later he described his experience in a letter to a friend:

I send you "Franklin" with the fullest belief that you will be pleased with it; and I shall be exceedingly disappointed if it proves otherwise. I am sure you are enough like me to warrant this opinion. I refer particularly to the life written by himself, though the essays are some of them excellent. I am willing to acknowledge, however, that I am not a very impartial judge in this case. The book fell very early into my hands. It delighted me so much that I read it several times over. I have not seen it till to-day for eleven years. I have been looking it over a little with a very strange combination of thoughts and feelings. It revived most vividly a train of associations which, though melancholy, were not entirely unpleasant. It was this book which first roused my mental energies, such as they are, and directed them to nobler objects than they seemed destined by fortune and the fates to be engaged in. It promoted me to resolutions, and gave me strength to adhere to them. It inspired me with an ardor, which I had not felt before, and which never afterwards forsook me. It taught me that circumstances have not a sovereign control over the mind. But I have no time to say more about Franklin, or the effect it had on my character and destiny. I know you will like it.[42]

"Mental energies" and "nobler objects" indeed. Born in a humble family in Connecticut, Sparks later became one of the leading scholars in the nation and served as president of Harvard College from 1849 to 1853.

In Boston and Philadelphia, mechanics and artisans not only learned moral lessons from Franklin's example, they also had a concrete reason to appreciate his legacy. As a result of his bequest of £1,000 each to the two cities, young journeymen could apply for loans designated to help them. By the mid-1820s some two hundred and fifty craftsmen in Philadelphia had borrowed money from the fund. These beneficiaries came from as many as thirty different trades and professions.[43]

In 1831 a series of lectures was established to educate young men in Boston. Called the Franklin lectures, they were inaugurated by a prominent politician and orator, Edward Everett. He emphasized that, as far as happiness was concerned, no goal was greater than the enrichment of the mind. For those who lacked formal education,

---

42. Herbert B. Adams, *The Life and Writings of Jared Sparks* (Boston, 1893), 1: 6–7.
43. American Philosophical Society, *Dr. Franklin's Legacy* (1791–1870), 4 vols. References here are from vols. 1 and 2.

Franklin's story could not be told too often, because his humble origins never discouraged him from educating himself.[44]

Everett's assertion was not an exception. In fact, throughout this period whenever people talked about self-determination and self-improvement, Franklin's career was always a handy reference. In 1840 an audience at the College of William and Mary was reminded that the days of Franklin's youth and "the gradual steps which led to his unparalleled success" should not be overlooked, although the achievements during his more advanced years were brilliant.[45]

A year later Henry Howe published *Memoirs of the Most Eminent American Mechanics*, in which he proposed that the name Franklin was the most distinguished in the annals of self-education. Franklin's example proved that the only obstacle to one's advancement was a lack of will, not low economic and social conditions.[46] In 1856 Henry D. Gilpin observed that Franklin became a successful printer in Philadelphia "with only the smallest pittance in his pocket; without a companion to cheer him—without a relative, a friend, even an acquaintance, to assist or even counsel him."[47] Freeman Hunt, the enthusiastic compiler of a selection of business ethics, further declared that as far as the morals and manners of trade and the rationale of business management were concerned, Franklin's writings covered "the true philosophy of business life, in giving tone and direction to the mercantile mind of America."[48]

About the same time in 1856, speaking in front of a huge gathering of artisans at the unveiling ceremonies of a Franklin statue in Boston, Robert C. Winthrop also exhorted his audience:

---

44. Everett, *An Address Delivered as the Introduction to the Franklin Lectures, in Boston, November 14, 1831* (Boston, 1832), 4, 14, 18. This address, under the title "Advantage of Scientific Knowledge to Working Men," is more easily available in his *Orations and Speeches on Various Occasions* (Boston, 1879), 1: 307–28.

45. John Tyler, Jr., *An Oration on the Life and Character of Benjamin Franklin, Delivered before the Franklin Society of William and Mary College, on the 17th January, 1840* (Norfolk, Va., 1840), 6.

46. Howe, *Memoirs of the Most Eminent American Mechanics* (New York, 1841), 37.

47. Gilpin, *The Character of Franklin: Address Delivered before the Franklin Institute of Pennsylvania, on the Evening of the Fourth of December, 1856* (Philadelphia, 1857), 13.

48. Hunt, *Worth and Wealth: A Collection of Maxims, Morals and Miscellanies for Merchants and Men of Business* (New York, 1856), vi–vii.

Behold him, mechanics and mechanics' apprentices, holding out to you an example of diligence, economy, and virtue, and personifying the triumphant success which may await those who follow it! Behold him, ye that are humblest and poorest in present condition or in future prospect, —lift up your heads and look at the image of a man who rose from nothing, who owed nothing to parentage or patronage, who enjoyed no advantages of early education which are not open —a hundred fold open—to yourselves, who performed the most menial offices in the business in which his early life was employed, but who lived to stand before kings, and died to leave a name which the world will never forget. Lift up your heads and your hearts with them, and learn a lesson of confidence and courage which shall never again suffer you to despair, —not merely of securing the means of an honest and honorable support for yourselves, but even of doing something worthy of being done for your country and for mankind![49]

No matter how widespread it might be, emulation of Franklin's path was not a guarantee for success. About the late 1840s or early 1850s, a printer, Orion Clemens, acquired the Hannibal (Missouri) *Journal*, with a goal to change that small weekly newspaper into a powerful organ of Western journalism. Having previously learned the printing business and studied Franklin's life in St. Louis, he wrote to his mother that he was "closely imitating" the great Franklin. For a while he lived on bread and water, and was amazed to discover how clear his mind had become on such a low diet. He worked hard and often drove his helpers to do the same, sometimes until midnight. Serving as an apprentice, his teenage brother often complained. Then the printer would quote Poor Richard's proverbs, which not only failed to ease his brother's tears but also led to more resentment. Clemens's paper failed in 1853. The younger brother, who was never paid a penny, left him to explore a different life. This young boy was Samuel Clemens, a literary giant later known to the world as Mark Twain.[50]

The myth of Franklin's success persisted, however. One advocate of the legend was Horace Greeley, editor of the *New York Herald* and alleged author of the most infectious words of his time: "Young man, go west. Go west!" Not only did he thus promote individual mobility; his face, many believed, resembled remarkably that of the beloved

---

49. Winthrop, "The Inauguration of the Statue of Franklin," *Addresses and Speeches on Various Occasions* (Boston, 1852–86), 2: 287.

50. Clemens, *Mark Twain's Autobiography*, 2 vols. (New York, 1924), 2: 268–69, 274–75, 285–86; Albert Bigelow Paine, *Mark Twain: A Biography*, 3 vols. (New York, 1912), 1: 27–28, 84–85, 92–93; Margaret Sanborn, *Mark Twain: The Bachelor Years* (New York, 1990), 62, 72.

Franklin. Therefore, many contemporaries called Greeley "the late Franklin." "Of the men whom the world currently terms *Self-Made*," Greeley lectured the public, "that is, who severally fought their life-battles without the aid of inherited wealth, or family honors, or educational advantages, perhaps our American *Franklin* stands highest in the civilized world's regard." He even went on to say, "I think I adequately appreciate the greatness of Washington; yet I must place Franklin above him as the consummate type and flowering of human nature under the skies of colonial America."[51]

In his book entitled *Self-Made Men*, Charles C. B. Seymour provided more than sixty biographical sketches, which included a wide range of domestic and foreign figures such as John Smith, Roger Williams, David Rittenhouse, Benjamin West, Andrew Jackson, Henry Clay, Daniel Webster, Stephen Girard, Robert Fulton, James Watt, Richard Arkwright, Charles Dickens, and Immanuel Kant. One of the author's favorite stories was none other than Franklin:

> It must not be supposed that Franklin's character is one of such extreme complexity that it can not be understood by ordinary intelligences. On the contrary, its utter simplicity is what is apt to confuse. . . . Franklin had what is called by phrenologists a well-balanced organization. Every faculty was largely formed and assiduously cultivated. He knew exactly his own strength, and consequently, never failed of success in what he undertook. . . . His life is remarkable for two things, great ambition and great virtue. He determined to be famous and to be good. He succeeded in both.[52]

There can be little doubt that to a significant extent Franklin's remarkable popularity hinged on his image as the embodiment of the self-made man, if not its synonym. Thus, in one of the few plays concerning Franklin during this period, John Brougham portrayed him as a poor printer who ultimately stood before kings. A biographical dictionary edited by John L. Blake and published in 1859 called Franklin "a philosopher and statesman, and emphatically a self-made man."[53]

---

51. From an unpublished lecture on self-made men by Greeley. Quoted in Parton, *Life*, 1: 677–78.
52. Seymour, *Self-Made Men* (New York, 1858), 429.
53. John Brougham, "Franklin: A New and Original Historical Drama in Five Acts," in [Samuel] *French's Standard Drama*, no. 166 (New York, 1856); John L. Blake, ed., *A Biographical Dictionary* (13th ed.: Philadelphia, 1859), 467.

V

Americans' emphasis on Franklin's rise did not diminish their interest in knowing about his particular personal traits. Early editors of his anthologies often included such works as "Dialogue between Franklin and the Gout," "A Petition of The Left Hand," and "The Handsome and the Deformed Leg," most of which revealed his light and humorous temperament.

Moreover, collecting anecdotes of Franklin became such a vogue that not only popularizers, such as Mason L. Weems and Samuel G. Goodrich (better known as Peter Parley),[54] but also famous Americans, such as Jefferson and Madison, were deeply involved. Readers seemed to be especially delighted when they could learn intimate details about Franklin from some of his most eminent colleagues. Jefferson contributed several of the most widely circulated anecdotes about Franklin. Soon after the latter's death he recalled:

> The succession to Dr. Franklin, at the court of France, was an excellent school of humility. On being presented to any one as the Minister of America, the common-place question, was. . . . "Is it you, Sir, who replace Doctor Franklin?" I generally answered—"No one can replace him, Sir, I am only his successor."[55]

Although he did not become acquainted with Franklin until 1785, Madison felt that he "never passed half an hour in his company without hearing some observation or anecdote worth remembering." Madison repeated some episodes so often that when he finally decided to write them down, he was confident that his record was "accurate."[56] For example:

> Whilst the last members were signing [the Constitution] Doctor FRANKLIN looking towards the President's Chair, at the back of which a rising sun

---

54. [Goodrich], *The Life of Benjamin Franklin: Illustrated by Tales, Sketches, and Anecdotes* (New York, 1832).

55. Jefferson to the Rev. William Smith, 19 February 1791, in Julian P. Boyd et al., eds., *The Papers of Thomas Jefferson* (New York, 1974), 19: 113. This anecdote was quoted in William Smith, *Eulogium on Dr. Franklin* (London, 1792), 33. The most recent selection of anecdotes by and about Franklin is P. M. Zall, ed., *Ben Franklin Laughing* (Berkeley, 1980).

56. Elizabeth Fleet, ed., "Madison's 'Detached Memoranda,'" *William and Mary Quarterly*, 3rd ser., 3 (October 1946): 536.

happened to be painted, observed to a few members near him, that painters
had found it difficult to distinguish in their art, a rising from a setting sun. . . .
but now at length, I have the happiness to know, that it is a rising and not
a setting sun.[57]

In addition to these prominent Americans, editors of Franklin's
manuscripts also included anecdotes in their selections, as William
Temple Franklin did in his 1817 edition of his grandfather's writings.
In order to prepare for his ten-volume edition of Franklin's works,
Jared Sparks visited Philadelphia several times and met with Franklin's descendants, friends, and admirers. Delighted with his undertaking, many obliged him in every conceivable way. They introduced
him to the Franklin papers in Charles P. Fox's possession, allowed
Sparks to use Franklin's autograph papers owned by their families,
and fed him with "the little anecdotes and bits of family gossip and
tradition they relate."[58] Sparks heard of this incident:

[On the occasion of signing the Declaration of Independence], "We must
be unanimous," said [John] Hancock, "there must be no pulling different
ways; we must all hang together." "Yes," replied Franklin, "we must, indeed,
all hang together, or most assuredly we shall all hang separately."[59]

Little stories like these were exceedingly popular. Gradually they
became part of the shared perception of Franklin, even though anecdotal accounts are not entirely credible.[60] Because of the widespread popularity of those familiar stories, Americans appeared to
have possessed more insight of Franklin's personal characteristics
than those of other Revolutionary heroes. No matter how much Americans idealized Franklin, they were also aware of the human side of
him. Unlike George Washington's or John Adams's image, Franklin's
amiable reputation was not associated with rigidness and loftiness,
but with warmth, wit, and benevolence. He was never a noble saint,
but a wise and beloved patriarch. His renowned common sense and

---

57. Henry D. Gilpin, ed., *The Papers of James Madison* (Mobile, [Alabama] 1842),
    3: 1642.
58. Whitfield J. Bell, Jr., "Franklin's Papers and the Papers of Benjamin Franklin,"
    Pennsylvania History 22 (January 1955): 1–17.
59. Sparks, ed., *Works of Franklin* 1: 408. Anecdotes of Franklin can also be found
    in this volume, 85, 91, 373, 430.
60. For instance, Van Doren argued that the "hang separately" story was without
    historical foundation (*Franklin*, 551–52).

humorous outlook drew people to him. Even during this golden era of his fame, he was treated as a hero who was not above his people, but remained one of them.

Many knew that Franklin's life was not flawless because he had openly admitted his errors in the *Autobiography*. While his image was venerated, it is interesting to know how admirers explained his weaknesses. To begin with, not all people appreciated Franklin's candor in acknowledging his shortcomings. Rather, some critics found his admissions to be the source of his defective characteristics. John Adams believed that Franklin's "reputation was more universal than that of Leibnitz and Newton, Frederick or Voltaire, and his character more beloved and esteemed than any or all of them." At the same time he lamented:

Had he been blessed with the same advantages of scholarly education in his early youth, and pursued a course of studies as unembarrassed with occupations of public and private life, as Sir Isaac Newton, he might have emulated the first philosopher.[61]

Years later Charles Francis Adams declared that Franklin was "the embodiment of one great class of New England character." But he agreed with his grandfather adding:

The errors of Franklin's theory of life may be detected almost anywhere in his familiar compositions. They sprang from a defective early education, which made his morality superficial even to laxness, and undermined his religious faith. His system resolves itself into the ancient and specious dogma, of *honesty the best policy.* That nice sense which revolts at wrong for its own sake, and that generosity of spirit which shrinks from participating in the advantages of indirection, however naturally obtained, were not his.[62]

Nevertheless, for most of the first half of the nineteenth century, it was a general practice not to focus on the darker side of a public figure. Franklin's admirers did not have a conscious plan to protect his reputation. But most seemed to avoid mentioning his flaws. For example, except for his political enemies, few Americans publicly discussed the issue of his illegitimate son. Instead, Franklin was depicted

---

61. Charles Francis Adams, ed., *Works of John Adams* (Boston, 1850–56), 1: 660, 664.
62. Ibid., 319.

as a reputable family man who maintained warm relations with his wife, children, and relatives. When Jacob Abbott wrote a series of popular stories for *Harper's New Monthly Magazine,* he particularly drew readers' attention to Franklin's domestic life, for unlike many great men who owed their fame almost entirely to their public career, Franklin's reputation chiefly rested on "the power of his private and personal character"[63] (Fig. 5).

In some instances, however, discussion of Franklin's shortcomings was essential to a complete description of his experience. For example, Franklin broke his indenture with James and ran away from Boston. When discussing this, most observers were more lenient than critical; a common defense was to attribute that incident either to the older brother's harshness or to circumstances. In one of his public lectures on Franklin's youth Edward Everett told his audiences that Franklin was "worked hard, chid, and beaten," because James was "a harsh and unreasonable brother."[64]

On the other hand, while James Herring and James Barton Longacre believed that Franklin's escape from his brother was meant to take advantage of the latter, they explained it: "He, like many other distinguished characters, was much indebted to circumstance. It must be admitted, too, that he had many conceits, or fancies; that he was by no means without his foibles; and that, in his own phrase, he committed some great errors in the early part of his career."[65] When under the auspices of the American Academy of the Fine Arts Herring and Longacre compiled *The National Portrait Gallery,* a multi–volume project of portraits and biographies of famous Americans, they used Franklin and his portrait to head the second volume and gave him one of the longest biographies in their series. This was an unusual gesture of respect for Franklin, because all the rest of the leading figures in each volume were either presidents or war heroes.

Still, the most striking defense of Franklin came from printers, who were facing a chronic problem of runaway apprentices in their own

---

63. Abbott, "Early and Private Life of Benjamin Franklin," *Harper's New Monthly Magazine* 4 (January 1852), 145; "Public Life of Benjamin Franklin," 4 (February 1852), 299.

64. Everett, "Franklin the Boston Boy," *Orations and Speeches* 4: 126, 122.

65. Herring and Longacre, comps., *The National Portrait Gallery of Distinguished Americans* (New York, 1834–39), 2: 1, 3. Some Englishmen held a similar view of Franklin's escape, but their defense of his character was less vigorous than their American counterparts. Charles Knight, ed., *The Gallery of Portraits: With Memoirs* (London, 1833–37), 3: 78, 84–85.

HARPER'S
NEW MONTHLY MAGAZINE.

No. XX.—JANUARY, 1852.—Vol. IV.

EARLY AND PRIVATE LIFE OF BENJAMIN FRANKLIN.

BY JACOB ABBOTT.

IT is generally true in respect to great statesmen that they owe their celebrity almost entirely to their public and official career. They promote the welfare of mankind by directing legislation, founding institutions, negotiating treaties of peace or of commerce between rival states, and guiding, in various other ways, the course of public and national affairs, while their individual and personal influence attracts very little regard. With Benjamin Franklin, however, the reverse of this is true. He did indeed, while he lived, take a very active part, with other leading men of his time, in the performance of great public functions; but his claim to the extraordinary degree of respect and veneration which is so freely awarded to his name and memory by the American people, rests not chiefly upon this, but upon the extended influence which he has exerted, and which he still continues to exert upon the national mind, through the power of his private and personal character. The prevalence of habits of industry and economy, of foresight and thrift, of cautious calculation in the formation of plans, and energy and perseverance in the execution of them, and of the disposition to invest what is earned in substantial and enduring possessions, rather than to expend it in brief pleasures or for purposes of idle show—the

Vol. IV.—No 2.—K

prevalence of these traits, so far as they exist as elements of the national character in this country—is due in an incalculable degree to the doings and sayings and history of this great exemplar. Thus it is to his life and to his counsels that is to be attributed, in a very high degree, the formation of that great public sentiment prevailing so extensively among us, which makes it more honorable to be industrious than to be idle, and to be economical and prudent rather than extravagant and vain; which places substantial and unpretending prosperity above empty pretension, and real comfort and abundance before genteel and expensive display.

A very considerable portion of the effect which Franklin has produced upon the national character is due to the picturesque and almost romantic interest which attaches itself to the incidents of his personal history. In his autobiography he has given us a very full and a very graphic narrative of these incidents, and as the anniversary of his birth-day occurs during the present month, we can not occupy the attention of our readers at this time, in a more appropriate manner than by a brief review of the principal events of his life —so far as such a review can be comprised within the limits of a single article.

The ancestors of Franklin lived for many generations on a small estate in Northamptonshire, one of the central counties in England. The head of the family during all this time followed the business of a smith, the eldest son

from generation to generation, being brought up to that employment.

The Franklin family were Protestants, and at one time when the Catholics were in power, during the reign of Mary, the common people were forbidden to possess or to read the English Bible. Nevertheless the Franklin family contrived to get possession of a copy of the Scrip-

time.[66] Many printers must have known Franklin's escape. But it might have seemed unwise to note that this celebrated colonial printer was on the list of early runaways. Under these awkward circumstances, a printer named John L. Jewett not only sought to defend Franklin's name but also attempted to discover a virtue in his errant behavior.

He said that Franklin lived in an age when children were treated with "great harshness and severity." More than once James, who was a man of "irritable and violent temper," inflicted "heavy blows upon the embryo philosopher".[67] Therefore, Franklin only left his brother because of the unbearable conditions. Here, Jewett even failed to mention what Franklin himself had admitted: that he was, at least sometimes, "too saucy and provoking."[68] Furthermore, sounding like a self-appointed didact, Jewett added: "No man ever made a better use than Franklin of the injuries done him. He permitted them to remain vivid in his mind, only that they might nerve his resolution never in his turn to inflict like injuries upon others." According to this account, it seemed that a misdeed done to Franklin became an opportunity for him to demonstrate his moral strength.

Finally, the most troubling aspect of Franklin's life was his religious beliefs. As indicated before, Americans' firm commitment to republicanism did not erase all other traditions, including their religious heritage. Thus, no matter how much people admired Franklin, few would go so far as to say that his Christian faith and practice were flawless.

As the dominant religious tradition in the country, however, Protestantism was never monolithic. It was divided into numerous denominations, such as Congregationalists, Presbyterians, Quakers,

---

66. See Ethelbert Stewart's pioneer study, "A Documentary History of the Early Organization of Printers," in U.S. Department of Commerce and Labor, *Bulletin of the Bureau of Labor* 11 (November 1905), 929–30, 933–34, 967, 972. Also George A. Tracy, comp., *History of the Typographical Union* (Indianapolis, 1913), 34–36, 58–59, 64–70, 82–83, 107–08; and George A. Steves, *New York Typographical Union No. 6* (Albany, N.Y., 1913), 65–70, 143–46.

67. Jewett, *Franklin—His Genius, Life, and Character; An Oration Delivered before the N. Y. Typographical Society, on the Occasion of the Birthday of Franklin, at the Printers' Festival, Held January 17, 1849* (New York, 1849), 13, 14. Harsh treatments of apprentices seemed to continue into the early nineteenth century; see Rollo G. Silver, *The American Printers, 1787–1825* (Charlottesville, Va., 1967), 1–27.

68. *Autobiography*, 70. Franklin also wrote: "It was not fair in me to take this Advantage, and this I therefore reckon one of the first Errata of my life."

Methodists, Baptists, and Episcopalians. Under these circumstances, it was hard to say on whose tenets Franklin's religious life should be judged. On the other hand, Franklin was known for his detachment from sectarian disputes and his insistence on religious tolerance. Therefore, no matter how unorthodox his own religious beliefs and practice were, they did not necessarily threaten any particular religious institutions. As a matter of fact, among the most enthusiastic advocates of Franklin were many clergymen from different denominations, such as Weems and Horatio Hastings Weld.

Weems accepted Franklin's own assertion that the best way to serve God is by doing good to men. He pointed out that Franklin's benevolence and philanthropy were sufficient proofs of his devotion to Christ's teachings on love and kindness. Deeply aware of the numerous religious controversies of his own time, Weems added: "I know there are some in the world who cannot believe that God will ever give grace and salvation to men but in one way; and this way always happened to be their own way. . . . This made no part of doctor Franklin's religion."

He emphasized that Franklin's greatness lay in his extraordinary tolerance toward different sects and his indiscriminate love of man, both of which showed his understanding of one of the highest principles of Christianity—God's "infinite love." Weems further observed that even though Dr. Franklin had cared little for religious tenets, he must have received the sublime ideas of tolerance and love from Christ. There was little doubt, therefore, that because Franklin understood the foundation of the Christian religion so perfectly, he could be among the few who were qualified for eternal life[69] (Fig. 6).

It was true that few people, whether cleric or layman, were willing to defend Franklin's faith as explicitly as Weems, whose own religious practice was often regarded as non-orthodox. Still a permissive attitude was common. Many cautiously emphasized that they wished that Franklin had given more thought to his faith. In the meantime they tried not to miss any evidence of good will, to balance his perceived indifference toward religion. The Reverend Horatio Hastings Weld wrote in his biography of Franklin:

---

69. Weems, *The Life of Benjamin Franklin* (Philadelphia, 1818), 265. This was Weems's most outspoken defense of Franklin's faith. He modified his tone in subsequent editions. His book was still in print until 1884. Additional revisions regarding Franklin's religion were added in those posthumous editions, but little is known about who revised them. Emily Ellsworth Ford Skeel, ed., *Mason Locke Weems: His Works and Ways* (New York, 1929), 1: 128–41.

130   THE LIFE OF

CHAPTER XXII.

BEN, as we have seen, was never without a knot of choice spirits, like satelites constantly revolving around him, and both receiving and reflecting light. By these satelites I mean young men of fine minds and fond of books. He had at this time a *trio* of such. The first was of the name of Osborne, the second Watson, and the third Ralph. As the two first were a good deal of the nature of wandering stars, which though bright soon disappeared again, I shall let them pass away in silence. But the last, that's to say Ralph, shone so long in the same sphere with Ben, both in America and Europe, that it will never do to let him go without giving the reader somewhat at least of a telescopic squint at him.— James Ralph, then, was a young man of the first rate talents, ingenious at argument, of flowery fancy, most fascinating in his manners, and uncommonly eloquent. In short, he appears to have been built and equipped to run the voyage of life with as splendid success as any. But alas! as the seamen say of their ships, "*he took the wrong sheer*." Hence, while many a DULL GENIUS, with only a few plain-sailing virtues on board, such as honest industry and prudence, have made fine weather through life, and come into port at last laden *up to the bends* with riches and honors, this gallant PROA, this stately GONDOLA, the moment he put to sea was caught up in a Euroclydon of furious passions and appetites that shivered his character and peace, and made a wreck of him at the very outset.

According to his own account, it appears that Ben was often haunted with fears that he himself had some hand in Ralph's disasters. Dr. Franklin was

certainly one of the wisest of mankind. But with all his wisdom he was still but a man, and therefore liable to err. Solomon, we know, was fallible; what wonder then young Franklin?

But here lies the difference between these two wise men, as to their errors. Solomon, according to Scripture, was sometimes overcome of Satan, even in the bone and sinew of his strength; but the Devil was too hard for Franklin only while he was in the gristle of his youth. The case was thus: Among the myriads of books which came to his eager tooth, there was a most unlucky one on Deism, written, 'tis said, by Shaftsbury, a man admirably calculated to pervert the truth; or as Milton says of one of his fallen spirits, to make "*the worse appear the better reason*." Mark now this imposing writer—he does not utter you a word against Religion; not he indeed: no, not for the world. Why, sirs, he's the best friend of Religion. He praises it up to the skies, as the sole glory of man, the strong pillar of his virtues and the inexhaustible fountain of all his hopes. But then he cannot away with that false religion, that detestable superstition called Christianity. And here, to set his readers against it, he gives them a most horrible catalogue of the cruelties and bloody persecutions it has always occasioned in the world; nay, he goes so far as to assert that Christians are the *natural enemies of mankind*; "vainly conceiting themselves," says he, "to be the FAVORITES of heaven, they look on the rest of the world but as "HEATHEN DOGS" whom it is "doing God service to kill," and whose goods it is right to seize on, as spoil for the Lord's People! Who," asks he cravingly, "filled Asia with fire and sword in the bloody wars of the Crusades? The Christians. Who depopulated the fine negro-coasts of Africa? The Christians. Who extirpated many of the once glorious Indian nations of America? The Christians; nay," continues he, "so keen are these Christians for blood, that when they cant get their "*Heathen Dogs*" to fall on, they fall on one another: witness the Papist

6. Calling him "Ben," Mason Weems set out to defend Franklin's religion in this and other chapters of *Life of Benjamin Franklin,* Philadelphia, 1818.

In some of his opinions upon theological subjects he was unsettled; in some points he acknowledges he had doubts. . . . But he never intruded his doubts or his speculative opinions upon others. He never attempted to disturb any man's faith; and he most earnestly urged the celebrated Thomas Paine to burn the manuscript of a deistical work which he submitted to Franklin for perusal—to burn it before it met the eye of any other person, and thus save himself a good deal of regret and repentance.[70]

In a similar vein, Winthrop also said that he wished Franklin had studied the Gospel of Christ more seriously. But he added:

The devout reliance upon a superintending Providence, attested by frequent prayer, which characterized him from his youth upwards, and which

---

70. Weld, *Benjamin Franklin* (New York, 1848), 528–29.

never failed him in private or in public life,—his intimacy with Whitefield and with the "Good Bishop" of St. Asaph, —his earnest religious advice to his daughter, and his strenuous remonstrance against the infidel publications of Paine, —furnish ample evidence of a reverence for sacred things and solemn observances, which might well put to shame the indifference of not a few of those who may be most disposed to cavil about his views of Christianity.[71]

To summarize, although many people still did not believe Franklin had a firm faith, his religious life, or lack thereof, was no longer a grave threat to his reputation. His weakness in religion was only marginally noticed; his insistence on doing good, however, was widely lauded and his assertion of religious tolerance and harmony was a clear indicator of his moral strength.

---

71. Winthrop, *Addresses and Speeches* 2: 275.

Chapter 3

"We All Unite to Honor Him"

"Character is this moral order seen through the medium of an individual nature." Ralph Waldo Emerson wrote this often quoted sentence in his discourse on character in *Essays: Second Series,* published in 1844. Earnestly seeking a reconciliation of man with nature, the Transcendentalist believed that "character is nature in the highest form" and an undiminishable force which "lies in the man." Great men's lives, therefore, "are documents of character," and "men of character are the conscience of the society to which they belong."[1]

Emerson's contemplation of the spiritual meanings in character was only one dimension of his contemporaries' concerns with the matter. When the young minister Lyman Beecher began his career at East Hampton, Long Island, one of the first things he did was to organize a moral society in 1803. A decade later after moving to Litchfield, Connecticut, he urged the authorities to pass state laws against immorality. He called for the establishment of a series of statewide organizations, while his proposed Connecticut Society for the Reformation of Morals would function as "the parent and patron of local auxiliary societies." "Let it once be known," Beecher declared, "that a fair private character is indispensable to the attainment of public suffrage."[2]

If Beecher's emphasis on character was a familiar exhortation on the close relations between private conduct and public good, more ingenuity and imagination would be needed to adopt the same concept in a different context. In order to promote the scheme of the Erie Canal, governor De Witt Clinton addressed the New York legislature,

---

1. Quoted in Alfred R. Ferguson et al., eds., *The Collected Works of Ralph Waldo Emerson* (Cambridge, Mass. 1971–), 3: 53–67.
2. Richard Rabinowitz, *The Spiritual Self in Everyday Life* (Boston, 1989), 81, 83, 142–43.

saying that "character is as important to states as to individuals, and the glory of a republic founded on the promotion of the general good, is the common property of all its citizens."[3]

Catharine Beecher, the eldest daughter of the Reverend Lyman Beecher, published her own discourse entitled *The Elements of Mental and Moral Philosophy, Founded upon Experience, Reason and the Bible* in 1831. Convinced that the book has demonstrated a shift of emphases from piety to morality, historian Kathryn Kish Sklar observed: "Catharine's decision to emphasize proper character formation rather than conversion may have arisen from her need to find a more inclusive and universal principle around which she could organize the studies of her class." Whereas Catharine Beecher admitted that she was "much engaged in moulding, correcting, and inspecting the character of others" in the 1830s, her sister Harriet Beecher Stowe later published one of the most explosive novels of antebellum America, *Uncle Tom's Cabin*. Speaking against the evil of slavery, Mrs. Stowe not only attempted to awaken the conscience of her readers in the North, but also passionately appealed to the "magnanimity and purity of character" of slave owners to reconsider their un-Christian behavior.[4]

It is clear that these frequent references to character served different spiritual, moral, social, and ideological purposes. Likewise, it would be misleading to suggest that widespread as people's praise was, their interest in Franklin's character originated only from economic motivations. In order to understand his popularity during this period, one needs further to analyze how Americans commemorated Franklin under different circumstances and in diverse forms.

I

Increasing admiration of Franklin coincided with a growing number of artifacts. Toward the end of the 1780s directors of the Library Company of Philadelphia began to plan a new building. They decided that a statue should be erected as a tribute to their most prominent founder, Benjamin Franklin. On April 4, 1792, they received a letter from the Philadelphia banker, and later senator, William Bing-

---

3. Quoted in Lionel D. Wyld, ed., *40′ x 28′ x 4′: The Erie Canal—150 Years* (Rome, N.Y., 1967), 12.

4. Sklar, *Catharine Beecher: A Study in American Domesticity* (Norton Library ed.: New York, 1976), 78–89; Stowe, *Uncle Tom's Cabin* (Cambridge, Mass., 1962), 453, 455.

ham, who informed them that their long awaited statue had finally arrived. The letter read:

Gentlemen,

The Respect I bore to the Memory of that deceased Patriot, Philosopher and Statesman, Dr. Franklin, induced me to engage to carry your Intentions, of erecting a Marble Statue to perpetuate, in the Minds of his Fellow-Citizens, the recollection of his public and private Virtues, into full Effect.

The Statue has, at length, arrived, and I have the honor of inclosing to you the Bill of Lading. —If I may credit the communications of my Correspondents, it is fashioned out from a beautiful block of Marble and is executed in a very masterly Stile, and is, in every respect, worthy of the distinguished Personage whom it is intended to represent: —As such I request your acceptance of it, and to believe me a sincere Friend to your Institution.[5]

His gift was happily accepted. Within a week it was placed in a huge niche over the front door of the new library on Fifth Street. It was a full-figure statue more than five feet high. A report in the *Universal Asylum and Columbian Magazine* told the public that the elegant sculpture, worth 500 guineas, had been executed by an Italian artist, François Lazzarini. The report went on to describe the latest embellishment of the city as follows: "The statue of Dr. Franklin is a full length figure, erect, clad with a Roman toga—the position easy and graceful—in the right hand is a sceptre reversed, the elbow resting on books placed on a pedestal—the left hand, a little extended, holds a scroll."[6]

This imported ornament pleased the directors of the library, who believed that as "the most finished Specimen of Sculpture America can exhibit," the statue was "much admired."[7] They did not exaggerate. As the first monument in the nation to honor Franklin, the statue became a distinctive landmark in Philadelphia and heralded a long history of using Franklin's image to promote contemporary interests.

Franklin once said that, because of the enthusiasm of continental artists, his face had become "as well known as that of the moon." It is true that when Franklin was alive, most of his portraits were painted by European artists. Nevertheless, when his autobiography initially appeared in France and England between 1791 and 1793, none of

---

5. Library Company of Philadelphia, *Minutes of the Proceedings of the Directors of the Library Company of Philadelphia*, 3: 301.

6. *Universal Asylum and Columbian Magazine* 8–9 (1792), 284.

7. *Minutes of the Library Company*, 3: 304, 306.

the publishers thought it necessary to include his portrait in these editions. It was in the first American editions printed at New York and Philadelphia in 1794 that a picture of Franklin was used as a frontispiece. Thereafter his writings were rarely published without a portrait.[8]

Through numerous engravings, the American public had the opportunity to encounter some of the most famous paintings of Franklin. In addition to Duplessis's "fur collar" portrait, two of the most frequently reproduced pictures were those by Charles Nicolas Cochin ("fur cap and spectacles" portrait, 1777) and by David Martin (depicting Franklin's chin resting upon his thumb, or "thumb" portrait, 1766). J. A. Houdon's bust of Franklin was very well known for it was copied in several replicas and in a great number of engravings. To a lesser extent, the public was also familiar with Franklin's portraits painted by Benjamin Wilson (1759), Mason Chamberlin (1762), Charles Willson Peale (1785), and Benjamin West (1784–85).[9]

To be sure, each of these artists had his own perspective, while all portrayed him with dignity. For example, the pictures painted by Cochin, Peale, and West stressed Franklin's simple dress and plainness, whereas Wilson and Martin presented him as a classical scholar in elegant clothes. Furthermore, those artists seemed to hold different views about improving Franklin's appearance. Thus, while Martin's and Wilson's portraits clearly showed the warts on Franklin's left cheek, others did not.

A portrait of Franklin should certainly present his likeness. Yet American publishers and editors seldom used those portraits for this purpose alone. In fact, for a long time the size of many engravings was so small and their quality so poor that his profile in those pictures was highly unreliable. Weems was among those booksellers who realized that illustrations could attract potential readers. He believed that if he had stories of patriotic heroes printed in small volumes, each of them with an interesting frontispiece, he would be able to sell "an immense number of them." Thus, when he published a life of Franklin, he repeatedly wrote to his publisher, Mathew Carey, requesting a

---

8. A conspicuous exception was William Temple Franklin's *Memoirs of the Life and Writings of Benjamin Franklin* (1817–18).

9. Historical Society of Pennsylvania, Benjamin Franklin, Society Portrait Collection; Charles Coleman Sellers, *Benjamin Franklin in Portraiture* (New Haven, 1962).

frontispiece of Franklin and sometimes asking for as many as a thousand copies of the picture.[10]

Some authors adopted an illustration of Franklin as a symbol of success. In his *Franklin Primer*, which included numerous woodcuts, Samuel Willard pointed out that he had "introduced the Bust of Dr. Benjamin Franklin, as a frontispiece; a man whose manner of life, from youth's first dawning morn to man's meridian day, is worthy the imitation of all who would wish to thrive upon this World's vast theatre"[11] (Fig. 7). Samuel G. Goodrich ascribed his success in selling children's books to the use of illustrations. He believed that the eye, as the master organ of the human senses, was the means to secure a child's interest.[12] His tactic was particularly useful when discussing such qualities as hard work, frugality, and economy. Depicting Franklin as a diligent young printer, Goodrich helped young readers to visualize those abstract economic virtues (Fig. 8).

The many European portraits of Franklin copied by American engravers and illustrators did not satisfy all of the nation's demand. For one thing, most depicted Franklin as an accomplished older man, whereas many Americans were interested in his youth. Some lesser-known native artists met the need. For example, artists like David Rent Etter and John Gadsby Chapman, and engravers like Reuben S. Gilbert and William B. Gihon, had often portrayed Franklin as a tallow-chandler and printer. Neither their artistic skill nor the authenticity of Franklin's likeness could match those of their European counterparts. But their pictures were adopted by several authors.[13]

There is little evidence that Franklin's image was caricatured during the first half of the nineteenth century.[14] Even in a pictorial broadside

---

10. Marcus Cunliffe, ed., *The Life of Washington by Mason L. Weems* (Cambridge, Mass., 1962), xiii–xiv; Skeel, ed., *Weems: His Works and Ways*, 1: 130, 131, 133, 135, 137.

11. [Willard], introduction, *The Franklin Primer: Containing a New and Useful Selection of Moral lessons, Adorned with a Great Variety of ELEGANT CUTS, Calculated to Strike a Lasting Impression on the Tender Minds of Children* (Boston, 1803).

12. Goodrich, *Recollections of a Lifetime* (New York, 1859), 2: 310–11.

13. [Horatio Hastings Weld? or John Frost?], *Pictorial Life of Benjamin Franklin* (Philadelphia, 1846). Weld, *Benjamin Franklin* (New York, 1848). Jacob Abbott, "Early and Private Life of Benjamin Franklin," "Public Life of Benjamin Franklin," *Harper's New Monthly Magazine* 4 (1852), 145–65, 289–309. Abbott, *Franklin, The Apprentice Boy* (New York, 1855).

14. His image was in some cartoons during the colonial period; see Coleman, *Franklin in Portraiture*, plates 6, 7; Martin P. Snyder, *City of Independence: Views of Philadelphia before 1800* (New York, 1975), 74–80.

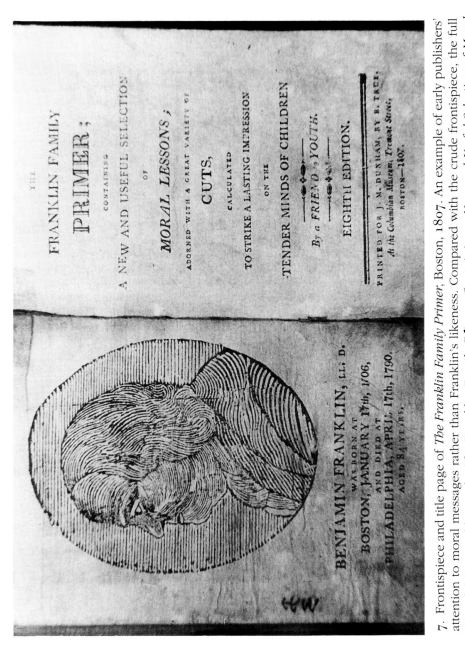

THE

FRANKLIN FAMILY

PRIMER;

CONTAINING

A NEW AND USEFUL SELECTION

OF

MORAL LESSONS;

ADORNED WITH A GREAT VARIETY OF

CUTS,

CALCULATED

TO STRIKE A LASTING IMPRESSION

ON THE

TENDER MINDS OF CHILDREN

By a FRIEND to YOUTH.

EIGHTH EDITION.

PRINTED FOR J. M. DUNHAM, BY B. TRUE,
At the Columbian Museum, Tremont Street,
BOSTON—1807.

BENJAMIN FRANKLIN, LL. D.
WAS BORN AT
BOSTON, JANUARY 17th, 1706,
AND DIED AT
PHILADELPHIA, APRIL 17th, 1790.
AGED 84 YEARS.

7. Frontispiece and title page of *The Franklin Family Primer*, Boston, 1807. An example of early publishers' attention to moral messages rather than Franklin's likeness. Compared with the crude frontispiece, the full title of this pamphlet reads: *The Franklin Family Primer; Containing a New and Useful Selection of Moral Lessons; Adorned with a Great Variety of CUTS, Calculated to Strike a Lasting Impression on the Tender Minds of Children.* Previously in an 1803 edition, the phrase was "a Great Variety of ELEGANT CUTS." (By permission of the Houghton Library, Harvard University)

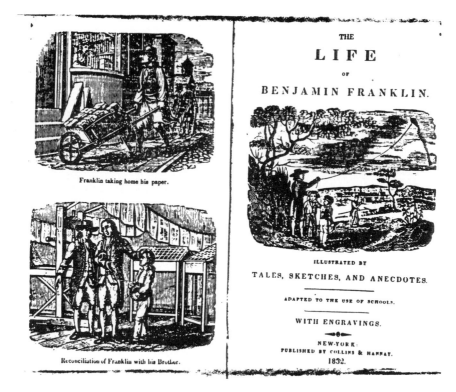

8. Frontispiece and title page of Samuel Goodrich's *Life of Benjamin Franklin*, New York, 1832.

such as *Bowle's Moral Pictures*, which was aimed at a less-educated audience, his formal portrait occupied the center of the page. A typical self-made man and a symbol of frugality, his portrait frequently appeared in commercial offices and on business certificates. The federal postal service, in memory of their first postmaster general, adopted his portrait on one of the first stamps issued in the United States in 1847. About the same time, as many as twenty-six states, including not only those in the Northeast but also Illinois, Tennessee, Mississippi, and Florida, printed bank notes bearing his likeness.[15]

Finally, the proliferation of Franklin's portrait reflected a wish to cherish his image as an icon. Sometimes the *Historical Magazine* received several letters within a few months, asking the whereabouts of particular Franklin portraits, such as the one painted by the Abbé

---

15. John A. Muscalus, ed., *An Index of State Bank Notes That Illustrate Washington and Franklin* (Bridgeport, Penn., 1938).

de Saint Non ("Dr. Franklin Crowned by Liberty," 1778), and the one that Franklin bequeathed to the Supreme Executive Council of Pennsylvania.[16] When George Bancroft wanted to use Franklin's portrait to decorate the third volume of his history of the United States, he instructed his agent in London to have an engraving of Franklin made, with the warts on the face erased.[17] Bancroft was not alone. A few years later at a convention of the National Typographical Union in 1859, a delegate from New York named Charles W. Colburn moved that the picture of the head of Franklin be omitted from the union's traveling card. His proposal caused "an animated discussion." Apparently, an overwhelming majority of the delegates believed that Franklin's picture was a valuable symbol to maintain; the motion was rejected by a vote of 24 to 2.[18]

II

Franklin's memoirs, publicly known as his *Autobiography*, had a special place in people's memories. Some regarded it as an influential handbook for success. Others believed that it was a masterpiece of American literature. In either case, few would deny that Franklin's *Autobiography* was one of his most important legacies.

Within a month after Franklin's death in May 1790 the *Universal Asylum and Columbian Magazine* began to publish Henry Stuber's serialized "History of the Life and Character of Benjamin Franklin." Two months later Mathew Carey, in his *American Museum*, issued "Memoirs of the Late Benjamin Franklin."[19] In this piece Carey informed the public that the deceased had written an account of his own life.[20] From Franklin's publicized will people learned that his

---

16. *Historical Magazine, and Notes and Queries Concerning the Antiquities, History and Biography of America* 3 (1859), 252; 4 (1860), 369; 8 (1864), 147.

17. Russel B. Nye, *George Bancroft: Brahmin Rebel* (New York, 1945), 126.

18. George A. Tracy, comp., *History of the Typographical Union* (Indianapolis, 1913), 183.

19. For extensive descriptions of early publications of Franklin's memoirs see Max Farrand, ed., *Benjamin Franklin's Memoirs: Parallel Text Edition* (Berkeley, 1949), xiii–xxxvii; J. A. Leo Lemay and P. M. Zall, eds., *The Autobiography of Benjamin Franklin: A Genetic Text* (Knoxville, [Tenn.] 1981), xlviii–lviii.

20. Some of Franklin's friends already knew his plans. Thomas Jefferson recalled that "since his return to America [from France in 1785], he had been preoccupied in preparing for the world the history of his own life." Merrill D. Peterson, ed., *Thomas Jefferson: Writings* (Library of America ed.: New York, 1984), 99. Franklin wrote to Mathew Carey on 10 August 1786, and declined publication

grandson, William Temple Franklin, had inherited his papers and manuscripts and would thus become his literary executor.[21] Informed people then anticipated Temple Franklin's publications, including his grandfather's autobiography.

Claiming that he would publish his grandfather's works as soon as he could, Temple Franklin nonetheless sold Franklin's library and left the country for England before the end of 1790. For the next twenty years he failed to publish anything. This inaction not only caused deep concern about the fate of one of the nation's most treasured literary assets, it also led to speculation about the grandson's integrity.

The uneasiness of Franklin's admirers was further aggravated when foreign critics began to exploit the situation. In 1791 the first part of Franklin's memoirs was translated into French by Jacques Gilelin and published by Buisson of Paris. Handsomely bound in hard covers, the Buisson edition was a fine example of French craftsmanship. The text was printed in fine type with generous margins, and the paper was exquisitely white, thin, and veined. Inside the lovely book, however, the publisher challenged the literary heir of the late Franklin. He pointed out that the later part of Franklin's career was closely connected to important political events which, to a large extent, had already made him famous. His volume therefore included "no more than the first period" of Franklin's life which, he suspected, Franklin's heirs might not have the courage to publish. "They will never," the

---

of his memoirs; see Albert Henry Smyth, ed., *The Writings of Benjamin Franklin* (New York, 1905–07), 9: 533–34.

21. *The Pennsylvania Mercury and Universal Advertiser*, 20 May 1790, p. 3; *The Pennsylvania Journal and the Weekly Advertiser*, 22 May 1790, p. 3.

William Temple Franklin (1760–1823) was the illegitimate son of William Franklin, who was appointed royal governor of New Jersey. He grew up under the protection of the famous Dr. Franklin, but his life was tormented as a result of the estrangement between his royalist father and his revolutionary grandfather. Eventually, he became a spoiled Philadelphia dandy, achieved little in his career, and died in obscurity in Paris. Over the years only scattered information about him could be found: J. Bennett Nolan, "The Only Franklin in Franklin's College," reprint from *The General Magazine and Historical Chronicle* (University of Pennsylvania, October 1939). But his frivolous life style has been a topic of literary satire for a long time; see, for example, Polan Banks's novel *The Gentleman from America* (New York, 1930). Biographical references to him are in Claude-Anne Lopez and Eugenia W. Herbert, *The Private Franklin: The Man and His Family* (New York, 1975). For the most recent discussion of his life see the series of articles by Claude-Anne Lopez, "On the Trail of the Last Franklin," *Franklin Gazette* (publication of the Friends of Franklin, Philadelphia), 2 (Summer 1991), n.p., and to date.

French editor asserted, "be prevailed upon to narrate the humble details of his early days and the simple but interesting anecdotes of his origin, the obscurity of which, although it enhances the talents and the virtues of this great man, may yet wound their own vanity."[22]

Two years after the first French edition, in July 1793, two English editions appeared in London. Both were retranslations from the French. Soon afterward two American editions were finally printed in 1794. After that numerous versions of Franklin's life were published almost annually on both sides of the Atlantic. Still, some people realized that none of these editions and reprints was based on either the author's native tongue or his original manuscript. All were pirated translations or retranslations from the French. By the end of the century, in 1798, a new French collection of Franklin's writings was published in Paris. The translator, Jean-Henry Castéra, also expressed his doubt by declaring, "It is not known why M. Benjamin Franklin Bache, who has them [the memoirs and other writings] in his possession, and is now residing in London, keeps them so long from the public. The works of a great man belong less to his heirs than to the human race."[23] Castéra, of course, confused grandson Bache with grandson Franklin.

In 1806 two London publishers, Johnson and Longman, issued three volumes of Franklin's writings. This time, an open attack was waged against Temple Franklin in a prefatory advertisement:

The proprietor, it seems, had found a bidder of a different description in some emissary of government, whose object was to withhold the manuscripts from the world, not to benefit it by their publication; and they thus either passed into other hands, or the person to whom they were bequeathed received a remuneration for suppressing them.[24]

When Francis Jeffrey (later Lord Jeffrey), the editor of the *Edinburgh Review*, commented on that edition in a long article, he disagreed with the accusation. He did complain, however, that "nothing, we think, can shew more clearly, the singular want of literary enterprize or activity, in the States of America, than that no one has yet been

---

22. Quoted in John Bigelow, ed., *The Life of Benjamin Franklin* (Philadelphia, 1874), 1: 41.

23. Quoted in John Bigelow, ed., *The Works of Benjamin Franklin*, 12 vols. (Federal ed.: New York, 1904), 1: vii.

24. [_____ Marshall and Benjamin Vaughan, eds.], *The Complete Works of Benjamin Franklin*, 3 vols. (London, 1806), 1: viii–ix.

found in that flourishing republic to collect and publish the works of their only philosopher."[25]

Neither the charge nor Jeffrey's commentary went unnoticed, especially after the latter's article was reprinted or quoted several times in a number of publications throughout the United States.[26] Perhaps a similar concern was in William Ellery Channing's mind when he lamented in 1815 that the country's reputation suffered for its want of literary distinction. He particularly noted that only foreigners succeeded in compiling excellent selections of American writers—"thus England boasts the first and best editions of our own Franklin."[27]

Waiting for an authentic edition of Franklin's works exhausted the patience of concerned citizens, and frustration led some of them to blame Temple Franklin. In an article printed in a newspaper in New York James Cheetham even went so far as to assert that "William Temple Franklin, without shame, without remorse, mean and mercenary, sold the sacred deposit, committed to his care by Dr. Franklin, to the British government. Franklin's works are therefore lost to the world."[28] About the same time, a similar charge was brought against Temple Franklin in the *National Intelligencer* of Washington. Its story hinted that he had transferred his copyright to a London publisher who, in turn, sold the copyright to the British government in order to suppress the publication.[29]

These speculations and allegations were groundless. For one thing, it was unlikely that the British government in the 1790s should feel a paramount need to suppress Franklin's writings or memoirs, which dealt with his life only up to 1757.[30] In fact, during the period

---

25. *Edinburgh Review* 8 (July 1806): 327.

26. See, for example, "Character of Dr. Franklin," *The American Register, or, General Repository of History, Politics, & Science* 1 (1806–07): 150–59.

27. [Channing], "Reflections on the Literary Delinquency of America," *North American Review* 2 (November 1815): 33.

28. *The American Citizen*, 8 September 1806. Six months later the article was reprinted in a tri-weekly called *The Argus or London Review in Paris* on 28 March 1807. On the same day Temple Franklin wrote a lengthy rebuttal to the editor, denying the accusation. At that time Thomas Jefferson subscribed to both *The American Citizen* and *The Argus*; it was not hard for him to notice the controversy. Bigelow, *Life of Franklin* 1: 62; Julian P. Boyd et al., eds., *The Papers of Thomas Jefferson* (Princeton, 1950–), 18: 88–89n.

29. Smyth, *Writings of Franklin* 1: 27.

30. Interestingly enough, it was Secretary of State Thomas Jefferson who believed that not all Dr. Franklin's papers, particularly his records of foreign negotiations, should be published. While he encouraged Temple Franklin's endeavor, he said to him that "I am sure your delicacy needs no hint from me against the

from 1790 to the end of the 1820s, a considerable part of his work was published in England. For example, fourteen editions of his *Autobiography* (out of a total of forty-one), and forty-one imprints of his works (out of sixty-four) were issued by English publishers. In other words, one-third of the autobiography and more than 60 percent of his selected writings were printed in England, not in America.[31] English publishers at this time were, to say the least, as active as their American counterparts in turning out Franklin's writings.

Furthermore, few people knew that the reason Temple Franklin promptly left for England was because he was engaged in a private business commissioned by Robert Morris, who had been a principal financier of the American Revolution.[32] As early as September 1790, Morris approached Temple Franklin and asked him to be his European agent in the sale of more than one million acres of land, which he had purchased from Oliver Phelps and Nathaniel Gorham. Within a few months after Temple Franklin arrived in England, he succeeded in making the sale. Three British gentlemen, Patrick Colquhoun, William Hornby, and Sir William Johnstone Pulteney, bought the land and agreed to pay a total of £ 75,000. On February 15, 1791, Colquhoun and Temple Franklin signed the preliminary articles of agreement. A month later a final agreement was reached (Fig. 9). According to the terms of his commission, Temple Franklin earned 10 percent of the sale or about £ 7,000.[33]

publication of such letters from Dr. Franklin as Minister Plenipotiary [*sic*] of the U.S. as might not yet be proper to put into the possession of everybody" (Jefferson to Temple Franklin, 27 November 1790, Boyd, *The Papers of Jefferson* 18: 87, 89n).

31. Numbers of the American and English editions are based on references registered in *The National Union Catalog: Pre-1956 Imprints* (London, 1971), 183: 100–81. This catalogue should be read along with Paul Leicester Ford's still valuable *Franklin Bibliography: A List of Books Written by or Relating to Benjamin Franklin* (Brooklyn, N.Y. 1889).

32. Ellis Paxson Oberholtzer, *Robert Morris: Patriot and Financier* (New York, 1903), 302–03.

33. Barbara A. Chernow's extensive investigation clearly shows Temple Franklin's agenda, "Robert Morris: Genesee Land Speculator," *New York History* 58 (April 1977): 195–220, esp. 195–207. See also her *Robert Morris: Land Speculator, 1790–1801* (New York, 1978), chap. 2, esp. 48–61. A transcript of the articles of agreement between William Temple Franklin and Patrick Colquhoun in March 1791 can be found in *Copies of Deeds of Conveyance and Agreements Relative to the Genesee Lands, 1790* in the Ontario Historical Society at Canandaigua, New York. In addition, numerous letters to and from Robert Morris, Gouverneur Morris, William Temple Franklin, and their British counterparts, are kept in the Gouverneur Morris Papers, Columbia University Libraries.

9. Transcript of the agreement signed between William Temple Franklin and Patrick Colquhoun in March 1791 for the sale of more than one million acres of land. The agreement shows that the total sale was 75,000 pounds. (By permission of the Ontario Historical Society, Canandaigua, New York)

Secretary of State Thomas Jefferson and Gouverneur Morris of New York were among the few who knew of Temple Franklin's engagement. In fact, when Robert Morris approached Temple, he also contacted Gouverneur Morris, hoping that the latter could represent him in England. Gouverneur Morris declined on the ground that he had previously accepted from Jefferson a mission to that nation. He felt it would be improper to become a private agent in the same country at the same time. His decision left Robert Morris with little choice but to rely on Temple Franklin. While in England, however, Gouverneur Morris not only maintained contact with Temple Franklin but advised Robert Morris about the entire transaction. It is likely that Gouverneur Morris informed Jefferson about Temple Franklin's activities in London. Thus Jefferson was able to report to President George Washington on March 27, 1791, "You knew of Mr. R. Morris's purchase of Gorham and Phelps of 1,300,000 acres of land of the state of Massachusetts, at 5d. an acre. It is said that he has sold 1,200,000. acres of these in Europe thro' the agency of W. Franklin, who it seems went on this business conjointly with that of printing his grand father's works."[34]

In any event, Temple was so excited about his successful business involvement that he wrote a letter from London to Louis-Guillaume Le Veillard in France on June 14, 1791, boasting about his handsome income.[35] Unfortunately, this letter was later discovered by John Bigelow. Not knowing the land speculation in which Temple Franklin had been involved, Bigelow seriously doubted that he could have reaped such a huge amount of money except as a payoff bribe from the British government. Comparing this with his father's acceptance of the royal governorship before the Revolution, Bigelow speculated that "it is not impossible that the grandson, after residing a while in London, succumbed to a similar weakness." He wrote:

When this [letter of June 14, 1791] was written, Dr. Franklin had been dead but about a year; the writer had been in London barely six months. He never pretended in his correspondence before to have any other business there than to edit his grandfather's works; he suddenly engages himself upon a salary; in less than six months finishes his business, and pockets a profit of £7,000, or say $35,000. While earning this handsome sum he was expecting

---

34. Boyd, *The Papers of Jefferson* 19: 626.

35. M. Le Veillard was an intimate friend of Dr. Franklin. He was mayor of Passy, where Franklin resided for several years during his mission to France. In the late 1780s Franklin sent a copy of his memoirs to him and to Benjamin Vaughan in England. Le Veillard died on the guillotine in the Reign of Terror in 1794 (*Autobiography* 27, 35).

to go in a few days or weeks to Paris, being only detained in London to finish his book. It is not easy to imagine any salaried employment, especially such a profitable one as this seemed to be, which imposed so light a restraint upon the movements of its beneficiary.

From whatever source this £ 7,000 came, and however little or much the acquisition of it had to do with the delay in the publication of his grandfather's works, it is certainly to be regretted that so little is known of the business engagement which was entered into so suddenly, was of such brief duration, and yet yielded such generous profits.[36]

Temple Franklin was certainly aware of the annoying rumors and suspicions about him.[37] But he could not possibly have imagined that one day records of his business income and private correspondence would be exposed as evidence against his reputation. In the public eye, he failed to make any convincing defense of his inaction, and the

---

36. Bigelow, *Life of Franklin* 1: 59–60; and his edition, *The Complete Works of Benjamin Franklin* (New York, 1887–88), 1: xx–xxii.

Three decades before Bigelow, another diligent student of Franklin, Jared Sparks, had been reluctant to follow most of those charges. Although he did not know Temple Franklin's private business at the time, he suggested that, instead of assuming the British government's involvement, readers could find the reason for the delayed publication within the family itself. He wrote that "[Temple Franklin's] father, William Franklin, died in 1813. He had been a pensioner on the British government, in consequence of the part he had taken in the Revolution; and it is probable that he may have been averse to the publication of his father's papers during his lifetime." After many years Bigelow was still unable to draw any conclusions for lack of further evidence. But he seemed to have modified his views and thus speculated in 1904:

The £ 7,000, if he ever received any such sum, may have been the proceeds of some job or contract which his father, towards whom the government no doubt felt kindly, may have procured, and in which he may have given his son an interest to indemnify him for deferring his publication. This, of course, is only conjecture, but it is far more probable than that the British government, several years after the peace, should have paid that or any other sum to stifle the utterances of any rebel American.

Spark's and Bigelow's skepticism about the father was not surprising, but two issues remained to be proved: first, William Franklin's unrestrained resentment against the deceased and, second, his extraordinary influence in obtaining profitable positions in England. Little proof has thus far been uncovered to sustain such "conjecture." Sparks, ed., *The Works of Benjamin Franklin* (Boston, 1836–40), 1: x–xi; Bigelow, *The Works of Franklin* 1: xviii. Biographer William Sterne Randall suggests that toward the end of his life William Franklin was delighted when, after a long time of separation, Temple suddenly wrote from Paris in 1813 that he would soon return to England and begin editing Franklin's papers (*A Little Revenge: Benjamin Franklin and His Son* [Boston, 1984], 496). The most recent study of William is Sheila L. Skemp, *William Franklin: Son of a Patriot, Servant of a King* (New York, 1990).

37. Sparks, *The Works of Franklin* 1: x–xi.

rumors continued.[38] When, in 1808, the first volume of a new publication of Franklin's works edited by William Duane appeared in Philadelphia, Temple Franklin realized that, even though he was the literary executor, others possessed a considerable portion of his grandfather's unpublished manuscripts as well.[39] It also became apparent that, if he still wanted to gain maximum benefit, he ought to have his edition ready soon, or else the sale of Duane's selections might greatly reduce his potential profits.

Henry Stevens, an American book dealer in London, later pointed out that the real reason for Temple Franklin's delay was that "he was unmethodical muddler" and "uncommonly dilatory in his habits." No matter how much the grandfather had trusted him, "for himself he was not born to finish anything."[40] Handicapped as an incompetent editor and under the pressure of his publisher Henry Colburn, Temple Franklin later hired a clerk to help him with the task. He and Duane also managed to make an arrangement by which they divided their market between London and Philadelphia.[41] Temple Franklin's selections finally came out in London in 1817 and 1818. The first edition was in three quarto volumes,[42] and the second was in six octavo volumes.[43]

---

38. For instance, W. MacDonald reiterated the charges in his introduction to *Benjamin Franklin's Autobiography* (Everyman's Library ed.: London, 1908), which was reprinted at least six times until the 1920s.

39. Duane had been the foreman and partner in Benjamin Franklin Bache's print shop in Philadelphia. Two years after Bache's death in 1798, Duane married his widow Margaret Markoe and gained access to some of Franklin's papers in that family. Claude-Anne Lopez and Eugenia W. Herbert, *The Private Franklin*, 312. For additional sources of Franklin's unpublished papers see *Papers* 1: xxi–xxiv.

40. Henry Stevens, *Stevens's Historical Collections* (London, 1881), 16of. Albert H. Smyth holds a similar view: "[Franklin] seems to have entertained an exaggerated notion of Temple's abilities, and to have believed him capable of properly sorting, arranging, and editing these multitudinous papers and giving them permanent literary form. But Temple Franklin had neither literary faculty nor historic sense; he was indolent and timid, and aghast at the magnitude of the task before him" (Smyth, *The Writings of Franklin* 1: 3).

41. For the business relationship between Temple Franklin, William Duane, and Colburn see Stevens, *Stevens's Historical Collections*, 16ok; Sparks, *The Works of Franklin* 1: xi; and Smyth, *The Writings of Franklin* 1: 30.

42. Temple had the grand idea of quarto form since the time of Franklin's death. See his letter to Thomas Jefferson from Philadelphia on 13 October 1790. Jefferson's advice, however, was to publish "Dr. Franklin's works in 8vo. otherwise I think you will find fewer purchasers." Temple only seemed to be persuaded; see his reply to Jefferson on 6 April 1791, Boyd, *The Papers of Jefferson* 17: 591; 18: 87; 20: 158.

43. Ford, *Franklin Bibliography*, nos. 561, 562.

However late it might be, many people welcomed the new publication, especially the new text of Franklin's memoirs included in the edition, a text believed to be genuinely based on the patriarch's original manuscripts. John Adams, not previously an enthusiastic advocate of Franklin, wrote a warm note to the editor:

> The volume of Dr. Franklin's Correspondence has seemed to make me live over again my Life at Passy. I rejoice that the Publick are to have a compleat Edition of his Works, for there is scarce a scratch of his Pen that is not worth preserving. —I am pleased to see you at length appearing on the stage of human Affairs.[44]

But others found little merit in the editorial style of the latest edition. An article in the *North American Review* seemed to suggest that the quality of the new edition was mediocre, for "there was not much to praise—or to censure." The review went on to complain that "where Dr. Franklin's own accounts of his life failed him, he [the editor] had supplied a narrative of his own; and he is but an indifferent writer. The transition to his style from Dr. Franklin's is rather abrupt and unpleasant."[45]

Above all, the old suspicions lingered and men as distinguished as Thomas Jefferson doubted the authenticity of the edition and the reliability of its editor. Jefferson called attention to a missing document that he had once possessed. It was written by Franklin about his negotiations in England up to the eve of the Revolution. This document, Jefferson believed, contained reports that revealed the unyielding attitude of the British ministry. Jefferson wrote in his autobiography in 1821:

> If this [document] is not among the papers published, we ask what has become of it? I delivered it with my own hands into those of Temple Franklin. It certainly established views so atrocious in the British government that its suppression would to them be worth a great price. But could the grandson of Dr. Franklin be in such degree an accomplice in the parricide of the memory of his immortal grandfather? The suspension for more than 20. years of the general publication bequeathed and confided to him, produced for a while hard suspicions against him: and if at last all are not published, a part of these suspicions may remain with some.[46]

---

44. Quoted from Lopez and Herbert, *The Private Franklin*, 309.
45. *North American Review* 7 (1818): 322.
46. Peterson, *Jefferson Writings*, 101.

In fact, Jefferson's memory deceived him, for there was no such record concerning what he believed was the stand of the British ministry in that piece of Franklin's writing, which Temple Franklin did include in his edition.[47] Jefferson nevertheless registered his personal speculation, and seems to have maintained until the end of his life the opinion that the grandson was bribed. He never bought the latter's American or English edition.[48]

III

The attention paid to Franklin's works came at a time when many Americans became increasingly interested in the nation's past. After the 1830s, as John Higham has pointed out, the nineteenth-century historical spirit gradually reached its height and history as a profession became the most remunerative, if not the most eminent, of all literary genres. Not only could popular history writers, like Charles A. Goodrich, Emma Willard, Salma Hale, John Frost, Jesse Olney, and Marcius Willson sell thousands of copies of their books, but so did such prominent authors as William H. Prescott, Washington Irving, and even the British historian Thomas Macaulay.[49] Among the leading authors in the nation some were great admirers of Franklin; the most distinguished was Jared Sparks.

Sparks was a pioneer in American historiography who devoted his life to studying the American Revolution. His ten-volume edition of *The Works of Benjamin Franklin* (1836–40) was a monumental tribute to the famous patriot. Several thousand copies were sold, and they remained the standard edition of Franklin's works for several decades.[50] Americans' experiences during the Revolution, Sparks believed, were the nation's most precious heritage; it was a historian's duty to record that heritage faithfully. He became increasingly irritated by mistreatment of Franklin. As early as 1830 he wrote in a book review:

---

47. William Temple Franklin, ed., *Memoirs of the Life and Writings of Benjamin Franklin* (London, 1817–18), 1: 223–83; and Sparks, *The Works of Franklin* 5: 1–82. For Jefferson's confusion about the said document see Boyd, *The Papers of Jefferson* 18: 87–97n.

48. Boyd, *Papers of Jefferson* 18: 89n.

49. Higham, *History* (Baltimore, 1983), 69.

50. Herbert B. Adams, *The Life and Writings of Jared Sparks* (Boston, 1893), 2: 525. P. L. Ford wrote in 1889 that "even now [Sparks's edition] is not entirely superseded," and severe criticism "cannot apply to his edition of Franklin" (*Franklin Bibliography*, liii).

The party rancor of the times, the personal jealousy of some of his coadjutors, and a combination of circumstances that may easily be explained, gave a currency to insinuations against his political character, which have been too readily incorporated into history. We shall only add, that we believe those insinuations to have been as ill founded in fact, as they have been unjust and hurtful in their effects.[51]

His opinions were shared by other Franklin advocates. Bancroft saluted him by saying that "your defense of Franklin was excellent; to every unprejudiced mind highly satisfactory. I read it with delight."[52] In fact, ever since the end of the 1820s Sparks had resolved "to bring out a complete collection" of Franklin's works in order to vindicate his name.[53] Some years later, in 1834, he began to publish *The Life and Writings of George Washington*, which secured his literary reputation.[54] Before long he was solicited to edit those papers written by a number of distinguished patriots, such as General Nathanael Greene, George Clinton, General William Eaton, and many others including Lafayette.[55] But his choice for the next subject was Franklin.

It should be pointed out, however, that, although Sparks resolved to defend Franklin's reputation, he approached the task as an editor, not as a writer. He believed that careful selections of Franklin's own words and the testimony of his contemporaries would be sufficient to do him justice. Therefore he chose those reports from newspapers and magazines that praised Franklin. He also used foreign sources, especially some French memoirs and histories, such as *Mémoires de L'Abbé Morellet, Mémoires de Madame Campan*, Charles de Lacretelle's *Histoire de France*, and Hilliard D'Auberteuil's *Essais historiques et Politiques sur la Révolution de l'Amerique*. Most of these authors held sympathetic views about Franklin.

Furthermore, Sparks seemed to be convinced that the most credible

---

51. [Sparks], "[Timothy] Pitkin's History of the United States," *North American Review* 30 (January 1830): 25.

52. Bancroft to Jared Sparks, 18 February 1830. John Spencer Bassett, ed., "Correspondence of George Bancroft and Jared Sparks, 1823–1832," *Smith College Studies in History* 2 (January 1917): 141.

53. H. B. Adams, *Life of Sparks* 2: 336.

54. Ibid., 334. By 1852 more than seven thousand sets of this work had been sold. National Historical Publications Commission, *A National Program for the Publication of the Papers of American Leaders: A Preliminary Report to the President of the United States* (Washington, 1951), 2–3

55. Adams, *Life of Sparks* 2: 334.

evidence to protect Franklin's reputation came from his closest colleagues. Hence he frequently quoted Washington, Adams, Jefferson, Jay, and Madison—all had appreciated Franklin at one time or another. For example, when he discussed a rumor charging that Franklin had neglected the country's claims for the right of boundaries and fisheries during the negotiations with Britain, he registered a first-hand account by Jay, who was a co-commissioner at the time. Jay wrote to Franklin:

> I have no reason whatever to believe, that you were averse to our obtaining the full extent of boundary and fishery secured to us by the treaty. Your conduct respecting them, throughout the negotiation, indicated a strong, a steady attachment to both those objects, and in my opinion promoted the attainment of them. . . . I do not recollect the least difference of sentiment between us respecting the boundaries or fisheries. On the contrary, we were unanimous and united in adhering to and insisting on them. Nor did I perceive the least disposition in either of us to recede from our claims, or be satisfied with less than we obtained.[56]

Without going into further details of the negotiations, Sparks was able to show that the charge against Franklin was without foundation, and that those who continued to spread the rumor, including the latest biographer of Jay, were, to say the least, ill–informed.[57]

Sparks's approach to history and, particularly, his method of editing original documents caused some controversy a few years after his selection of Washington's writings appeared. His edition of Franklin's works, however, did not. A contemporary reviewer, Francis Bowen, commented that "he has executed the work with his usual judgment, diligence, and ability, bringing together all the materials that the most extensive research, both in Europe and America, could supply." He further pointed out that because of Sparks's painstaking effort Americans could finally put to rest allegations from abroad that this country had little appreciation for Franklin's legacy.[58] Bancroft also said to Sparks that "I regard the firmness with which you have upheld the fame of Franklin as one of the most honorable incidents in your literary life." Sparks replied by expounding his opinions of Franklin:

---

56. Sparks, *The Works of Franklin* 1: 497–98.
57. Ibid., 498n.
58. [Bowen], "Sparks' Life and Works of Dr. Franklin," *North American Review* 59 (October 1844): 446.

Nothing could be more erroneous as touching the character of Franklin. He was cautious in counsel, reserved when wisdom dictated silence, quick and sagacious in detecting the hidden elements of any subject; but he never made a promise which he did not intend to fulfill, nor uttered insinuations designed to deceive or mislead. He was generous in every sense of the word, —generous to the faults, the foibles, and the weaknesses of others; generous in his kindly feelings and sympathies, large in his charities, constant to his friends, forbearing to his enemies; bland in his deportment, unpretending, unostentatious, proud of nothing, unless of having risen by his own industry and efforts from an humble station to one of dignity, influence, and greatness; faithful to every trust, true to every pledge. No man was more bold in declaring his opinions, or firm in maintaining them, when occasion required. A more ardent and devoted patriot never lived, nor one who loved his country more, or served it with a steadier zeal or more disinterested motives. Examining his voluminous writings from end to end, analyze the incidents of his long and varied career, and the traits here enumerated will show themselves everywhere.[59]

Many years later Bigelow, who pinpointed more than a thousand errors in Temple Franklin's edition of the autobiography, acknowledged that Sparks's edition was in the main satisfactory.[60] For most Franklin supporters, Sparks's great contribution to Franklin's legacy primarily lay in this edition. What was less known to the public, however, was his effort for nearly a decade to try to obtain and publish Franklin's unpublished manuscripts.

In 1840, the same year the last volume of Sparks's selection of Franklin writings was published, a great mass of papers in loose bundles was discovered in St. James Street, London. The person who had the possession said that he found those documents on the top shelf of the shop of a tailor, who was using them as paper patterns. Claiming that these papers belonged to the late Dr. Franklin, he attempted to sell them to the British Museum, to Lord Palmerston, and to successive American ministers to England. All of them declined. Early in 1850 a new American minister, Abbott Lawrence, referred the matter to Henry Stevens, who recognized the value of the collection and bought it within three days. A protégé of Jared Sparks, who assisted him to obtain a much-needed starting capital of $400 to go to England in 1847, Stevens immediately sought advice from his patron, who was then president of Harvard College and the best Franklin authority in the nation.

---

59. Adams, *Life of Sparks* 2: 353–54.
60. Bigelow, ed., *The Complete Works of Benjamin Franklin* (New York, 1887–88), 1: xxvi.

These papers, as it turns out, were owned by William Temple Franklin, after whose death his widow left them at her husband's bank in St. James Street. As early as 1829 when Sparks visited Paris, he attempted to get access to the papers, but the widow refused. Now that the papers once again came into light, he was eager to make a deal with Stevens so that he could select and publish them. At one point, he proposed to prepare the papers for the press, to supervise the work of publication, and to let Stevens have two-thirds of the profits. Sparks's explicit interest and repeated proposal only reconfirmed the value of the collection, for which Stevens was considering to ask $25,000. For eight years from 1850 to 1858 more than a dozen letters went back and forth between Sparks and Stevens. The former even went to London to examine the collection in 1857, but no deal ensued. When Sparks died in 1866, Stevens was deeply in debt and had to mortgage his Franklin collection to Charles Whittingham & Co. as security. This was not the first time that Stevens fell into debt, or that the Franklin manuscripts were deposited in a bank. Nothing was heard about these papers until several decades later, when they were offered for sale at auction in England.[61]

IV

Franklin's legacy was particularly dear to printers, who were proud that their patron saint enjoyed international renown. Using his name as an ornament, many printers believed that Franklin's fame might help to glorify their own trade. When he was alive, some printers in Philadelphia formed an institution called the Franklin Society, which was dissolved shortly after his death (1782–92). Several years later, in 1799, a group of printers in New York founded the Franklin Typographical Society of Journeymen Printers. In 1822 another Franklin Typographical Society was established in Boston, and in 1844 the

---

61. For more extensive discussions on the relationship between Sparks and Stevens see Whitfield J. Bell, Jr., "Henry Stevens, his Uncle Samuel, and the Franklin Papers," *Proceedings of the Massachusetts Historical Society* 72 (October 1957-December 1960): 143–47; Adams, *Life and Writings of Sparks* 2: 520–33; Stevens, *Stevens's Historical Collection*, 160I-160L. As a shrewd businessman, Stevens emphasized that Sparks's edition was "insufficient and defective," whereas his Franklin collection was enough to make at least "five additional volumes" to that "fullest and best" edition thus far. He, of course, did not mention that Sparks had negotiated with him about the collection throughout the 1850s.

Franklin Typographical Association in New York. These organizations were among the earliest benevolent societies within the craft.

If Franklin's name appealed to the imagination of printers, so did his works. In Auburn, a small town in central New York, a printer named Henry Oliphant purchased a newly-invented power press from Seth Adams & Co. of Boston in 1845. Pleased with the new equipment, the owner promised that his press could be "making books at a rate which only a few years since, would have been looked upon as altogether beyond belief."[62] In the same town an energetic publisher, James Cepha Derby, seized the opportunity and asked Oliphant to print books for him. One of the earliest that they launched was Franklin's autobiography, which they reprinted almost yearly from 1846 to 1853.[63]

Technical advances and entrepreneurial undertakings were by no means limited to Auburn.[64] When Frederick Follett, a long time printer at Batavia, in Genesee County, reviewed the progress of his trade, he pointed out that the changes and improvements for the last fifty years had been "truly wonderful." He wrote:

> Any one who will take the trouble to visit the magnificent Printing Establishments in Rochester and Buffalo, will admit the truthfulness of this remark. —This branch of business has fully kept pace with other improvements of the day, and added very greatly to the general, and I may add, the almost universal diffusion of knowledge and information among the people.[65]

Printers like Oliphant and Follett had good reason to believe that their struggle for progress transformed their humble profession into a real art, that their arduous work changed ordinary citizens into skilled craftsmen, and that their efforts to diffuse useful knowledge through the press helped the wilderness of western New York to grow into a

---

62. Oliphant, "The Past and Present," *Auburn Journal and Advertiser*, 25 June 1845, p. 2; his advertisement, ibid., p. 3; and *The Cayuga Patriot* (Auburn), 8 October 1845, p. 3.

63. Douglas C. McMurtrie, comp., *A Bibliography of Books, Pamphlets and Broadsides Printed at Auburn, N.Y. 1810–1850* (Buffalo, N. Y., 1938); Karl Sanford Kabelac, "Book Publishing in Auburn, New York: 1851–1876" (M.A. thesis, State University College at Oneonta, New York, 1969); *The National Union Catalog: Pre-1956 Imprints* (London, 1971), 183: 111–13.

64. The most illuminating study of this topic is Milton W. Hamilton, *The Country Printer: New York State, 1785–1830* (New York, 1936).

65. Follett, *History of the Press of Western New-York*, reprint of the 1847 ed. (Harrison, N. Y., 1973), 64.

promising land. As Follett summarized it: "The 'Press' and a 'Printer'! Who is not proud to be associated with the one, and classed with the other?"[66] This self-confidence and optimism generated a need for a common bond and expression. It was in search of such a common bond and expression that Franklin's name again loomed large: Printers in western New York decided to hold a festival to celebrate his birthday on January 17, 1846, which was the first of its kind among New York printers.

The festival was held in Rochester. Approximately eighty craftsmen and more than a hundred guests were present, many of whom came from neighboring towns and villages. A local newspaper reported: "For the *first time*, a large number of the Printers of Western New York, assembled at the Champion Hotel last evening, for the purpose of commemorating by an appropriate *Festival*, the birth-day of one who was not only an ornament to the profession, but who was proud to claim, even when surrounded by honors and greatness, that he was one of the craft—*BENJAMIN FRANKLIN*."[67]

The event was organized and presided over by printers. Participants included not only masters and journeymen, but also devils and apprentices. Throughout the evening Franklin's remarkable career and admirable achievements were repeatedly lauded. The president of the occasion, Derick Sibley, set the tone at the beginning of the celebration when he declared:

> While *Franklin* was himself the greatest honor to the craft with which we are connected, he gave the highest evidence that he felt himself honored in being associated with the great and intelligent fraternity of Printers. He prepared the epitaph for his own tombstone; and this document, which was to be as enduring as the marble upon which it was inscribed, made no allusion to the more public acts of his life, but took the simple designation of *Benjamin Franklin, PRINTER*.[68]

His speech was followed by a series of toasts. Many of them stressed an emotional link between tradesmen's pride and Franklin's glory, such as "Our Craft," "Printers," "The Press—The engine of Liberty," "Franklin—The self-made man," and "Once a printer, always a printer, and never ashamed of the craft"[69] (Fig. 10).

---

66. Ibid., ix.
67. *Rochester Daily Advertiser*, 17 January 1846, p. 2.
68. Ibid.
69. Ibid.

PRINTERS' FESTIVAL.

The first ever held in Western New York

For the first time, a large number of the Printers of Western New York, assembled at the Champion Hotel last evening, for the purpose of commemorating by an appropriate FESTIVAL, the birth-day of one who was not only an ornament to the profession, but who was proud to claim, even when surrounded by honors and greatness, that he was one of the craft—BENJAMIN FRANKLIN. The feast was one of reason—a pleasant commingling of sentiment and feeling. There were present on the occasion, Employer and Journeyman, Editor and Devil, as well as many of those who have long since abandoned the type-case, for more profitable if not more honorable occupations. Old and young —men who could tell us of a Printer's life in the wilderness, and youngsters who have hardly yet been initiated into the mysteries of the profession—all joined in doing honor to the memory of the man whose name stands second to only one, perhaps, on the bright page of our country's annals.

The assemblage was called to order by J. A. HADLEY, Esq., Chairman of the Committee of Arrangements; after which, the following officers were appointed:—

Hon. DERICK SIBLEY, President.
SAMUEL BLANCHARD, 1st Vice President.
PHILEMON CANFIELD, 2d   do.
ERASTUS SHEPARD, 3d   do.
C. B. THOMPSON, 4th   do.
George Dawson, ⎞
J. M. Patterson, ⎬ Secretaries.
H. L. Wigants, ⎠

10. Extensive report of the first printers' festival in western New York to celebrate Franklin's birth, in the *Rochester Daily Advertiser*, January 17, 1846, p. 2. The publisher acknowledged: "Much of the specimen prepared for this day's paper is crowded out by the proceedings of the Printers' Celebration."

Apparently, that evening was a delightful success,[70] for participating printers decided to hold the same festival in Rochester in 1847 (Figs. 11, 12, and 13), and later again in 1848 and 1849. What happened in western New York did not pass unobserved elsewhere. Only a few days later the *New-York Daily Tribune* reported on its front page that "the anniversary of Franklin's birthday was celebrated by the printers of Rochester in glorious style"[71] (Fig. 14). The Franklin Typographical Society in Boston began to hold its first printers' festival on January 15, 1848, and again in 1857 and 1858. In New York City the Typographical Society made a quiet but significant change. Hitherto it had maintained a tradition of celebrating Independence Day, on which it was founded in 1809. Starting in 1849, however, it shifted to observe Franklin's birthday (Fig. 15), and repeated the ceremony in 1850, 1851, 1853, and 1865. Evidence also suggests that in a place as remote as Keokuk, Iowa, local printers held a party on January 17, 1856, when Mark Twain gave his first after-dinner speech.[72]

The first printers' festival in Rochester in 1846 not only triggered a series of similar ceremonies; it also established a pattern that printers in other cities would adopt: A printers' festival was a memorial celebration held by printing craftsmen to commemorate Franklin's birthday. In most cases it was organized by a special committee, composed of eminent practitioners of the trade. The main event was a banquet, preceded by the delivery of a formal or informal speech. During the banquet a toast-master would propose regular toasts, and participants were allowed to volunteer sentiments. The number of participants might vary. Women were not necessarily excluded. In some instances, water rather than wine would be served.[73] After each festival, detailed proceedings were published in newspapers or pamphlets, which might also contain a brief history of the local printing industry or of the initiating organization.

In all the ceremonies, however, Franklin's career remained the

---

70. Hamilton, *The Country Printer*, 92.
71. *New-York Daily Tribune*, 21 January 1846, p. 1.
72. Margaret Sanborn, *Mark Twain: The Bachelor Years* (New York, 1990), 101.
73. Printers believed that female members of the Franklin family were among the first to work within the profession. Isaiah Thomas, *The History of Printing in America*, ed. Marcus A. McCorison (New York, 1970), 315–16. Printers also loved to recall the story that when young Franklin sojourned in England in the 1720s, he drank water rather than beer, and yet was able to carry heavier things than his English co-workers (*Autobiography*, 169–70, 99–100).

HISTORY

OF THE

PRESS OF WESTERN NEW-YORK;

PREPARED AT THE REQUEST OF A COMMITTEE,

BY FREDERICK FOLLETT, OF BATAVIA.

TOGETHER WITH THE

PROCEEDINGS OF THE PRINTERS' FESTIVAL,

HELD ON THE 141st ANNIVERSARY

OF THE

BIRTH-DAY OF FRANKLIN,

IN THE

City of Rochester, on Monday, Jan. 18, 1847.

ROCHESTER:
PRINTED BY JEROME & BROTHER, DAILY AMERICAN OFFICE.

1847.

11. Cover of Frederick Follett's *History of the Press of Western New-York*, Rochester, 1847. His undertaking was proposed at the second printers' festival in Rochester, January 18, 1847.

focal point and participants constantly stressed their connection with him. Because the ways of glorifying Franklin were so ritualized, little wonder that printers often referred to their celebrations as Franklin festivals.

of hours were spent in sharpening the appetite, by social converse. About six, the company, headed by Adams' Brass Band, moved to the dining room and organized as follows:

President—A. G. DAUBY, Esq., Utica.
1st V. Pres't—Dr. T. M. FOOTE, Buffalo.
2d do —L. H. REDFIELD, Syracuse.
3d do —F. FOLLETT, Batavia.
4th do —A. WARREN, Perry.

5th V. Pres't—G. M. DANA, Ithaca.
6th do —S. S. BLANCHARD, Warsaw.
7th do —C. W. DIBBLE, Dansville.
8th do —E. S. PALMER, Angelica.
1st Secretary—E. SCRANTOM, Rochester.
2d do —J. O. BRAYMAN, Buffalo.
3d do —D. D. WAITE, Batavia.

The following diagram will show the position of the guests at the table:

T. M. FOOTE, 1st V. P.			A. G. DAUBY, Pres't.		L. H. REDFIELD, 2d V. P.
P Canfield	A Strong	Rev A G Hall	E Scrantom	W A Welles	W S Falls
E Shepard	G R Davis	R v D C Houghton	J O Brayman	M L Greene	J A Hadley
M Patterson	J Rowley	Rev J Robie	D D Waite		J E Morey
H L Winants	J Steel	J D Bemis	D Mann	D McKay	D D T Moore
C Comens	M Hulett	E Peck	A Mann	P Barry	G T Frost
C Carver	G F Terrell	Dr S Hamilton			J W Benton
G Winn	J W Barber	Dr J Webster	I Butts	L Wetherell	H H Winants
G Beers	T Murmin	E Barnard	S P Allen	D Hoyt	A Bennett
W W Bruff	J Clough	A A Schenck			L Disbrow
C H M'Donald	B F Enos		H Cook	D M Dewey	N Sage
C A Waldo	W Gardner	W H Beach		M Purcell	W Alling
C Billinghurst	E St Jermain	F Cowdry	J Vick		G W Fisher
T C Schell	J Barnard	H Sanford	C A Gregory	W R Wells	W H Enos
J S Tryon	E R Andrews	{ G M Dana 5th V P }		J A Canfield	
C G Palmer	S K Reed		S S Blanchard 6th V P	R M Patterson	E S Palmer 8th V P
C W Dibble 7th V. P.	H K Walker	I Jerome	E Bridges	G Wilson	T Summers
J M Campbell	G S Walker	C Jerome	J B Clark	R H Benson	J Curtis
C B Thompson	C T Wilson	S M Raymond	J P Fogg	B W Mansfield	E Darrow
C Beach	G Holden	H Raymond	S B Stoddard	H Gaul	E D Ely
W B Clough	O Oleson	J Kinney	Dr A D Gordon	P Homan	G Barnard
L Chichester	J W Riggs	W McDermott	M M Mathews	C R Beach	E S Carpenter
J G Reed	R M Watts	R Bloss	S G Crane	W Lovett	W H Campbell
L Chapin	G J Lawrence	R S Parsons	H Parsons	J McMahon	J Martin jr
W C Foster	M A Fisher	H J Adams	J Scott		C Barnum
W A Sage	L W Jerome	J W Staring	Richardson	M Orr	G W Haskell
W Westbrook	I M Hall	W Dwyer	C J Howland		R M Colton
W Cowles	Lieut Lee	E Chipman	A Scott	P V Stoothoff	L E Gould
J G Moore	I Jerome		Carmichael	C H Sedgwick	M Miller
A M Clapp			R L Swift		
L B Swan					
W A Beaver					
F. FOLLETT, 3d V. P.		Capt. ADAMS.		A. WARREN, 4th V. P.	

12. Diagram of table arrangement for the 160 guests at the second printers' festival held in Rochester, from Frederick Follett's *History of the Press of Western New-York*, p. 2.

V

To most Americans, Franklin's renown was hardly separable from his writings, such as his essays, almanacs, memoirs, and discourses on electricity. His reputation within the literary circle, however, was an uneasy one almost from start, because many writers held ambiguous attitudes about him.

The following is the bill of fare:

OYSTER SOUP.

ROAST.

Alamode Beef,	Roast Turkeys,
Roast Beef,	Swans,
" Pork,	Partidges,
" Veal,	Chicken Pies,
" Pigs,	Chicken Curry,
" Venison,	Chicken Salad.

BOILED.

Ham,	Turkey, (Oyster Sauce,)
Tongues,	Chickens, (Celery ")
Mutton, (Caper Sauce.)	

VENISON STEAK, (Currant Jells.)

OYSTERS.

Oysters Stewed,	Oysters Scoloped,
" Fried,	" Pattes.

FISH.

Boiled Codfish, (fresh,)	Black Bass, (barbecued,)
Baked Codfish,	Perch.

PASTRY.

Lemon Pudding,	Mince Pies,
Plum do.	Apple do.
Carrot do.	Cranberry Tarts,
Apple do.	Peach Pies,
Flour do.	Squash do.

DESSERTS.

Apples,	Almonds,
Grapes,	Whip Cream,
Raisins,	Ice Cream.

While discussing the dessert, which consisted of the choicest variety of fruits in season and out, ALEXANDER MANN, Esq., the reader for the evening, announced the following regular toasts

---

13. Menu of the second printers' festival in Rochester, from Frederick Follett's *History of the Press of Western New-York*, p. 4.

Emerson was a cautious admirer of Franklin. Although his published works were mainly concerned with spiritual and literary matters, for several decades from the 1820s to the 1850s Emerson made numerous references to Franklin in his private journals.[74] An advo-

---

74. William L. Hedges, "From Franklin to Emerson," in J. A. Leo Lemay, ed., *The Oldest Revolutionary: Essays on Benjamin Franklin* ([Philadelphia], 1976), 139–56. For attitudes of Emerson and other Transcendentalists toward Franklin see Alexander C. Kern, "Emerson and Economics," *New England Quarterly* 13 (December 1940): 678–96; and Jesse Bier, "Weberism, Franklin, and the Transcendental Style," *New England Quarterly* 43 (June 1970): 179–92.

Celebration of Franklin's Birthday at Rochester.

The anniversary of Franklin's birthday was cele brated by the printers of Rochester in glorious style on the 16th inst. about eighty members of the craft being present, among whom were Vice Chancellor WHITTLE SEY formerly proprietor of the Republican—an old pa per published in the State ; EVERARD PECK, who pub lished the Rochester Telegraph as early as 1818, and a number of well known journalists. The whole number of guests amounted to one hundred and seven. Among the regular toasts were the following :—

The Typographical Profession—*Guided* by the pre cepts and examples of the immortal Franklin, we will always have a *clean case*, an abundance of *sorts*, a *correct proof*, and in the end be *justified* and *registered* on high.

Washington—A *leader* in the *columns* of Freedom, who *battered* a royal *imperial form*, and *set up a work* whose *pages* should never be *distributed*

The Union—A *form of twenty eights, locked up* in the *chase* of the People's affections.

The President of the United States—May he always *set a clean proof*.

Some well conceived compliments were paid to the memory of Franklin by the President, DERRICK SIBLEY, Esq.

The remarks of Mr. WILLIAM A. WELLES were very interesting. In his account of his experience as a mem ber of the craft he said that he served nearly 7 years' apprenticeship in the office of the late Alderman Sey mour, 49 John-st. N. Y ; associated as fellow-workmen, were the late Commissary General of this State— A. Chandler, ex-Mayor Harper, of New-York, Gen. George P. Morris of the " Mirror," John Winot, Elliott, the Fore man, (one of the notorious " Miranda Expedition,") and others. About this time, I *pulled* the first No. of the " New York American," then edited by Chas. King. James A. Hamilton and Gulian C. Verplanck. The first edition of " Salmagundi," was also printed in this office, about this time, from the MS. of Washington Irving, in the *composition* of which I assisted. In Boston, I worked upon the " Columbian Centinel" for " Old Ben Russell."

14. News of the cele bration of Franklin's birthday at Rochester in the *New-York Daily Tri bune*, January 21, 1846, p.1.

cate who emphasized the innocent stage of man's mental abilities, he deeply appreciated the "extraordinary ease" with which Franklin's mind worked, and attributed such a quality to the latter's remarkable "disinterestedness." Like many Americans, Emerson also acknowl edged that Franklin was a great man, even though he seldom praised him openly. He explained the reason:

If any apology be demanded for the seeming neglect in classical journals of a name so much the ornament of America as Franklin's, there is but one answer. It is not because we do not appreciate the manifold merits of this distinguished person or would ungratefully cancel the debt we owe to his phi losophy or political wisdom; but because his fame had wider circulation than our page & his character has that sort of commanding excellence which is as

---

FRANKLIN—HIS GENIUS, LIFE, AND CHARACTER.

AN

ORATION ·

DELIVERED BEFORE THE

N. Y. TYPOGRAPHICAL SOCIETY,

ON THE OCCASION OF

𝕮𝖍𝖊 𝕭𝖎𝖗𝖙𝖍𝖉𝖆𝖞 𝖔𝖋 𝕱𝖗𝖆𝖓𝖐𝖑𝖎𝖓,

AT THE

PRINTERS' FESTIVAL,

HELD JANUARY 17, 1849.

BY

JOHN L. JEWETT.

PUBLISHED BY ORDER OF THE SOCIETY.

NEW-YORK :
HARPER & BROTHERS, 82 CLIFF-STREET.
M.DCCC.XLIX.

---

15. Title page of John L. Jewett's oration, "Franklin—His Genius, Life, and Character," delivered before the New York Typographical Society on Franklin's birthday at the printers' festival held in New York on January 17, 1849.

undisputed as it is unrivalled, it was not worth while to beat the air in vindicating the justice of his claims to the veneration of mankind.[75]

---

75. William H. Gilman et al., eds., *The Journals and Miscellaneous Notebooks of Ralph Waldo Emerson* (Cambridge, Mass., 1960–82), 2: 222–23.

That Franklin belonged to the distinguished Revolutionary generation seemed always to command Emerson's veneration, for he asked: "Where is the master that could have instructed Franklin or Washington?" On the other hand, he regretted that "Franklin's man is a frugal, inoffensive, thrifty citizen, but savours of nothing heroic." As William L. Hedge has suggested, Emerson liked Franklin's proverbial wisdom, but he was also disturbed by the latter's content with "Common Sense," inclination to "vulgar Utilitarianism," and inability to express more explicit spiritual "Reason."[76]

Emerson's reserved appreciation was shared by other contemporary authors, who often felt it difficult to reconcile Franklin's amiable qualities with his less desirable ones. For example, some modern observers tend to categorize Nathaniel Hawthorne as a strong critic of Franklin, for he once said that Franklin's concern was "all about getting money or saving it." In fact, this phrase has been so frequently repeated that its context is generally ignored. In answering the question why Franklin should have grown very famous, Hawthorne wrote:

> I doubt whether Franklin's philosophical discoveries, important as they were, or even his vast political services, would have given him all the fame which he acquired. It appears to me that "Poor Richard's Almanac" did more than anything else towards making him familiarly known to the public. As the writer of those proverbs which Poor Richard was supposed to utter, Franklin became the counsellor and household friend of almost every family in America. Thus it was the humblest of all his labors that has done the most for his fame.[77]

It is clear that Hawthorne's view of Franklin was more complex than the previous quote might suggest. Keener than blind admirers and more subtle than acid detractors, Hawthorne understood that it would be misleading to identify Franklin with the *persona* he created in his almanacs. At the same time, if Hawthorne was not entirely convinced that Franklin's almanacs had overemphasized material gain, he was by no means so naive as to assume that readers' obsessions with the subject should be attributed to the compiler alone. In the end, Hawthorne pointed out that Franklin's sayings in those almanacs "were suited to the condition of the country; and their effect,

---

76. Hedges, "From Franklin to Emerson," in Lemay, ed., *The Oldest Revolutionary,* 146–47.

77. Hawthorne, "Benjamin Franklin," *Tales, Sketches, and Other Papers* (Riverside ed.: Boston, 1897), 202.

upon the whole, has doubtless been good, although they teach men but a very small portion of their duties."[78]

If Emerson and Hawthorne had mixed feelings about Franklin, the most troubling aspect of his life, according to the gifted writer Herman Melville, was his lack of aesthetic judgment and poetic imagination. The following segment from his novel *Israel Potter* represented Melville's dramatized portrayal of Franklin:

Having carefully weighed the world, Franklin could act any part in it. By nature turned to knowledge, his mind was often grave, but never serious. At times he had seriousness—extreme seriousness—for others, but never for himself. Tranquillity was to him instead of it. This philosophical levity of tranquillity, so to speak, is shown in his easy variety of pursuits. Printer, postmaster, almanac maker, essayist, chemist, orator, tinker, statesman, humorist, philosopher, parlor man, political economist, professor of housewifery, ambassador, projector, maxim-monger, herb-doctor, wit:—Jack of all trades, master of each and mastered by none—the type and genius of his land. Franklin was everything but a poet.[79]

For years, Melville's sarcastic description satisfied those who would like to mock Franklin. Twisting Franklin's versatility to a measure of shallowness, Melville's criticism was caustic indeed. Except for its rhetoric, the author's cynicism not only revealed his unwillingness to appreciate Franklin's varied genius, but also left an impression of a professional writer's uneasiness to come to terms with an amateur's accomplishment. Besides, humorous as it was, careful observers would find that Melville's fictional sketch was inadequate as an analysis. To be more precise, he did not mean to be analytical at all. He promised his publisher that his new novel was not meant to please or "shock the fastidious," but to provide what the public wanted, with "little reflective writing . . . nothing weighty."[80]

When the novel first appeared in *Putnam's Magazine* in 1856, Melville's "clear," "direct," and "manly" style pleased many magazine readers. They especially enjoyed his "stirring" narratives, "graphic" recitals, and "eccentric" comments, as newspaper commentators praised his "masculine vigor," "fantastical ruggedness," and "raciness

---

78. Ibid.

79. Melville, *His Fifty Years of Exile (Israel Potter)*, introd. Lewis Leary (New York, 1957), 66.

80. Hugh W. Hetherington, *Melville's Reviewers: British and American, 1846–1891* (Chapel Hill, N.C., 1961), 240.

of flavor."[81] Nevertheless, the novelist did so only at the expense of not telling history. Although his novel was claimed to have been based on Potter's own account, he totally ignored the latter's description:

My interview with Dr. Franklin was a pleasing one—for nearly an hour he conversed with me in the most agreeable and instructive manner, and listened to the tale of my sufferings with much apparent interest, and seemed to be disposed to encourage me with the assurance that if the Americans should succeed in their grand object, and firmly establish their Independence, they would not fail to remunerate their soldiers for their services—but, alas! as regards myself, these assurances have not as yet been verified!—I am confident, however, that had it been a possible thing for that great and good man (whose humanity and generosity have been the theme of infinitely abler pens than mine) to have lived to this day, I should not have petitioned my country in vain for a momentary enjoyment of that provision, which has been extended to so great a portion of my fellow soldiers.[82]

Instead, Melville portrayed Franklin as a mediocre moralist who lived brilliantly in Paris and cared little about rescuing American war prisoners. Like other critics of the time, he grossly underestimated Franklin's diplomatic services to the country. Only recently have scholars begun to realize that Franklin was one of the few Americans who had exerted themselves to help those unfortunate captives. In fact, Franklin had involved himself in efforts toward prisoner relief even before the Continental Congress specifically instructed him to do so. Furthermore, because official financial resources for prisoner relief were exceedingly limited, he tried to use his personal connections in England, especially his friendship with David Hartley and William Hodgson, to help American captives. Franklin's humanitarianism was such that among those who petitioned his assistance were not only American prisoners, their friends and relatives, but French and British prisoners and their loved ones as well.[83] Melville's fictionalized Franklin was so incompatible with his public image, it is no surprise that when the novel was published in England, a reviewer

---

81. Ibid., 240–46.
82. Israel R. Potter, *The Life and Remarkable Adventures of Israel R. Potter*, introd. Leonard Kriegel (New York, 1962), 50–51.
83. Catherine M. Prelinger, "Benjamin Franklin and the American Prisoners of War in England during the American Revolution," *William and Mary Quarterly*, 3rd ser., 32 (April 1975): 261–94.

said that Melville's Franklin "is selfish in his prudence, and icy in his calmness. Such, we take it was not the real Franklin."[84]

In 1856, the same year that Melville's *Israel Potter* appeared, Henry David Thoreau published his *Walden; or Life in the Woods.* Because of his strong skepticism of the prevailing emphasis on business and success, and because of his cynical view of conventional belief in wealth, comfort, and luxury, some modern students consider him one of the most acute critics of Franklin during this period. They also suggest that, since Thoreau was seeking a life that was drastically different from Franklin's, *Walden,* especially its first chapter on economy, was perhaps written in an attempt to satirize Franklin's *Autobiography.*

But a closer review of Thoreau and the ideas represented in *Walden* indicates otherwise. To be sure, Thoreau disliked the commercial world of his day and attacked railroads, banks, and corporations on numerous occasions. Nevertheless, considering that he never unequivocally used Franklin as a prime target, the assertion that Thoreau was one of the strongest of Franklin's critics seems hard to sustain. Thoreau did write the following words in his journal while he was preparing *Walden*:

There is little or nothing to be remembered written on the subject of getting an honest living. Neither the New Testament nor Poor Richard speaks to our condition. I cannot think of a single page which entertains, much less answers, the questions which I put to myself on this subject. How to make the getting our living poetic![85]

Thoreau's dissatisfaction with Poor Richard's almanacs did not necessarily mean that he was writing *Walden* in order to ridicule Franklin. Nor was it profound to discover that Franklin had no accomplishment in poetry, for Franklin had confessed that in his autobiography. The point is that, immediately following the above statement, Thoreau further complained that society "with all its arts," including literature, answered little of his question.

Thoreau's *Walden* was launched against many norms and traditions. His friend and patron Emerson keenly observed: "He wanted a fallacy to expose, a blunder to pillory, I may say required a little sense

---

84. Hetherington, *Melville's Reviewers,* 247.
85. Bradford Torrey and Francis H. Allen, eds., *The Journal of Henry D. Thoreau* (Cambridge, Mass., 1949), 2: 164.

of victory, a roll of the drum, to call his powers into full exercise. It cost him nothing to say No; indeed he found it much easier than to say Yes."[86]

Thoreau never married. He lived alone. He never went to church. He never voted. He refused to pay a tax to the state. He stood for the abolition of slavery, of tariffs, and almost of government. His quest for the so-called poetic life was only another expression of his yearning for a complete freedom and a total realization of the self. It seemed "as if he did not feel himself except in opposition."[87] Thus, when Thoreau lost faith in western religion, he studied Brahmanism. Convinced that conventional wisdom was no longer useful, he stopped reading books and began to hoe beans. Believing that the contemporary business world was filled with pitfalls, he ignored it and turned to nature. Only nature pleased him and provided the ultimate passage to his self-fulfillment.

Because Thoreau's perceptions of life were so different from those of the majority of his contemporaries, no sooner had his book been published than he was labeled as a "Yankee Diogenes," an "eccentric person," and an "oddity."[88] The book may have been at odds with Franklin's doctrines, but its publication failed to influence popular concepts of Franklin. For the first edition of *Walden* only two thousand copies were printed. They did not sell well for years, as Thoreau's publisher informed him: "We have never been out of the book but there is very little demand for it."[89]

In the end, if Emerson's ambivalent opinions of Franklin represented his contemporaries' ambiguity, if Hawthorne's subtle observations fell into obscurity, if Melville's satire only pleased the reader's senses, the regrettable misinterpretations of Thoreau's exquisite book only revealed that throughout the first half of the nineteenth century no literary masterpiece, or other mode of ideal, could challenge Franklin's popularity.

---

86. Emerson, "Thoreau." Quoted in Walter Harding, ed., *Thoreau: A Century of Criticism* (Dallas, 1954), 25.

87. Ibid., 24, 25, 27.

88. See "A Massachusetts Hermit," *New-York Daily Tribune,* 29 July 1854, p. 3; "A Yankee Diogenes," *Putnam's Monthly Magazine* 4 (October 1854), 443; "Town and Rural Humbugs," *The Knickerbocker* 45 (March 1855), 235. Years later another reviewer called him a "skulker": R[obert] L[ouis] S[tevenson], "Henry David Thoreau: His Character and Opinions," *The Cornhill Magazine* 41 (June 1880): 666.

89. *Walden* finally became popular during the last decades of the nineteenth century. See Thoreau, *Walden,* ed. J. Lyndon Shanley (Princeton, 1971), 368.

VI

For a long time European visitors to the United States had complained that they did not see a major Franklin statue, although they noticed that many streets, banks, and companies adopted the name Franklin. From their point of view, only a work of art could be regarded as the ultimate tribute to a hero. Furthermore, for those Europeans who "identified national greatness with artistic maturity" and who insisted that sculpture was the most elevated of all the arts,[90] the lack of such a monument indicated the barren condition of the arts in America.

Though there was a small Franklin statue at the Library Company of Philadelphia, those European observers were partially correct, because until the early 1850s there had been neither a Franklin statue by an American artist, nor a bronze of him, in the nation. Well–informed people, such as Jared Sparks and Robert C. Winthrop, felt that such an omission was an embarrassment. Thus, toward the end of 1853 Winthrop spoke before the Massachusetts Charitable Mechanic Association and urged its members to consider erecting a Franklin statue. Convinced that the statue was more important to the city's reputation than anything else, he stressed:

> Not, then, because Franklin is in any danger of being forgotten, —not because his memory requires the aid of bronze or marble to rescue it from oblivion, —not because it is in the power of any of us to increase or extend his pervading and enduring fame, —but because, in these days of commemoration, it is unjust to ourselves, unjust to our own reputation for a discriminating estimate and a generous appreciation of real genius, of true greatness, and of devoted public service.[91]

A statue of Franklin, therefore, was more than a tribute to the hero; it should show artistic taste and achievement in the city. It was then proposed that "the statue should be an American work, and, as far as possible, a Massachusetts work, designed and executed upon the soil

---

90. Neil Harris, *The Artist in America: The Formative Years, 1790–1860* (New York, 1966), 20.

91. Robert C. Winthrop, "Archimedes and Franklin," *Addresses and Speeches on Various Occasions* (Boston, 1852–86), 2: 138; [Nathaniel Bradstreet Shurtleff], ed., *Memorial of the Inauguration of the Statue of Franklin* (Boston, 1857), 346.

of Massachusetts, and they were desirous, too, that Boston, the native place of Franklin, should furnish the artist."[92]

Subsequently Richard S. Greenough, a native of Jamaica Plain, Massachusetts, was chosen as the sculptor. He understood that Bostonians wanted a Franklin of their own, not some classical, toga-draped saint. In order to satisfy these desires the artist expressed his vision:

The strength of portraiture lies in fidelity of likeness and truth of character. . . . His mind was too rich, and his pursuits too liberal, to find their expression in a single act. I have accordingly endeavored to treat my statue in harmony with his character simply. I would have it thoughtful, dignified, of kindly expression, and unconscious [sic; unselfconscious?]. In pursuing this course I am gratified to feel that the same principle was observed in the most eminent portrait statues of antiquity.[93]

Fidelity and simplicity indeed. Cast in rich golden bronze eight feet high, the finished statue depicted neither a philosopher nor a statesman, but a respectable citizen in his later age: bare-headed and dressed in a long coat trimmed with fur, Franklin stood holding an old crab-tree walking stick in the right hand and a continental hat in the left. The sculptor modeled his statue after Houdon's original bust, which showed Franklin's placid and benign countenance. Greenough's Franklin, however, looked downward to the left, seemingly lost in contemplation and unaware of the public gaze. Thus, anyone standing in front of the statue could easily meet Franklin's eye from the ground, and was able to have a close view of the aged and thoughtful Franklin who, with virtuous tranquillity and plain costume, appeared to be a hero without pretentious grandeur (Fig. 16).

William James Stillman, an art critic from New York, happened to see the statue in Greenough's studio. He declared that it was a "noble work, unaffected and thoroughly full of common-sense." This common sense, he believed, was "a quality not by any means so usual in modern Art as men might suppose in these practical times. . . . Indeed, it is the rarest of all artistic traits; . . . . [The statue is] a genuine work of Art—the realization of an idea."[94] This Franklin statue was one of the most successful sculptures that Greenough had ever modeled.

---

92. Shurtleff, ed., *Memorial*, 358.
93. Ibid., 359.
94. *The Crayon* (New York), 7 March 1855, p. 155.

16. Richard Greenough's 1856 statue in School Street in Boston was the first full-figure bronze of Franklin in the nation. Four bas-reliefs on the pedestal presented Franklin at the press, his kite experiment, his signing the Declaration of Independence, and his signing the peace treaty with Great Britain.

Thousands of lead and chalk copies were made; a century later some of them could still be found in New England antique shops.[95]

Greenough's Franklin statue was further distinguished by its grand unveiling ceremonies, which promoted the city as much as glorified Franklin. His sculpture attracted far more public attention than had earlier memorials, such as Charles Bulfinch's memorial urn and building in Franklin Place (1794) (Fig. 17), the renovation of the grave of Franklin's parents in the Granary Burial Ground (1827) (Fig. 18), and Thomas Bowse's memorial monument in honor of Franklin at Mount Auburn Cemetery in Cambridge (1854) (Fig. 19). In fact, not since the

---

95. Thomas B. Brumbaugh, "The Art of Greenough," *Old-Time New England* 53 (1963): 68.

Vol. XXXVI. No. 1   JULY, 1945   Serial No. 121

Old-Time New England

THE BULLETIN OF

The Society for the Preservation of New England Antiquities

Antique Urn, formerly in Park at Franklin Place, Boston
Since 1855 at Grave of Charles Bulfinch, 1763 1844. Mt. Auburn Cemetery, Cambridge, Mass.

17. Cover of *Old-Time New England* (July 1945) featuring a photograph, by Arthur C. Haskell, of Charles Bulfinch's memorial urn for Franklin. Originally located at Franklin Place in Boston in 1794, Bulfinch's monument was many years later removed to Mount Auburn Cemetery in Cambridge, Massachusetts, where it is currently under restoration. (By permission of the Society for the Preservation of New England Antiquities)

railroad jubilee in 1851 had Bostonians witnessed such an elaborate celebration.[96] Sunny and pleasant, September 17, 1856 began with church bells ringing and cannon being fired. Throngs of people from

---

96. Boston City Council, *The Railroad Jubilee; An Account of the Celebration Commemorative of the Opening of Railroad Communication between Boston and Canada, September 17th, 18th and 19th, 1851* (Boston, 1852).

18. Tomb of Franklin's parents, Josiah and Abiah Franklin, in Granary Burial Ground behind Boston Athenaeum. Unless people, such as the two in this photograph, move close enough to read the inscriptions, visitors, especially young ones, sometimes mistake this monument as Benjamin Franklin's.

all parts of the city intermingled with hundreds of school boys and girls on the street. Dressed in their best clothes, many of the pupils held a small card printed with this lyric:

> We come! we come! our music bringing, —
> Our hearts are with our voices singing:
> Rejoice! Rejoice! our spirits say,
> And hail with us this happy day.

It was the two hundred and twenty-sixth anniversary of the founding of Boston, when Greenough's statue was to be unveiled in front of City Hall in School Street.[97] The day was designated as a general

---

97. The most detailed record of the ceremony is Shurtleff, ed., *Memorial.* See also [Joseph Tinker Buckingham], *Supplement; Annuals of the Massachusetts Charitable Mechanic Association, 1852–1860* (n.p., n.d.), 437–38, 450, 500, 504–15, 572–73; W[illiam] J. Knowles, *Features of Inauguration of the Franklin*

19. Granite obelisk memorial for Franklin donated by Thomas Dowse in 1854, Mount Auburn Cemetery, Cambridge, Massachusetts. Inscriptions on the back read: "To The Memory/of/Benjamin Franklin/The Printer/The Philosopher/The Statesman/The Patriot/Who/By His Wisdom/Blessed His Country & His Age/And/Bequeathed to the World/an Illustrious Example/of Industry/Integrity/and/Self-Culture."

holiday (Fig. 20), and organizers were determined to have one of the most impressive municipal ceremonies in the city's history. By special arrangement with railroad companies, they mobilized thousands of people from nearby towns and cities. Participants in the celebration

Statue in Boston (Boston, 1856); [Benjamin Penhallow Shillaber], *A Very Brief and Very Comprehensive Life of Ben: Franklin, Printer, Done into Quaint Verse, by One of the Types* [Boston, 1856]; and John Clyde Oswald, *Benjamin Franklin in Oil and Bronze* (New York, 1926), 38–40.

ORDER OF EXERCISES

AT THE

INAUGURATION OF THE STATUE

OF

BENJAMIN FRANKLIN,

SEPTEMBER 17, 1856.

VOLUNTARY BY THE BAND.

CHORUS BY PUPILS OF THE GRAMMAR SCHOOLS,
UNDER DIRECTION OF PROF. CHAS. BUTLER.

PRAYER, BY REV. GEORGE W. BLAGDEN, D.D.

INAUGURAL ORATION, BY HON. ROBERT C. WINTHROP.

ORIGINAL ODE,

WRITTEN FOR THE OCCASION BY JAMES T. FIELDS, ESQ., AND ADAPTED TO MUSIC BY MR. NATHANIEL RICHARDSON.

Give welcome to his sculptured form!
Art's splendid triumph here is won;
Thus let him stand, in light and storm,
Our sea-girt city's greatest son.

His genius stamped the Press with power;
His glance the glowing future saw;
His science curbed the fiery shower;
His wisdom stood with Peace and Law.

His lineage sprung from honest Toil,
Swart Labor trained his youthful hand;
High with the brave who freed our soil,—
Where first he breathed let FRANKLIN stand.

The world his story long has shrined,—
To Fame his spotless deeds belong—
His homely Truth, his ample Mind,
His Saxon hate of human Wrong.

Room for the gray-haired patriot-sage!
For here his genial life began;
Thus let him look from age to age,
And prompt new Thought ennobling Man.

ADDRESS OF PRESENTATION, BY FRED. W. LINCOLN, ESQ., PRESIDENT OF THE MASSACHUSETTS CHARITABLE MECHANIC ASSOCIATION.

ADDRESS OF RECEPTION, BY HIS HONOR ALEXANDER H. RICE, MAYOR OF THE CITY.

MASONIC CEREMONIES OF INAUGURATION,

BY WINSLOW LEWIS, M. D., GRAND MASTER, ASSISTED BY JOHN T. HEARD AND CHARLES R. TRAIN, ESQRS., GRAND WARDENS, AND OTHER OFFICERS OF THE GRAND LODGE.

HYMN. Tune—"Old Hundred."

IN THE SINGING OF WHICH THE AUDIENCE ARE INVITED TO UNITE.

From all who dwell below the skies,
Let the Creator's praise arise;
Let the Redeemer's name be sung,
Through ev'ry land, by ev'ry tongue.

Eternal are thy mercies, Lord;
Eternal truth attends thy word;
Thy praise shall sound from shore to shore,
Till suns shall rise and set no more!

BENEDICTION BY RIGHT REV. BISHOP EASTBURN.

The Grand Piano used on this occasion, is from the Celebrated Manufactory of CHICKERING & SONS.

Geo. C. Rand & Avery,   Printers to the City.

20. City of Boston: "Order of Exercises at the Inauguration of the Statue of Benjamin Franklin, September 17, 1856." (By permission of the Boston Athenaeum)

procession included craftsmen from almost every major trade in the city as well as members of the American Academy of Arts and Sciences and students from Harvard College.

    Along the route of the procession, Tremont, Washington, Union,

Milk, Federal, and many other streets were richly decorated. Among hundreds of signs, flags, and posters one slogan that captured the general mood of the day read: "Franklin—We All Unite to Honor Him." After four hours the five-mile-long procession finally came to City Hall, where Winthrop was to deliver an oration. Stressing the hero's birth in Boston, the orator praised Franklin's greatness and carefully related his achievements to his New England heritage, by using such phrases as "native son," "native Bostonian," "native energy," and "native genius."[98]

Winthrop understood how much the statue meant to the pride of Bostonians. The new work of art, he emphasized, was "the product of New England industry and invention" and represented "the latest and best efforts of American genius and American skill."[99] If Franklin was "the man of the people," the orator declared, let his statue be unveiled and receive the daily salute of all who would pass it by.[100]

Not all New Englanders appreciated this sort of fanfare. In a personal letter James Russell Lowell observed satirically that the purpose of the entire event was "to invent something—in order to encourage sculptors."[101] But public spirit was not affected. Local newspapers reported that the celebration was a "Festival of the People" and "the first Franklin Day." The ceremony was "brilliantly successful" and the populace's reaction to the statue was "a universal sentiment of satisfaction, pleasure and delight"[102] (Fig. 21). The enthusiasm amazed outside observers as well. The *New York Times* commented that, though Bostonians had been regarded as "a people, usually esteemed economic," on the inauguration day "the city seems mad."[103]

Indeed, more than one hundred and thirty years after Franklin's escape from the city, Bostonians, concerned with their own reputation, honored him with lavish ceremony.[104] But the unprecedented

---

98. Shurtleff, ed., *Memorial*, 218, 223, 228, 233, 240, 251, 253, 257, 258, 259.
99. Ibid., 220.
100. Ibid., 223, 263.
101. To Miss [Jane] Norton, 9 September 1856, in Charles Eliot Norton, ed., *Letters of James Russell Lowell* (New York, 1894), 1: 271–72.
102. *Daily Evening Traveller* (Boston), 18 September 1856, pp. 1, 3; *Boston Daily Advertiser*, 19 September 1856, pp. 1, 2; *Salem Register*, 22 September 1856, p. 2.
103. *New York Times*, 19 September 1856, p. 1.
104. *Cambridge Chronicle* (Cambridge, Mass.), 20 September 1856, p. 2. *Illustrated Magazine of the Eighth Exhibition under the Direction of the Massachusetts Charitable Mechanic Association at Faneuil and Quincy Halls, Boston, September, 1856* (Boston), no. 4 (26 September 1856), viii.

A VERY BRIEF AND VERY COMPREHENSIVE LIFE

— OF —

BEN: FRANKLIN, PRINTER,

DONE INTO QUAINT VERSE, BY ONE OF THE TYPES.

B. P. Shillaber.   (was)   Mrs. Partington.

SEPTEMBER 17th, 1856.

KIND friends, just list to our ditty
 Of one whom the world loves to talk about,
Who was born in our tri-mountain city,
 And through its streets used to walk about.

In Boston he first saw the light,
 'Neath the shade of the Old South steeple,
And his parents, all say, were quite
 Respectable sort of people.

Old Mr. Franklin, his dad,
 Made candles to light all creation;
And naturally destined the lad
 To follow the same avocation—

To deal in candles and soaps,
 Thus light and cleanness dispensing;—
Our sight to the wisdom opes
 Of this way of Franklin's commencing:

Those candles prefigured the mind
 To break through the darkness o'ershading;
Those soaps the wisdom refined
 To cleanse men of errors pervading.

He was much as other boys are,
 And loved to play with the rest of 'em;
In all of their sports took a share,
 And wrestled and ran with the best of 'em.

We are told that he stole some stone
 To make a wharf to his wishing,
Where Haymarket Square has grown,
 The better to do his fishing.

He drew down his father's ire,
 On a string, because he made it,
Just as he did heaven's fire
 In after years as he bade it.

He read in his bed at night,
 And studied summer and winter,
When, seeing his Benny so bright,
 His father made him a printer.

He bound him out to his brother,
 A churlish fellow, they say,
And one quarrel followed another,
 Till Benjamin ran away.

He went to the Quaker city
 In a Philadelphia packet,
His mind undimmed and witty,
 And a true heart 'neath his jacket.

He printed, and spouted, and throve,
 And nobody could but like him;
He went overhead in love
 With a Read that chanced to strike him.

Then rascally Governor Keith
 Sent him on a fool's errand to London,
But in spite of the Governor's teeth,
 The boy printer wasn't undone.

For though in a stranger land,
 The youngster wasn't scared at it,
But to printing he turned his hand,
 And very respectably fared at it.

We'll not say he never was "hard"—
 There was some little flaw in his quality;
And he lost his friend Ralph's regard,
 And his cash, by a lapse of morality.

He returned and soon became great,—
 Got married—was made legislator—
Took very high rank in the state,
 And none with the people was greater:

Set a trap for the fires of heaven,
 And made the philosophers wonder;
The lightning's power was riven,
 And cut were the peals of the thunder.

Then "Poor Richard's" maxims he made,
 In language both prudent and funny,
And if all his voice had obeyed,
 They all would have rolled in money.

In Congress then he was placed,
 As England made new demonstrations,
And his name was soon after traced
 To that greatest of declarations.

And then when the bond was rent,
 And the patriots made resistance,
He over to France was sent,
 To ask King Louis' assistance.

His name before him had gone,
 And the King was delighted to meet him;
He even stepped from his throne,
 In his earnestness to greet him.

And the Queen frowned not in check,
 When this plain republican Mister
Threw his arms about her neck,
 And very gallantly kissed her:

Should ever occasion arise
 That we are in like situation,
This act of our brother wise
 We'll remember for imitation.

When long abroad he had staid,
 And had ceased our revolution,
He returned to the nation he'd made,
 And helped frame its constitution:

An instrument still revered,
 Though some there be who assail it;
Our country has long by it steered,
 And to our mast head we nail it.

Young married tradesmen to aid,
 He willed 'em a loan of his dollars,
And ordered medals made
 For all of our medalsome scholars.

But the great of the world must die,
 And Franklin had no immunity;
Though he wished to come back by and by,
 Should fate grant opportunity.

And here his wish is allowed,
 And here he is with us standing;
His fame and position proud,
 Our homage and love commanding.

And now, with our bosoms elate
 With pride we will not smother,
We join the grateful honors that wait
 To crown our "wholesome brother."

The world will cherish his name,
 And spread abroad his glory,
When yonder bram that tells his fame
 Shall be but a thing of story.

21. Benjamin Penhallow Shillaber's *Very Brief and Very Comprehensive Life of Ben: Franklin, Printer* is an animated depiction of Franklin's life and of the inauguration of Richard Greenough's statue in 1856. (By permission of the Boston Athenaeum)

public participation served another purpose. The Massachusetts Charitable Mechanic Association had scheduled its eighth industrial exhibition at the same time, and was therefore able to attract much of the crowd to their shows. The organization estimated that a record num-

22. Contemporary sketch of Greenough's statue, *Illustrated Magazine of the Eighth Exhibition under the Direction of the Massachusetts Charitable Mechanic Association*, September 1856, p. 16. The *Illustrated Magazine's* report on Greenough's statue was a prelude to a catalogue that contained advertisements of hundreds of industrial and consumer products. (By permission of the Houghton Library, Harvard University)

23. Franklin's bust in a niche of a dental office building on Milk Street in Boston, indicating his (1706) birthplace. The Old South Church where he was baptized was just around the corner. A few years later the family moved to another house at Union and Hanover Streets.

ber, more than one hundred and fifty thousand people, visited their exhibition, which was a "decided success"[105] (Fig. 22). Commercial motivations were also apparent when two years later, in 1858, the house where Franklin's family used to live at the corner of Union and

---

105. *Illustrated Magazine of the Eighth Exhibition; The Eighth Exhibition of the Massachusetts Charitable Mechanic Association; At Faneuil and Quincy Halls, In the City of Boston, September, 1856* (Boston, 1856), x, xi; *Annals of the Massachusetts Charitable Mechanic Association, 1795–1892* (Boston, 1892), 10.

Hanover Streets was demolished in order to make room for an increasing volume of traffic (Fig. 23). No one, including Edward Everett, could do anything to stop the demolition other than to lament the permanent loss of a historical site.[106] These events suggest that depending on the city's circumstances, Franklin's legacy could be either an asset on which to capitalize or a liability to be sacrificed.

---

106. Edward Everett, *The Mount Vernon Papers* (New York, 1860), 21–31; *The New York Times*, 16 November 1858, p. 2.

Interlude, 1861–1869

By the mid-nineteenth century Franklin's life had become a frequent lecture topic on the lyceum circuit, which was one of the most popular cultural institutions of the time.[1] The prominent public speaker Edward Everett, who often addressed "nationalistic themes" and who was once called by Robert C. Winthrop "our American Cicero,"[2] recorded:

On the 17th of January of the present year [1859], I delivered an address on the "Early Days of Franklin," at the invitation of the Association of the Franklin Medalists of the city of Boston; which has since been repeated at New York, Philadelphia, Baltimore, Richmond, and the University of Virginia.[3]

In fact, within a two-year period from January 1859 to February 1861 Everett's speech "Franklin the Boston Boy" and its various versions were delivered twenty-eight times. The places where he gave the speech included Abington, Massachusetts; Rutland, Vermont; Manchester, New Hampshire; Biddeford, Maine, and Troy, New York.[4] These small town audiences enthusiastically welcomed him, for his reputation as a famous orator often generated high expectations. An advertisement in a Manchester newspaper read:

Hon. Edward Everett is to deliver an address on the Early Days of Franklin at Smyth's Hall this evening. Mr. Everett is the man of all others that has

---

1. Donald M. Scott, "The Popular Lecture and the Creation of a Public in Mid-Nineteenth-Century America," *Journal of American History* 66 (March 1980): 791–809.
2. Quoted from Ronald F. Reid, "Edward Everett: Rhetorician of Nationalism, 1824–1855," *Quarterly Journal of Speech* 42 (October 1956): 273, 278.
3. Everett, *Orations and Speeches on Various Occasions* (Boston, 1879), 4: 16.
4. Ibid. 4: 129.

embalmed the memory of Washington, and as Franklin is next to the "Father of his Country" in the heart of the people, Mr Everett is just the orator to do justice to his memory.[5]

On the other hand, the orator understood that, regarding Franklin as a great patriot, his listeners were eager to hear everything relating to him, no matter how trivial it might be. He satisfied their patriotism and curiosity by revealing that the ancestors of Washington and Franklin had lived only miles apart in England.

Everett's melodious voice, commendable knowledge of the local history of Boston, unusual ability to incorporate anecdotes into a grand theme, and firm grasp of minute details, all seemed to have pleased his audiences. At the same time, he reminded them that Franklin's humble birth was only a prelude to his glories. His toiling childhood only toughened his will and sharpened his mind, and hence became an unusual preparation for future greatness. Although his stories and assertions were not entirely original, the speaker's "rich imagery, abundance of detail, and the clearness of narration and description made them intensely interesting."[6]

Newspapers in the North were almost overwhelmingly appreciative of his performance. But one of the most convincing testimonies can be found in a long article that appeared in the issue of the *Daily Richmond Enquirer* for April 11, 1859. With Everett's celebrated oration, "The Character of Washington," still fresh in memory, the reporter characterized Everett as "the noble orator" and went on to say:

A large audience assembled at the Mechanics' Institute, on Friday evening last, to listen to an orator who is about the only one we know who never fails to draw a crowd, and never fails to delight them when assembled. —His "Franklin" differs from his "Washington" in tone and general features, just as the two great men differ one from the other. But we should hardly venture to call the discourse on "Franklin" a production inferior to the eulogy on "Washington." Indeed, the former contains bursts of electrifying eloquence

---

5. *Manchester Daily Mirror* (Manchester, New Hampshire), 19 November 1860, p. 2. For similar reactions to his lecture on Franklin see Paul Revere Frothingham, *Edward Everett: Orator and Statesman* (Boston, 1925), 386; *Atlas and Daily Bee* (Boston), 18 January 1859, p. 2; 18 January 1860, p. 2; *Rutland Courier* (Rutland, Vermont), 13 April 1860, p. 2; *Bristol Ph[o]enix* (Bristol, Rhode Island), 1 December 1860, p. 2; *Waltham Sentinel* (Waltham, Massachusetts), 16 November 1860, p. 2; and *Vermont Phoenix* (Brattleboro, Vermont), 10 January 1860, p. 2.

6. Reid, "Edward Everett," 280, 281.

that almost surpass the most stirring passages of the "Washington." The powerful, yet poetic, description of the birth of Franklin, roused the audience to a high pitch of enthusiasm. —The whole discourse abounded with interesting facts, unfamiliar to most persons, and presented strong pictures of human life, dashed upon the canvas with a master's boldness and consummate skill—the interest throughout was unflaggingly sustained.

The last time Everett gave his speech on Franklin was in Troy, New York, on February 28, 1861. Less than two months later, the Civil War broke out. One might expect this to hamper efforts to promote the reputation of Franklin, whose inclinations, it is believed, were more closely associated with harmony and peace-making than with confrontation and war. Through a series of historical coincidences, however, the war facilitated the activities of his several important advocates.

After Charles Sumner was violently assaulted by Preston Brooks of South Carolina on the Senate floor in 1856, his injuries required time for recovery. He twice went to Europe where he had the leisure to write an article entitled "Monograph from an Old Note-Book," which was published in the *Atlantic Monthly Magazine* in 1863.[7] In it Sumner investigated extensively the origin of Turgot's Latin verse on Franklin, and went so far as to assert: "This verse was no common event. It was a new expression of the French alliance, and an assurance of independence."[8]

The bloody war dragged on and James Parton, who could not wait to see its end, published his two-volume *Life and Times of Benjamin Franklin* in 1864.[9] The most comprehensive account of Franklin's life written during the nineteenth century, Parton's biography remained very popular for several decades.[10] For the first time in a volume readily available Parton revealed the contents of Hutchinson's letters, and stated that "they were written by public men to a public man, for the information of public men, upon public topics." Therefore he

---

7. Sumner, "Monograph from an Old Note-Book," *Atlantic Monthly* 12 (November 1863): 648–62.

8. Sumner revised the article and changed its title to "Benjamin Franklin and John Slidell at Paris"; it was included in *The Works of Charles Sumner* (Boston, 1874), 8: 1–38. The quote is from page 5.

9. *Historical Magazine* 8 (March 1864): 127.

10. Max Farrand believed that even Carl Van Doren's informative *Benjamin Franklin* in the twentieth century had not superseded Parton's biography ("Self-Portraiture: The Autobiography," reprint from *General Magazine and Historical Chronicle* [July 1940], 4).

concluded that Franklin did nothing wrong in passing them along for the sake of the public.[11]

Parton obtained, from Henry Stevens, a transcript of *A Dissertation on Liberty and Necessity, Pleasure and Pain*. He included the piece in his appendix and later deposited the copy in the New-York Historical Society.[12] Written by Franklin in London at the age of nineteen, the tract was such a rare specimen that even the indefatigable Sparks failed to find it. Parton mildly criticized Franklin's personal life in France by pointing out that unlike Thomas Jefferson, Franklin did not travel around the nation. Franklin indulged himself in the luxury of Paris, and contented himself with the society of the celebrated. Thus, according to Franklin's own written record, he seemed unaware of the poor, and of disturbing social conditions in France.[13]

Numerous as Parton's own contributions were, he remained deeply indebted to Sparks. When he discussed Franklin's discovery of electricity, Parton benefited from Sparks's edition, which had printed for the first time in the United States more than seventy letters and numerous valuable footnotes written by Franklin himself. Parton paid a tribute to his predecessor, saying that "Dr. Sparks's edition is a monument, at once, to the memory of Benjamin Franklin, and to his own diligence, tact, and faithfulness."[14]

The most significant event concerning Franklin's legacy during the 1860s, however, was John Bigelow's discovery of the invaluable original manuscripts of Franklin's memoirs. Bigelow served as American consul in Paris in 1864 and became minister to France the next year. Learning that the manuscript of Franklin's autobiography might be in that country, he looked for it, but to no avail. Before he left for home, via England, in January 1867, he visited his friend Professor Édouard Laboulaye and requested his help. No sooner had Bigelow arrived in London than Laboulaye reported that the manuscripts were in the hands of Paul and Georges de Senarmont, grand-nephews of M. Le Veillard. The owners demanded 25,000 francs to part with them. Bigelow agreed. Through the dedicated help of his friend William Henry Huntington, the manuscripts were delivered to him in London on January 28, 1867.

In the summer of the same year, Bigelow started collating the original manuscript with Temple Franklin's edition of the autobiog-

---

11. Parton, *Life and Times of Benjamin Franklin* (New York, 1864), 1: 562.
12. Stevens, *Stevens's Historical Collections* (London, 1881), 161–62.
13. Parton, *Life and Times of Franklin*, 2: 412–13.
14. Ibid. 2: 639.

raphy. His oldest daughter read the original slowly so that he could discern any discrepancy between the two documents: he found twelve hundred errors in Temple Franklin's edition. Bigelow also discovered that the original draft of Franklin's autobiography contained a fourth part, which had never been published in English, and an outline, which had never appeared in print. It became clear that Temple Franklin's edition of the autobiography was, in fact, based not on the original manuscripts but on a fair copy, which his grandfather had provided to M. Le Veillard in 1789. When Temple Franklin went to Paris in the early 1790s, he exchanged the autograph manuscripts with M. Le Veillard's copy, which was easier to read and prepare for the press. If the old rumors that Temple Franklin had been bribed proved to be false, his own action, especially his indifferent treatment of his grandfather's manuscripts, ultimately jeopardized his reputation.

When Bigelow's edition of the autobiography was published in the spring of 1868, it immediately superseded previous editions. It was the first time that Franklin's memoirs had been printed in full.[15] Declaring that Bigelow had rescued the autograph manuscript of Franklin's autobiography from foreigners, the *New York Times* asserted: "Mr. Bigelow is entitled to the warmest gratitude of all Americans—and, indeed, to that of the world."[16]

---

15. The most detailed account of this episode is Bigelow's *Retrospections of an Active Life* (New York, 1909–13), 3: 596–97, 4: 6–30. See also Margaret Clapp, *Forgotten First Citizen: John Bigelow* (New York, 1968), 261; John Bigelow, ed., *The Life of Benjamin Franklin* (Philadelphia, 1874), 66–71; Max Farrand, ed., *Benjamin Franklin's Memoirs* (Berkeley, 1949), xxi–xxxii; J. A. Leo Lemay and P. Zall, eds., *The Autobiography of Benjamin Franklin* (Knoxville, [Tenn.] 1981), lxv.
16. *New York Times*, 6 June 1868, p. 3.

Part II:
Personality
1870–1938

Chapter 4

The Spell of Personal Traits

In the years following the Civil War, America was rapidly changed into an industrialized society. This profound social and economic transformation led to new cultural conditions under which many Americans gradually shifted their interest from character to personality. Within such a historical context many people also began to perceive Franklin's image from a new angle. The changing perceptions of his image will be the subject of chapters 5 and 6; this one analyzes those changing cultural conditions.

I

The emergence of a new emphasis on personality was a gradual and complex process. Toward the end of the 1860s there were signs that some people began to see "character" and "characteristic men" as different concepts.[1] As mentioned earlier, in a society preoccupied with character people were deeply concerned about the propriety of conduct. Because the basic principle of morality was to discern good and evil, or to distinguish between right and wrong, there could be no middle ground, and character was often categorized in a dichotomy.

Americans generally assumed the existence of two types of people whose character was either good or bad, strong or weak, high or low.[2] They believed that only those of good and high character would

---

1. Edwin P. Whipple, *Character and Characteristic Men* (Boston, 1877). Most essays in this volume were written in the 1860s. For articles reflecting the public's growing interest in personality after the 1860s, see A[braham] A[aron] Roback, comp., *A Bibliography of Character and Personality* (Cambridge, Mass., 1927).

2. A[braham] A[aron] Roback, *The Psychology of Character; With a Survey of Personality in General* (3rd ed.: London, 1952), 6. As a psychologist who

demonstrate strong moral strength, which should be the model for others to follow. A small number were perceived as having the consummate type of character, whose sublimity inevitably placed them above their countrymen. When a new emphasis on personality began to develop, the public's attitudes toward their heroes changed accordingly. People began to think less about a commonly accepted mode of conduct their heroes represented, and became more and more inclined to emphasize individual traits.

From the early 1870s Thomas Jefferson's appearance, habits, manners, and tastes became a focal point of discussion. Merrill D. Peterson illustrates that this shift of attention from Jefferson's public activity to his private experience could be found in Sarah Nicholas Randolph's book, *Domestic Life of Thomas Jefferson*, published in 1871. Miss Randolph characterized Jefferson as "a beautiful domestic character."[3] Concurrently, James Parton emphasized Jefferson's charm and romance in a biography in which he devoted an entire chapter to his marriage.[4]

A similar trend occurred after some leading scholars called for a reappraisal of George Washington. John Bach McMaster asserted in 1885 that "his true biography is still to be prepared. General Washington is known to us, and President Washington. But George Washington is an unknown man." Such a suggestion generated some furious protest from Washington's enthusiastic advocates, who were seriously concerned about where those personal investigations would

---

treated and advised several thousand people about personality problems, Henry C. Link wrote: "When people say that a man has a good character, they frequently mean that he is honest, does not steal, is true to his word, is steady in his habits. . . . Personality is the extent to which the individual has learned to convert his energies into habits or actions which successfully influence other people" (*The Return to Religion* [New York, 1937], 89). The author thought that his book could have been renamed as *How to Develop Your Personality*; see Dale Carnegie, *How to Win Friends and Influence People* (New York, 1937), 86–87.

3. The public did not cease to use the word *character* after the 1870s. Whereas personality rarely carried the moral implication that character often suggested, within certain contexts *character* could mean a person or his personal trait. Therefore, in some cases, when people continued to use the word *character*, what they actually meant was personality. Psychologists and sociologists also used the two words interchangeably. As scientists, they did not pay particular attention to the moral dimension of character; they emphasized the psychological, social, or cultural *structures* of personality.

4. Peterson, *The Jefferson Image in the American Mind* (New York, 1962), 231–36.

lead. Leonard Irving declared: "The towering excellence and nobility of George Washington is too much for some people. . . . It is silly to suppose or maintain that Washington was faultless. . . . But it is mean to be anxious to show that he possessed traits of meanness."[5]

Convinced that traditional portrayals of Washington ought to be reexamined, however, McMaster insisted that people "shall read less of the cherry-tree and more of the man," who had "many human frailties and much common sense." He predicted that "we shall also hear his oaths, and see him in those terrible outbursts of passion to which Mr. Jefferson has alluded," or "we shall know him as the cold and forbidding character with whom no fellow-man ever ventured to live on close and familiar terms."[6]

Although new studies could reveal the "true" characteristics of old heroes, not all investigations would enhance their reputations. In 1892 Paul Leicester Ford wrote an article, "Thomas Jefferson in Undress," in which he suggested that Jefferson was not immune to human vices, such as gambling and spending lavishly beyond his income. Around the turn of the present century University of Virginia professor William Mynn Thornton asked in an address, "Who Was Thomas Jefferson?"[7] Though Abraham Lincoln's reputation as a great president soared after he was assassinated, the search for his personal qualities persisted, reflected in such books as Francis Fisher Browne's *Every-Day Life of Abraham Lincoln* (1886), Eleanor Gridley's *Story of Abraham Lincoln, Including His Jokes and Anecdotes* (1900), William Eleroy Curtis's *True Abraham Lincoln* (1902), Charles L. C. Minor's *Real Lincoln* (1904), William E. Barton's *Women Lincoln Loved* (1927), and Dale Carnegie's *Lincoln the Unknown* (1932).

II

Many public figures' personal lives were scrutinized, in some cases vulgarized, and Franklin's reputation was not exempt from this sort of

---

5. Irving, "Do We Know George Washington?" *Magazine of American History* 29 (March 1893), 223. For discussions of the renewed interest during this period in digging out details of Washington's personal life see Karal Ann Marling, *George Washington Slept Here* (Cambridge, Mass., 1988), 115–50.

6. McMaster, *A History of the People of the United States* (Philadelphia, 1883–1915), 2: 452–53.

7. Ford, "Thomas Jefferson in Undress," *Scribner's Magazine* 12 (October 1892), 509–16; Thornton's address was delivered before the Virginia Bar Association on 12 August 1909, see Peterson, *The Jefferson Image*, 232–60.

reevaluation. What made his case singular, however, was its close relation with the fundamental transformation in American society.

When much of the nation remained in the pre-industrial stage, it was reasonable for a tradesman to expect success that was based on his skill, thrift, and industry. The prevailing concern with character, therefore, was also deeply interwoven with the work ethic. Many Americans believed that hard work and its subsequent outcome of prosperity were manifestations of inner goodness, which should lead to success almost anywhere under most circumstances:[8] work was honor and glory; diligence was crucial to economic advancement.[9]

As a well-known self-made man, Franklin represented this kind of mentality. For many years prior to the Civil War most Americans did not explicitly link his story with wealth, but tried to use his example to emphasize the importance of moral goodness. In post-Civil War America, however, the premise that a man's success depended primarily on his own merits was gravely shaken. Richard Hofstadter observed that "with its rapid expansion, its exploitative methods, its desperate competition, and its peremptory rejection of failure, post-bellum America was like a vast human caricature of the Darwinian struggle for existence and survival of the fittest."[10] While businessmen, especially new entrepreneurs, openly accepted social Darwinism as a guiding doctrine in their enterprise, many also began to re-think the importance of character in their lives and to reevaluate the relevance of ethics in their business practices. Although ethical concerns did not suddenly disappear, a number of traditional values became increasingly incompatible with reality.

Like Victorians during the same period, many Americans believed that in the battle for economic advancement "the greatest and the strongest must of necessity be the most unscrupulous." Whenever survival was at stake, honor, truth, and virtue could be "sacrificed together."[11] The notions of success, industry, and frugality became gradually dissociated. Hard work remained fundamental for an hon-

---

8. Sigmund Diamond, *The Reputation of the American Businessman* (Cambridge, Mass., 1955), 178.

9. Samuel Smiles, *Character* (New York, 1876), 97.

10. Hofstadter, *Social Darwinism in American Thought, 1860–1915* (Philadelphia, 1945), 30.

11. Quoted in Walter E. Houghton, *The Victorian Frame of Mind, 1830–1870* (New Haven, 1957), 192n. For the Victorians' perspective of character see Stefan Collini, "The Idea of 'Character' in Victorian Political Thought," *Transactions of the Royal Historical Society*, 5th ser., 35 (1985): 29–50.

est living; success, however, was no longer an immediate consequence of diligence. On the contrary, as Alan Trachtenberg has described, "The public knew well enough that virtue was the easiest victim in the hard world of competition."[12] Perhaps many underprivileged people, such as the blacks in the South, dispossessed farmers from the countryside, or newly-arrived immigrants, might still consider themselves successful, if success meant no more than earning a salary or obtaining a job in a factory. Booker T. Washington, for example, a strong believer in the Yankee value of self-help, insisted on educating his students at Tuskegee Institute in Alabama mainly through "character building."[13] Yet Tuskegee Institute could provide its black pupils with no more than basic vocational training, such as sewing, cooking, brick-laying, and carpentry. An even greater number of people painfully realized that

industrialization upset the certainty that hard work would bring economic success. Whatever the life chances of a farmer or shop hand had been in the early years of the century, it became troublingly clear that the semiskilled laborer, caught in the anonymity of a late-nineteenth-century textile factory or steel mill, was trapped in his circumstances—that no amount of sheer hard work would open the way to self-employment or wealth.[14]

Not surprisingly, Mark Twain, the man who gave the period its name, the Gilded Age, despised Franklin's story. He bitterly charged that Franklin's agitation for success in his autobiography "was of a vicious disposition," which was "to inflict suffering upon the rising generation of all subsequent ages." Convinced that Franklin's rosy picture of striving for success through hard work was an illusion, Twain continued to satirize:

His simplest acts, also, were contrived with a view to their being held up for the emulation of boys forever—boys who might otherwise have been happy. . . . With a malevolence which is without parallel in history, he would work all day, and then sit up nights and let on to be studying algebra by the

---

12. Trachtenberg, *The Incorporation of America: Culture and Society in the Gilded Age* (New York, 1982), 80.
13. Washington, *Character Building; Being Addresses Delivered on Sunday Evenings to the Students of Tuskegee Institute* (New York, 1902).
14. Daniel T. Rodgers, *The Work Ethic in Industrial America, 1850–1920* (Phoenix ed.: Chicago, 1979), 28.

light of a smouldering fire, so that all the boys might have to do that also, or else have Benjamin Franklin thrown upon them (Fig. 24).[15]

Moreover, when success was no longer regarded as a manifestation of virtue, it was frequently equated with the accumulation of wealth and money. During the post-Civil War era literature that promoted success sounded more and more like Mammon worship.[16] From P. T. Barnum's exceedingly popular lecture, "The Art of Money-Getting," to Andrew Carnegie's highly acclaimed article, "The Gospel of Wealth," Americans were daily advised that pecuniary pursuits were goals in their own right. Russell H. Conwell, the clergyman, insisted: "I say that you ought to get rich, and it is your duty to get rich." When some people questioned whether or not it was appropriate for a Christian clergyman to say so, he replied: "Yes of course I do. . . . Because to make money honestly is to preach the gospel."[17] Little wonder that when Walt Whitman summarized the situation, he noticed that all of "the extreme business energy" and the "almost maniacal appetite for wealth prevalent in the United States" were praised by his contemporaries as indispensable "parts of amelioration and progress."[18]

Not only did the dissociation of success from serious concern about morality pave the way for modern business practice; more important, the separation of virtue from modern industrial activity called for a different kind of personality. If a businessman wanted to be successful in a highly competitive world, traditional merits—such as craft, thrift, and diligence—were far from adequate. He must be a person of ambition, power, energy, and ability, as John D. Rockefeller plainly stated:

It is my belief that the principal cause for the economic differences between people is their difference in personality, and that it is only as we can

---

15. Mark Twain, "The Late Benjamin Franklin," *Galaxy* 10 (July 1870), 138–39.
16. Irvin G. Wyllie, *The Self-Made Man in America: The Myth of Rags to Riches* (New Brunswick, N.J., 1954), 55– 74.
17. P[hineas] T[aylor] Barnum, *The Life of P. T. Barnum Written by Himself* (New York, 1855) and *The Art of Money-Getting* (New York, 1882); Carnegie, *The Gospel of Wealth and Other Timely Essays*, ed. Edward C. Kirkland (Cambridge, Mass., 1962). Speaking of the popularity of his lecture, "Acres of Diamonds," Conwell claimed that he had delivered it almost five thousand times (*Acres of Diamonds* [New York, 1915], 18, 180).
18. Whitman, *Democratic Vistas* (Library of Liberal Arts ed.: New York, 1949), 24n.

26   *NAST'S ALMANAC FOR* 1872.

THE LATE BENJAMIN FRANKLIN.

BY MARK TWAIN.

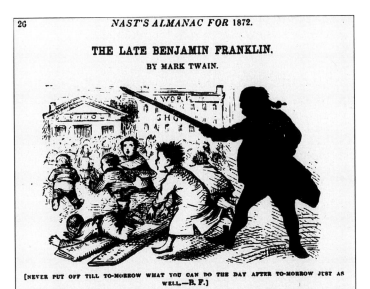

[NEVER PUT OFF TILL TO-MORROW WHAT YOU CAN DO THE DAY AFTER TO-MORROW JUST AS WELL.—B. F.]

THIS party was one of those persons whom they call philosophers. He was born twins, being born simultaneously in two different houses in the city of Boston. These houses remain unto this day, and have signs upon them worded in accordance with the facts. The signs are considered well enough to have, though not necessary, because the inhabitants point out the two birthplaces to the stranger anyhow, and sometimes as often as several times in the same day. The subject of this memoir was of a vicious disposition, and early prostituted his talents to the invention of maxims and aphorisms calculated to inflict suffering upon the rising generation of all subsequent ages. His simplest acts, also, were contrived with a view to their being held up for the emulation of boys forever—boys who might otherwise have been happy. It was in this spirit that he became the son of a soap-boiler, and, probably, for no other reason than that the efforts of all future boys who tried to be any thing might be looked upon with suspicion unless they were the sons of soap-boilers. With a malevolence which is without paral-

lel in history, he would work all day, and then sit up nights, and let on to be studying algebra by the light of a smouldering fire, so that all the boys might have to do that also, or else have Benjamin Franklin thrown upon them. Not satisfied with these proceedings, he had a fashion of living wholly on bread and water, and studying astronomy at meal-time — a thing which has brought affliction to mil-

lions of boys since, whose fathers had read Franklin's pernicious biography.

His maxims were full of animosity toward boys. Nowadays a boy can not follow out a single natural instinct without tumbling over some of those everlasting aphorisms, and hearing from Franklin on the spot. If he buys two cents' worth of pea-nuts, his father says, " Remember what Franklin has said, my son—'A groat a day is a penny a year ;' "

24. Thomas Nast's cartoons further dramatized Mark Twain's sarcastic "Late Benjamin Franklin," *Thomas Nast's Almanac for 1872*, p. 26.

assist in the wider distribution of those qualities which go to make up a strong personality that we can assist in the wider distribution of wealth.[19]

In the whirlpool of modern business the belief that skill and hard work would bring success became obsolete. Modern business was a storm of warfare. In this struggle self-exertion and self-discipline were hardly as critical as the ability to manipulate others and manage hundreds.

In addition, modern entrepreneurs suggested that a crucial condition for their success was not diligence, but capital investment, as Carnegie's and Rockefeller's memoirs clearly indicated. The former revealed that in order to give him "a start," the family mortgaged their house for him to purchase ten shares of Adams Express Company stock, worth fifty dollars each. The latter recalled that he got his first loan of a thousand dollars from his father at an interest rate of 10 percent.[20] After comparing a number of prominent businessmen in both the eighteenth and nineteenth centuries, Sigmund Diamond concluded that the age when "character determines destiny" was gone. Business success in the late nineteenth century depended heavily on the whole economic system.[21]

As a final word, if a businessman did continue to consider his moral character, his personal reputation would lie primarily in spheres other than business activity, such as charity or philanthropy. Business was not directly linked with morality, which became important only after businessmen had achieved their success: Andrew Carnegie believed that rich men were stewards of wealth, and John D. Rockefeller characteristically described "The Art of Getting" and "The Art of Giving."[22]

These profound changes forced people as perceptive as Henry Adams to admit that the society was demanding "a new type of man."[23] Even though Franklin's life remained an inspiration for those who continued to believe in the myth of the self-made man, his story was no longer the classic example in the market of agitating individual success. His simple virtues sounded increasingly insufficient in a world that relied heavily on modern technology and capital invest-

---

19. Rockefeller, *Random Reminiscences of Men and Events* (Garden City, N.Y., 1933), 154.
20. Carnegie, *Autobiography* (Cambridge, Mass., 1920), 75–76; *The Gospel of Wealth*, 9–10; Rockefeller, *Random Reminiscences*, 41.
21. Diamond, *The Reputation of the American Businessman*, 178.
22. Carnegie, *The Gospel of Wealth*, 14–49; Rockefeller, *Random Reminiscences*, 31–52, 137–62.
23. Adams, *The Education of Henry Adams* (Sentry ed.: Boston, 1961), 499.

ment. More popular materials were as easily available as his *Autobiography*, from Horatio Alger's novel, *Ragged Dick*, to Thomas Louis Haines's manual, *Worth and Wealth; or, The Art of Getting, Saving, and Using Money*.[24] In an age of a frantic Mammon cult Franklin's famous tract, *The Way to Wealth*, was only sporadically printed as an independent work. Although it was included in many anthologies, the reason was more for its literary value than because of its usefulness as a practical guide.

III

Although Americans' concerns with character were closely related to their Protestant heritage, their new interest in personality was deeply involved with the development and influence of modern science.

Throughout Western civilization from Theophrastus' *Characters* to Immanuel Kant's *Anthropologie*, various methodologies had been adopted to explain personality. Ancient palmistry tried to determine man's experience by interpreting the meaning of lines on his hands. Phrenology attempted to project man's characteristics by examining the external shape of the skull.[25] Biology revealed that in order to survive, human beings were constantly adjusting themselves to the environment, and that the pattern of their behavior was quite similar to the instinctive life of the higher animals.

None of these explanations made a more profound impact on the understanding of personality than modern psychology, psychiatry, psychoanalysis, and neurology. These studies flourished toward the end of the nineteenth century,[26] especially after Sigmund Freud postulated that human behavior had an intrinsic relationship with the nervous system and mental condition.[27]

---

24. Many of Alger's successful stories stressed luck more than industry, for example *Ragged Dick* (Boston, 1868), which was reprinted about a hundred and thirty times within the next few decades. See Frank Luther Mott, *Golden Multitudes: The Story of Best Sellers in the United States* (New York, 1947), 158–59. About handbooks and manuals on success see Louis B. Wright, "Franklin's Legacy to the Gilded Age," *Virginia Quarterly Review* 22 (Spring 1946): 268–79; and Wyllie, *The Self-Made Man*, 116–32.

25. Alexander Bain, *On the Study of Character, Including an Estimate of Phrenology* (London, 1861).

26. Abraham Myerson, *The Foundations of Personality* (Boston, 1927).

27. Freud, *The Interpretation of Dreams* (London, 1913), which was first published in German in 1899.

The American public was much attracted to new discoveries in psychology and related subjects. In professional lectures and in the literature of popular science, scholars and self-appointed experts frequently informed Americans that they should pay close attention to the condition of their brains and nervous systems, because they were more apt to suffer from mental diseases than ever before. These diseases were generated by anxiety, fear, frustration, and insecurity, all of which were phenomena peculiar to an industrialized society.[28] Without proper treatment, these symptoms might utterly destroy man's well-being. To prevent this the public needed to know more about personality—the working mechanism of the human psyche.

As early as 1871 Silas Weir Mitchell, a physician in Philadelphia, warned the public: "The nervous system of certain classes of Americans is being sorely overtaxed."[29] Americans were "overworked and overworried," Dr. Mitchell concluded. Two years later, another physician, George M. Beard, confirmed that neurasthenia or nervous exhaustion was a typically American disease.[30] Mitchell's and Beard's views were confirmed by Professor William Mathews who wrote: "Everywhere men are killing themselves by overwork, —by intense, exhausting labor of hand and brain."[31]

These warnings indicated that overwork was a much more serious problem than idleness, and that hard work often brought physical and psychological strains rather than happiness. In her best selling book entitled *Power through Repose*, Miss Annie Payson Call insisted that, like the air and food, relaxation and rest were indispensable conditions for a healthy human being. Soon after the book was published, the distinguished psychologist, William James, highly commended it in an address entitled "The Gospel of Relaxation."[32]

---

28. Freud did not deny that "economic conflicts" could contribute to the intensified relationship between what he called the id and the ego, *An Outline of Psycho-analysis* (New York, 1949), 62.

29. Mitchell, *Wear and Tear, or Hints for the Overworked* (5th ed.: Philadelphia, 1887), 9, 22–26. Using the latest statistics, Mitchell revealed that diseases related to disorders in the nervous system were increasing rapidly in some crowded cities in the United States. In Chicago, he noted, a city that had grown "from a country town to a vast business hive within a few years," its death rate as a result of nervous breakdowns increased faster than its population growth.

30. Ibid., 39, 71. Beard, *American Nervousness* (New York, 1881).

31. Mathews, *Getting on in the World; or, Hints on Success in Life* (Chicago, 1873), 329–30.

32. Call, *Power through Repose* (Boston, 1892). Also Donald Meyer, *The Positive*

In order to maintain personal identity and mental health, each individual needed to know when to relax and how to develop his personality. Fortunately, there was hope of accomplishing this since personality differed from character. To change character from bad to good or from weak to strong, could take a lifetime, because good character was a gift of nature.[33] Modern science demonstrated, however, that with empirical methodology, well-monitored tests, and closely-examined data, personality could be studied rationally. Modern science could not only cure patients with mental diseases, but also be of great help to those who were eager to improve their personalities. As long as an individual case was studied and treated scientifically, personality was malleable and could be altered within a relatively short period of time.

IV

Modern America was a society of mass production and mass consumption, and both depended on mass or effective communication.[34] Happiness now depended not only on how hard one worked and how much one would consume, but also on how well one could relate to other members of society. Thus the new interest in personality complemented a growing awareness of the importance of sociability.

Ernest R. Groves, a professor of sociology and a prolific author on social relations, asserted in his book, *Personality and Social Adjustment*, that "our happiness in life largely depends upon our having pleasant associations with the people about us," such as family members, friends, neighbors, and fellow-workers. He pointed out that

in every field of human behavior, business, arts, politics, teaching and the rest, the commanding importance of psychological and psychiatric investigations is being recognized. Goods are bought and sold by psychological

---

Thinkers (revised ed.: Middletown, Conn., 1988), 32; Daniel T. Rodgers, *The Work Ethic in Industrial America*, 94–124.

33. Rudolf Eucken, "Character," *Encyclopaedia of Religion and Ethics* (New York, 1960), 3: 364–65.

34. How modernity broke traditional isolation in American society is the theme of Robert H. Wiebe's perceptive synthesis, *The Search for Order, 1877–1920* (New York, 1967).

methods. A political campaign is now largely a psychological struggle between rival parties.[35]

"Recent psychology has been tested by experience," he went on to say, "and the successful man of business and affairs is the most outspoken in his appreciation of the advantage there is in having a scientific interpretation of mental behavior."[36]

When Americans talked about character, they concentrated on a person's inner goodness. Character spoke of integrity and recognized consistency between one's internal feelings and outward expressions. That good character was appreciated had little to do with other persons, except as examples. Virtue benefited only those who possessed it. As Richard Grant White said, "Character is like an inward and spiritual grace, of which reputation is, or should be, the outward and visible sign."[37] In fact, those who were believed to have good character would not expect immediate recognition. Personality, by contrast, emphasized outward appearance, including physical and verbal expression and refinement of manners. An outstanding personality had the ability to attract, please, and influence people. In short, if the goal of character was self-righteousness, that of personality was popularity—the crux of social intercourse in modern society.[38] "Success is measured by how well one fits in, how well one is liked by others, how well others respond to the roles one is playing," the historian Warren I. Susman observed.[39]

Little wonder that after years of such emphasis, many began to perceive Franklin differently. When the self-appointed authority on human relations and effective speaking, Dale Carnegie, urged his audiences to improve themselves, he pointed out that Franklin's *Autobiography* was an excellent textbook for those who were interested in personality. Listen to what the famous Franklin said about "dealing with people and managing yourself." Buy a copy of the *Autobiography*. If you could not find one in a nearby bookstore, he sug-

35. Groves, *Personality and Social Adjustment* (New York, 1924), 1, 10–11. Henry C. Link insisted that the most important factor in successful selling was the study of a consumer's personality and buying habits (*The New Psychology of Selling and Advertising* [New York, 1938], 2).

36. Groves, *Personality and Social Adjustment*, 11.

37. White, *Words and Their Uses* (revised ed.: Boston, 1899), 86.

38. A[braham] A[aron] Roback, *Personality: The Crux of Social Intercourse* (Cambridge, Mass., 1931).

39. Susman, *Culture as History: The Transformation of American Society in the Twentieth Century* (New York, 1984), 200.

gested, send sixty-eight cents to order one, and don't forget to enclose ten cents for postage.[40]

The new attention on personality did not happen overnight, nor did it completely erase traditional convictions. The popular English author Samuel Smiles declared as late as in 1886 that "the crown and glory of life is character."[41] Americans, similarly, did not cease to believe that some of Franklin's characteristics represented fundamental Americanness, such as his philosophy of life and his attitudes toward work and success. Generally speaking, after the Civil War Americans gradually began to perceive him as one who possessed a charismatic personality. They now stressed those singular characteristics that differentiated him from the rest of his countrymen, not the moral qualities that might be emulated. In some cases, cynical critics stripped away his moral greatness and scrutinized his private life to such a degree as to expose his dark side and personal weaknesses.

---

40. Carnegie, *How to Win Friends and Influence People*, 149. More than fifteen million copies have been sold since the 1930s, and the book is still in print.
41. Smiles, *Self-Help* (revised ed.: New York, 1884), 416.

Chapter 5

"He Was a Great Humane Man"

❧

Unlike many great Americans whose fame faded as time went by, Franklin remained one of the nation's most familiar names almost a century after his death. As has been indicated, the vicissitudes of his legacy were not politically or ideologically related. Franklin continued to interest Americans largely because of his fascinating personal traits. His native humor, varied genius, and remarkable achievements captivated Americans' imaginations as they began to move into a modern age. Most people no longer referred to him as "illustrious," and many began to call him Ben Franklin instead of Dr. Franklin.[1]

To Americans of the late Victorian period he was not the consummate hero but increasingly a real human being. Despite his self-confessed mistakes and the increasing exposures of his shortcomings, Franklin's overall good reputation remained intact until the end of the nineteenth century. Skeptical as they were, most people tolerated his errors and avoided open criticism of his shortcomings. Their interest in Franklin culminated in the bicentennial celebration of his birth in 1906.

I

Artistic representations of Franklin attracted admirers, who used literary descriptions, sculpture, and paintings to form their perceptions about him. Some of his biographers, such as Sydney George Fisher and Paul Leicester Ford, reconstructed his profile and carefully analyzed his physical and mental health.

Franklin himself left few clues concerning his appearance. In the

---

1. As far as surviving evidence shows, in the early nineteenth century Mason Locke Weems seemed to be one of the few who occasionally dared to call him Ben Franklin.

Autobiography he indicated that from his father's side he inherited "an excellent Constitution of Body." He described himself in his early sixties as "a fat old fellow," and sometimes humorously referred to himself as "Dr. Fatsides." He once said to his sister Jane: "For my part I wish the house was turned upside down; 'tis so difficult (when one is fat) to go upstairs."[2]

Franklin's unfriendly critics and some contemporary cartoonists used to portray him with a wrinkled forehead, a double chin, a large nose, and several warts on his face,[3] but these portrayals were overshadowed by Franklin's dignified portraits through most of the nineteenth century. In 1857 the English writer William Makepeace Thackeray adopted Franklin as a fictional figure in his novel *The Virginians*, which was reprinted numerous times in the United States. When he referred to Franklin as "a little gentleman,"[4] this casual depiction offended quite a few Franklin admirers, who insisted he was a tall man.[5]

In fact, enthusiasts tended to agree with Jared Sparks, who described him thus: "Dr. Franklin was well formed and strongly built, in his latter years inclining to corpulency; his stature was five feet nine or ten inches; his eyes were grey, and his complexion light."[6] Based on James Parton's record, admirers also believed that Franklin's head was so large that no suitable wig could be found when he was to meet the King of France in 1778. In the end Franklin dressed without a wig, but "in a suit of plain, black velvet, with the usual snowy ruffles at wrist and bosom, white silk stockings and silver buckles."[7]

Between 1870 and 1872 the sculptor Ern[e]st Plassman[n] modeled a new Franklin statue, which would be dedicated by a successful merchant named Albert De Groot to printers and publishers in New York City. When the artist invited a number of printers and publishers to his studio, seeking their opinions of his work, many gladly responded. Some visitors told Plassman that, in their judgment, the

2. *Autobiography*, 54; Paul Leicester Ford, *The Many-Sided Franklin* (New York, 1899), 57; John Clyde Oswald, *Benjamin Franklin in Oil and Bronze* (New York, 1926), 8.

3. Oswald, *Franklin in Oil and Bronze*, 7; Charles Coleman Sellers, *Benjamin Franklin in Portraiture* (New Haven, 1962), plates 6, 7.

4. Thackeray, *The Virginians: A Tale of the Last Century* (New York, 1899), 72.

5. *Record of the Proceedings and Ceremonies Pertaining to the Erection of the Franklin Statue in Printing-House Square* (New York, 1872), 84, 88 (hereafter cited as *Record of Franklin Statue*); Oswald, *Franklin in Oil and Bronze*, 7.

6. Sparks, ed., *The Works of Benjamin Franklin* (Boston, 1836–40), 1: 534.

7. Parton, *Life and Times of Benjamin Franklin* (New York, 1864), 2: 311.

Franklin statue modeled by François Lazzarini in Philadelphia showed "an imbecile desire" on the face and the one by Richard S. Greenough in Boston had "a silly smirk."[8] Plassman's plaster model, however, seemed to have pleased the viewers. It would be a colossal statue of twelve feet, more than twice the height of the real person. The sculptor presented Franklin as a printer, dressed like an ordinary citizen and standing with a newspaper held in the left hand. His graceful face was looking down and the figure was marvelously at ease.[9]

As one of the frequent observers in Plassman's studio, Peter Carpenter Baker was particularly proud of his contribution to the new sculpture and recorded his experience:

I was accustomed to go [to Plassman's studio] every morning, for a good while, to hear what was said. I felt, in a certain sense, responsible for the truthfulness of the statue, and was determined that only a creditable work of art should be placed in Printing-House Square [in New York]. I may fairly say that some important changes were made by my direction. And the face was made more like Franklin's by my persistent efforts to have the sculptor change and change till it suited me.[10]

It is unclear to what extent Baker had specific influences on the artist. But comments from people like him convinced Plassman to destroy this first model and make a second one in order to satisfy his patrons.

Plassman's finished work emphasized Franklin's impressive bare head, with locks falling over his ears. Such a configuration was representative of several Franklin statues during the post-Civil War period, for example, those by Plassman in Washington in 1889, by Richard H. Park in Chicago in 1896 and its replica in New Orleans, and by John J. Boyle in Philadelphia in 1899.[11]

In spite of the increasing number of new Franklin statues, American

---

8. *New York World*, 10 May 1870. Quoted from *Record of Franklin Statue*, 18.

9. *Record of Franklin Statue*, 18, 21, 22, 83.

10. Ibid., 98.

11. Many statues of Franklin characterized him differently: wearing a hat; Hiram Powers on Capitol Hill in 1863 and its replica in New Orleans in 1873, and the one by R. Tait McKenzie in the University of Pennsylvania in 1914. In addition, Carl Rohl-Smith modeled a young Franklin flying a kite, which was exhibited at the World's Fair in Chicago in 1893, and John J. Boyle made a similar one for the St. Louis Exhibition of 1904; neither one was preserved. See [Brad Stephens, ed.], *The Pictorial Life of Benjamin Franklin* (Philadelphia, 1923), n.p.; Oswald, *Franklin in Oil and Bronze*, 38–58.

artists were still deeply indebted to several famous Franklin busts modeled by Jean Antoine Houdon, Jean Jacques Caffiéri, and Giuseppe Ceracchi. In a series of articles entitled "Life Portraits of Great Americans" for *McClure's Magazine* in 1897, Charles Henry Hart, a leading expert in historical portraits, chose and reviewed a total of fifteen Franklin pictures painted from life by various artists, from Patience Wright's wax model and Jean Baptiste Nini's medallion, to oil paintings by Mason Chamberlin, David Martin, Joseph Siffred Duplessis, and Charles Willson Peale.

Above all the others, Hart appreciated Ceracchi's characterization, which highlighted Franklin's firmly closed mouth, his square and lean face, and deep wrinkles on a huge forehead. Hart declared that "Ceracchi's bust of Franklin is truly the head of a philosopher." Popular as it was, the critic added, Houdon's bust of Franklin lacked definite characteristics because he attempted to present a warmer Franklin by softening the lines of his face, forehead, and wrinkles.[12]

It should be pointed out, however, that because all the fifteen portraits that Hart had selected were reprinted in black and white, readers could not detect subtle differences among the works. For example, David Martin's and Charles W. Peale's pictures presented Franklin with a dark complexion, which contradicted Sparks's description of a light one. Furthermore, the sophisticated color in the portrait painted by Joseph Siffred Duplessis revealed that Franklin's eyes were hazel and only in some lights seemed to be gray. Finally, although Hart highly praised the Italian artist Ceracchi's bust, he later realized that in reality Ceracchi's work was a copy after the original bust modeled by the French sculptor, Jean Jacques Caffiéri.[13]

In addition to sculptors like Ernst Plassman, and art critics like Charles Henry Hart, several new biographers also appeared to be seriously concerned with Franklin's likeness. After a close examination of three Franklin portraits by Robert Feke, David Martin, and Joseph Siffred Duplessis, Sydney George Fisher concluded that what most characterized Franklin's appearance was the smooth lines of the overall contour, like his corpulent body and rounded shoulders. Fisher observed:

---

12. Hart, "Life Portraits of Great Americans: Benjamin Franklin," *McClure's Magazine* 8 (January 1897), 271, 267.

13. Sellers, *Franklin in Portraiture*, 2–4, plates 16, 17; Hart, "Bust of Franklin, Attributed to Ceracchi the Work of Caffiéri," *Pennsylvania Magazine of History and Biography* 30 (1906), 241.

Franklin's figure was a series of harmonious curves, which make pictures of him always pleasing. These curves extended over his head and even to the lines of his face, softening the expression, slightly veiling the iron resolution, and entirely consistent with the wide sympathies, varied powers, infinite shrewdness, and vast experience which we know he possessed.[14]

Fisher also noticed that despite a vigorous look in many of Franklin's pictures, there was a certain lassitude in his manner. This suggested Franklin's even temperament—he seldom abused others, nor was he easily irritated. "He was never in a hurry," the biographer said, "and this was perhaps one of the secrets of his success." Fisher added, however, that Franklin "was one of those stout, full-blooded men who the doctors say are peculiarly liable to gout, and his tendency to it was evidently increased by his very sedentary habits."[15]

Like Fisher, Paul Leicester Ford's interest in Franklin's appearance went beyond his likeness. As an enthusiastic collector of Franklin materials, Ford carefully charted Franklin's physical history by highlighting his early obsession with diet and vegetarianism, long-time fondness for fresh air, decaying eyesight during his advanced years, and repeated attacks of gout in old age.

What is more, Ford also revealed how Franklin's physical condition had affected his public service. He pointed out that because of a severe attack of gout, Franklin was unable to do much while he served as a member of a special committee to prepare the Declaration of Independence. During the years when he was minister to the French court, his gout "seriously interfered with his ministerial duties." Finally, in order to show that the old Franklin "had become intellectually idle," Ford quoted a statement by Franklin himself, which went as follows:

For my own part, everything of difficult discussion, and that requires close attention of mind and an application of long continuance, grows rather irksome to me, and where there is not some absolute necessity for it, as in

---

14. Fisher, *The True Benjamin Franklin* (Philadelphia, 1899), 17. Before the authorship of the painting by Feke was identified, Fisher and many others had generally called that picture by its owner's name, the [Thomas Waldron] Sumner portrait, which was in the possession of Harvard University as early as 1856. See Sellers, *Franklin in Portraiture*, 39–45, 281, plate 1.

15. Fisher, *The True Franklin*, 21, 35. Incidentally, one of the illustrations that Fisher selected for the book was Otto Grunmann's portrait of Franklin, who, holding a book and sitting in an arm chair, looked tired.

the settlement of accounts, or the like, I am apt to indulge the indolence usually attending age, in postponing such business from time to time; though continually resolving to do it.[16]

Thus, Sydney G. Fisher's and Paul L. Ford's new investigations not only drew attention to the subtle details of Franklin's appearance, but also revealed his intimate inclinations. While Franklin always seemed to represent vigor, diligence, and youthfulness, Fisher and Ford reminded readers that the accomplished Franklin had a habit of indolence, and fell easily into idleness after he passed the prime of life.

II

Franklin's *Autobiography* was no doubt his best self-advertisement. Within the thirty years between 1880 and 1910 new editions of the *Autobiography* were issued more than a hundred times, the highest number for any period during the last two hundred years. John Bach McMaster estimated that in 1885 alone readers at the Cooper Union Library in New York City called for Franklin's *Autobiography* more than four hundred times, and for James Parton's biography nearly a thousand times.[17] For well–informed people, however, that was not enough. George Bancroft stated as early as before the Civil War:

Not half of Franklin's merits have been told. He was the true father of the American Union. It was he who went forth to lay the foundation of that great design at Albany; and in New York he lifted up his voice. Here among us he appeared as the apostle of the Union. It was Franklin who suggested the Congress of 1774; and but for his wisdom, and the confidence that wisdom inspired, it is a matter of doubt whether that Congress would have taken effect. It was Franklin who suggested the bond of the Union which binds these States from Florida to Maine. Franklin was the greatest diplomatist of the eighteenth century. He never spoke a word too soon; he never spoke a word too much; he never failed to speak the right word at the right season.[18]

Bancroft was one of the earliest and most talented American historians who were trained in Europe. He was determined in the 1830s to investigate Franklin's diplomatic missions during the Revolution,

---

16. Ford, *Many-Sided Franklin*, 61, 63, 58.
17. McMaster, *Benjamin Franklin As a Man of Letters* (Boston, 1895), 269.
18. Quoted in Epes Sargent, ed., *The Select Works of Benjamin Franklin* (Boston, 1857), on a quotation page preceding the frontispiece.

and his multi–volume American history published through the 1870s played a special role in establishing Franklin's reputation as a great diplomat. Bancroft viewed the achievement of independence by the thirteen colonies as the outcome of a series of complex struggles from an international perspective. Thus he conceived the year 1783, when the treaty between France and the United States was signed, as a turning point in the war not only for the Americans, but for the Europeans and British as well. He wrote:

The alliance of France with the United States brought the American question into the heart of Europe, where it called new political aspirations into activity, waked the hope of free trade between all the continents, and arraigned the British ministry at the judgment-seat of the civilized world. England could recover influence in the direction of external affairs only by a peace with her colonies. American independence was to be decided, not by arms alone, but equally by the policy and the sympathies of foreign princes and nations.[19]

Within such a context Bancroft began to praise Franklin's diplomatic activities. His description started with enthusiasm:

Franklin reached Paris on the twenty-first of December [1776], and was welcomed with wonderful unanimity. His fame as a philosopher, his unfailing good-humor, the dignity, self-possession, and ease of his manners, the plainness of his dress, his habit of wearing his straight, thin, gray hair without powder, contrary to the fashion of that day in France, acted as a spell.[20]

More familiar with European politics and culture than many of his contemporaries, Bancroft paid considerable attention to Franklin's manners because he understood that in eighteenth-century France, court etiquette had a subtle but important role in the success or failure of diplomacy. He wrote that "Franklin's manner was frank; and yet, when he had spoken, his silence raised [the] expectation that he had still weightier words to utter." He adulated Franklin in this way:

His charm was simplicity, which gave grace to his style and ease to his manners. No life-long courtier could have been more free from vulgarity; no diplomatist more true to his position as minister of a republic; no laborer

---

19. Bancroft, *History of the United States* (Boston, 1837–74), 10: 35.
20. Ibid. 9: 287.

more consistent with his former life as a working-man; and thus he won respect and love from all.[21]

Believing that Franklin was "a man of the best understanding," Bancroft highly appreciated his mind and wrote:

[Franklin was] never disturbed by recollections or fears, with none of the capricious anxieties of diseased minds, or the susceptibilities of disturbed self-love. Free from the illusions of poetic natures, he loved truth for its own sake, and looked upon things just as they were. As a consequence, he had no eloquence but that of clearness.[22]

Finally, he concluded:

The initiating of the negotiation, equal sincerity, benignity of temper, an intuitive and tranquil discernment of things as they were, wisdom which never spoke too soon and never waited too long, belonged to Franklin, who had proceeded alone to the substantial conclusion of the peace.[23]

After Henry Adams read the last volume of Bancroft's history, he wrote in a review: "It is in the diplomatic history of this period that Mr. Bancroft's success is most striking, and here no candid critic can deny that he has rendered in this volume an immense service to his countrymen."[24] On January 10, 1885 the reviewer wrote to the author:

My own unqualified admiration has always been given to Franklin above all his rivals, not so much because he was the best of them, but because he had the marvellous skill to carry on—even to initiate—his private and personal negotiation behind Vergennes' back, and to conclude a treaty without Vergennes' knowledge,—and then, after doing everything precisely as he wanted it, he stood aside and threw on his colleagues the burden of Vergenne's [sic] wrath. I call this masterly diplomacy.[25]

---

21. Ibid., 286, 491.
22. Ibid., 490.
23. Ibid. 10: 558.
24. *North American Review* 120 (April 1875), 426.
25. J. C. Levenson et al., eds., *The Letters of Henry Adams* (Cambridge, Mass., 1982), 2: 568–69.

Henry Cabot Lodge seemed to agree with Adams. Many years later he expressed his admiration for Franklin in the following manner:

Franklin was the greatest American of his time, with the exception of Washington, but he was also one of the very greatest men of the eighteenth century both at home and abroad. He was a great man of science, great in literature, his autobiography is a masterpiece, he had a thorough knowledge of politics and diplomacy. He was not only a thinker and a philosopher, but he was a man of action, a very great man, and he made that treaty.[26]

In addition to Bancroft, Adams, and Lodge, other eminent Americans frequently praised Franklin, including Charles William Eliot and Woodrow Wilson. The latter, while as a history professor at Princeton University, especially appreciated Franklin's literary gift. "The firm, clear strokes define and clarify everything he touches." His style, Wilson claimed, "is letters in business garb, literature with its apron on," and "stands typical and significant of our whole intellectual history as a nation."[27] In 1900, when a poll was taken to survey the names of candidates for the Hall of Fame for Great Americans, Franklin was one of the top four, following only George Washington, Abraham Lincoln, and Daniel Webster.[28]

III

New economic conditions and technologies, while fast changing the printing business, did not diminish the practitioners' interest in Franklin. Through the last several decades of the nineteenth century printers reemerged as the most active promoters of his fame. The Typothetae of New York City, for example, held an annual dinner to celebrate his birthday every year from 1884 to 1896 (Fig. 25). On a less frequent basis, printers in Chicago, Boston, St. Louis, and Springfield, Ohio, had held similar celebrations during the same period.[29]

---

26. Henry Cabot Lodge to James M. Beck, 17 July 1923, Henry Cabot Lodge Papers, box 71, Massachusetts Historical Society.

27. Eliot, *Four American Leaders* (Boston, 1907); Wilson, ed., *The Autobiography of Benjamin Franklin* (Century Classics ed.: New York, 1901), vii, x.

28. *New York Times*, 13 October 1900, p. 7; Albert Firmin, *The Hall of Fame and Benjamin Franklin* ([New York], 1918), 3–5.

29. *New York Tribune*, 29 January 1880, p. 5; *Chicago Tribune*, 16 January 1881, p. 7; 18 January 1881, p. 3; 21 January 1883, p. 5; *New York Times*, 18 January 1872, p. 8; 9 January 1895, p. 10; 18 January 1895, p. 8.

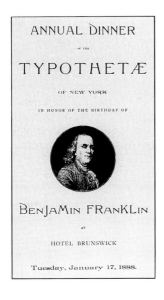

ANNUAL DINNER
or the
TYPOTHETÆ
OF NEW YORK
IN HONOR OF THE BIRTHDAY OF

BENJAMIN FRANKLIN
AT
HOTEL BRUNSWICK

Tuesday, January 17, 1888.

25. Cover of the proceedings of the *Annual Dinner of the Typothetae of New York in Honor of the Birthday of Benjamin Franklin at Hotel Brunswick, Tuesday, January 17, 1888.* (Courtesy of The Papers of Benjamin Franklin, Yale University Library)

Unlike practices before the Civil War, the apprenticeship system disappeared and celebrations were no longer held as a harmonious symbol of fraternity, embracing all members of the trade from masters and journeymen to apprentices. Because the profession was clearly divided into employers and employees, those celebrations became an exclusive occasion for the leading figures of the business.[30]

One of the first post-Civil War annual dinners in New York, in 1884 is a good example. Guests included people from established printing offices in the city, Theodore Low De Vinne, Martin Bartholomew Brown, and Joseph James Little; influential editors and journalists, Whitelaw Reid (editor of the *New York Tribune*), Bernard Peters (editor of the *New York Times*), Horace White (editor of the *New York Evening Post*), Amos J. Cummings (president of the New York Press Club), John Albert Sleicher (editor of the *Albany Evening Journal*); and important publishers like Stilson Hutchins (founder of the *Washington Post*), Henry Oscar Houghton (of the Riverside Press), John Bishop Putnam (of G. P. Putnam's Sons), and Arthur Hawley Scribner (of Charles Scribner's Sons).

Few of the participants in those events had any desire to boast of

---

30. The Typothetae of New York was an organization of master printers. Records of their numerous parties have indicated that apprentices were never mentioned by the participants, and only once was a single toast given in honor of the journeymen printers. *Annual Dinner of the Typothetae of New York* (New York, 1886), 13.

their rise from apprentice to master. Throughout these dinner parties virtually no person related his hard-working experience as an apprentice or a journeyman. One guest said flatly: "I supposed I was invited as a master printer. My first experience was as a master printer. I don't pretend I ever was an apprentice or a journeyman. I started as a master printer."[31]

The main purpose of the dinner parties was for master printers and their friends to have a good time. As a veteran in the industry and long-time organizer of the event, Theodore L. De Vinne advised his audience at a party:

> Ours is a wearing business and we need an occasional night of relaxation to help us through the worries of the day and year. . . . We love our business, but there comes a time when we don't want to think of shop, nor talk shop. This is the time.[32]

Most participants seemed to agree with De Vinne. They considered their annual dinners to be one of the few entertainments in the profession. One participant declared that the dinner party was not only a nice occasion, it was also "something we remember very kindly after we have left it" and "something to look back to with great pleasure."[33]

Preoccupied with seeking pleasure and not recalling toil, some printers felt that January was really not a good month for celebration, and only wished that Franklin had been born in May or June when flowers and fruits could be plentiful. Nonetheless, organizers suggested that the annual dinner was the time to forget all business concerns, for "we do propose to be merry and wise after the fashion of Benjamin Franklin. The frosty night without tells us that we should have some cheer within [the hotel where the dinner party was taking place]."[34] A Chicago businessman, Charles Richard Williams, concurred. After complaining about the whirling activities, feverish demands, and strange diseases of modern time, he cheered his fellow attendants at an annual banquet of the Chicago Typothetae: "The business of life, gentlemen, is not business but life!"[35]

---

31. Ibid., 13.
32. Ibid. (1893), 4.
33. Ibid. (1894), 4.
34. Ibid. (1892), 5.
35. Williams, *Benjamin Franklin* (Chicago, [1911]), 3, 21.

Occasionally, participants' concerns about business did surface, particularly when there was a serious internal dispute between management and labor. Instead of calling for reconciliation, some members of the profession did not hesitate to stand firm. At one time R. R. Donnelly, a guest from Chicago at a New York dinner party, told his audience in a very assertive fashion: "The position I took was that I had often acceded to an unreasonable demand because I thought it was policy to do it; but when it was presented as a strike, they had known that never in the past twenty-five years had I acceded."[36]

Most of the dinner parties were characterized by jubilant spirits, however. Delicate gourmet food was an indispensable feature for the occasion. Compared with the roast whole ox at the first printers' festival in 1846, specially prepared French cuisine showed taste and class. After a delightful meal, dancing might begin, which, as a report of a banquet in Chicago described, "was much enjoyed by the gay company."[37]

Many parties featured after-dinner speeches. The guest speakers varied from mayors, ex-governors and ex-senators, to distinguished authors or publishers. Most of them seemed eager to entertain the party, but some failed to pay attention to Franklin. On a few occasions the party did not offer its first toast to Franklin. Sometimes the guests of honor, such as Mark Twain in 1886, did not bother to mention Franklin's name at all.[38]

When Franklin's name was mentioned, the light-hearted response from the participants could be described as less respectful than humorous. Invited to speak at a dinner in 1887, Stilson Hutchins missed no time to amuse the audience and said:

I know very little about Franklin. . . . I think that he was a great printer. I am sure that he was a great philanthropist and I know that he was a great inventor. He never ran a daily newspaper, and has not survived the test. (Laughter.) I shall not attempt either to defame his memory by any knowledge of mine or explain his shortcomings. The chairman [of the dinner committee and the president of the Typothetae, William C. Martin] said that he was the nonpareil of statesman [*sic*]. I don't know what you mean by

---

36. *Annual Dinner of the Typothetae of New York* (New York, 1890), 17.

37. A report on a banquet and ball held by the Association of International ex-Delegates of Typographical Unions at the Palmer House, *Chicago Tribune*, 18 January 1881, p. 3. In the same year the Press Club in Chicago began to hold its first annual evening banquet in mid-January. Little was said there about Franklin.

38. *Annual Dinner of the Typothetae of New York* (New York, 1886), 8–9.

nonpareil. I understand that he did not wholly behave himself in France. (Laughter.)[39]

At times, such a casual reference to Franklin and lively response from the audience could become a high point of the party. Whitelaw Reid, editor of the *New York Tribune*, made the following remarks in 1885:

> I do not think that Benjamin Franklin would be a popular man to-day; I do not think for an instant that my enemy on the New York *Evening Post* would admit it; he would say that there was something wrong with his private life—(applause and laughter)—and I do not believe that the editor of the Albany *Evening Journal* would support him for Senator of the State of New York. . . . His public record was too bad—you would not elect him Senator from any State in the Union to-day; he had a bad habit of putting his relatives in office. He had other bad habits; but after all, gentlemen, he was a great, big, manly, humane man. (Applause.)[40]

IV

Clearly, one reason that people were attracted to Franklin was that many did not feel any significant distance from him. There seems to be a special closeness that later generations could share with him.

Americans liked his humor and enjoyed his wit. His ingenuity and innovation spoke for common sense, not for lofty ideas and theories. Thomas Edison, for example, became the greatest American inventor of the late nineteenth century. But for quite some time, especially after he set up his first experimental laboratory at Menlo Park, New Jersey in 1876, he was frequently portrayed as a mysterious loner, a ghostly isolationist, a modern alchemist, and a midnight wizard.[41]

The public's suspicion of the first professional experimental scientist was in sharp contrast with their familiar views of Franklin, an experimentalist and amateur inventor. As a gifted natural observer, Franklin's achievement in science was based on his extraordinary common sense and highly observant nature, not on any elaborate apparatus. His unsophisticated method and simple devices, such as

---

39. Ibid. (1887), 6.
40. Ibid. (1885), 6.
41. David E. Nye, *The Invented Self: An Anti-Biography, from Documents of Thomas A. Edison* (Odense University Press, 1983), 75–118; Wyn Wachhorst, *Thomas Alva Edison: An American Myth* (Cambridge, Mass., 1981), 17–128, 169–202.

the Leyden jars, the kite experiment, and the lightning rod, enabled lay people to understand his scientific concepts. In an age of increasing technological advancement and professionalization, Franklin's past invoked a nostalgic feeling, because his scientific interest was not for profit, but for the enjoyment of life.[42]

Yet the claim that Franklin was a great humane man was made with thoughtfulness. While many people still considered Franklin a highly accomplished man, they acknowledged that his greatness was associated not only with his exceptional merits, but also with his courage and honesty to admit his failings. Although some rigid critics insisted that Franklin's flaws degraded him as a hero, more people thought that knowing his faults made his life interesting.

Reports in newspapers and magazines often highlighted less admirable aspects of his life. Using whatever information was available from foreign sources, from fictional materials, or sometimes, from rumors and gossip, those journalistic accounts were not always reliable. The *New York Evening Mail* carried an article, extracted from a translation of a German novel, which discussed the origin of the glass harmonica. The novelist apparently knew about Franklin's close relationship with Mrs. Margaret Stevenson of London and her daughter Mary (Polly), and decided to adapt this material into fiction. In the story Franklin, while in England, often visited a widow named Mrs. Davis, whose two daughters, Mary and Cecilia, were passionate admirers of him. Cecilia liked to sing for Franklin. One of her favorite songs was a Scottish melody, which began with the following lyrics: "Then fare thee well, my dear, dear love!" One day Franklin learned that Cecilia had lost her voice. He was so concerned about her that he invented the harmonica in the hope that the new instrument would sound as wonderful as the young lady, for whom he had great affection.[43]

If this fictional Franklin appeared to be sensitive and romantic, other sources portrayed him as insensitive and rude. After an American named Albert Rhodes, who lived in Europe for a long time, published a book called *The French at Home* in 1875, the *New York Times* quickly published an excerpt from the book, which described Franklin's behavior in France as follows:

Mme. De Créquy's criticism of Franklin's Manners—"That which I saw most remarkable in him was his mode of eating eggs. He emptied five or six

---

42. Critics would say that his achievements were so simple and unsophisticated that he was no more than a tinkerer.
43. *New York Evening Mail*, 19 March 1873.

into a goblet, mingling salt, pepper, and butter, and thus made a *joli ragout philadelphique*. He cut with his knife the pieces of melon he wished to eat; and he bit the asparagus, in place of cutting off the point with his knife on the plate, and eating it properly with a fork. You perceive it was the mode of a savage."[44]

This record of Franklin's manners was subsequently adopted by others, such as the novelist Lion Feuchtwanger in *Proud Destiny* (1947). [Many years later in 1966 Claude-Anne Lopez pointed out that the account based on *Memoirs of the Marquise de Créquy* was a forgery.[45]] For those who relished sensations and social gossip, however, truth did not matter. Reprinted from a newspaper in Connecticut, an article in the *New York Times* asserted that Franklin had had a serious argument with his son, William, at the end of the Revolutionary War, not over the dispute with the mother country, but over the family's property.[46] This story was another dubious account that modern scholarship does not support.

A genuine curiosity about history was one thing, but using history for revisionist purposes was another. Worse, the degree to which Franklin's flaws were exposed revealed some individuals' relentless efforts to dig out the dirt of the past. Horace Wemyss Smith published in 1880 the life and correspondence of his great-grandfather the Reverend William Smith, which contained numerous vigorous attacks on Franklin.[47] In 1889 Paul Leicester Ford reissued a colonial tract, which alleged that Franklin had an affair with his housemaid who subsequently gave birth to William Franklin. This little pamphlet was not reliable, because it was originally published in 1764 when political animosity was high. Soon afterward, Charles Henry Hart defended Franklin's reputation in an article addressing the same issue, "Who Was the Mother of Franklin's Son?"[48] In 1897 Lewis Burd

---

44. Albert Rhodes, *The French at Home* (New York, 1875), 69; *New York Times*, 11 July 1875, p. 4.

45. Lopez, *Mon Cher Papa* (New Haven, 1966), 14.

46. *New York Times*, 6 November 1875, p. 3. The date in the account seemed to be unreliable, because William Franklin left America for England in 1782 and never came back. Nevertheless, people at Perth Amboy, New Jersey, believed that Franklin did quarrel with his son over the family's land property when the two met there in 1774. See Willard Sterne Randall, *A Little Revenge: Benjamin Franklin and His Son* (Boston, 1984), 359–63.

47. Smith, ed., *Life and Correspondence of the Rev. William Smith* (Philadelphia, 1880), 2 vols.

48. Ford, *Who Was the Mother of Franklin's Son?* (1971: New York, 1889); Hart,

Walker published a selection from the papers of the colonial chief justice William Allen of Pennsylvania. It included extensive materials concerning the election of 1764, when Franklin's integrity was viciously denounced.[49]

The revitalized attempt to defame Franklin did not escape his admirers' attention. In a public speech to an audience in Philadelphia, James M. Beck asked: "Why has our city failed to fully recognize the honor done her, or to show her pride in the achievements of her mighty son?" "There were Philadelphians in his time who disliked him," he continued, "Time was when in Philadelphia it was not 'fashionable' to visit Franklin. Time *is* when in a small and ever decreasing circle it *is* not fashionable to praise him." After hearing these comments, the mayor of the city, Samuel H. Ashbridge, who was at the same gathering, felt compelled to respond. He insisted that "the memory of Franklin has never been forgotten. It never can." "In their patriotism and in their pride," the mayor explained, Philadelphians "have not forgotten to honor Franklin and do justice to his memory. They have been lax only in outward demonstrations."[50]

Similar ambiguities seemed to have permeated to a younger generation. After the 1870s an increasing number of schoolbooks began to include extended stories of Franklin's life. Between the 1880s and 1890s various essay contests were conducted in his honor, organized by institutions ranging from schools and banks to patriotic organizations. Although those contests were aimed at promoting Franklin's reputation, some teenage contestants unintentionally revealed a nonheroic view of Franklin.

Under the auspices of the Missouri Society of the Sons of the American Revolution, a contest took place in 1896 with the designated topic "Franklin, the Patriot." Among numerous entries from schools across the state, three prize essays were finally chosen. Ralph P. Swofford, the silver medalist from Kansas City, wrote in his opening paragraph: "He was a very mischievous and wilful boy, unable to get along with his brother, to whom he was apprenticed." He suggested

---

"Who Was the Mother of Franklin's Son?" *Pennsylvania Magazine of History and Biography* 35 (1911): 308–14.

49. Lewis Burd Walker, ed., *The Burd Papers; Extracts from Chief Justice William Allen's Letter Book* (Philadelphia, 1897).

50. *Ceremonies Attending the Unveiling of the Statue of Benjamin Franklin, June 14, 1899, Presented to the City of Philadelphia by Mr. Justus C. Strawbridge* (Philadelphia, 1899), 42–43, 57.

that Franklin's youth, "stained with many errors, pointed to a sinful future"; only later did he become a respectable citizen.

The gold medalist, Miss Elinor Jones of St. Louis, praised Franklin's "industry, perseverance, and self-control." But when she discussed his foreign mission during the Revolution, the young essayist commented in a slightly different tone:

This was no easy task, for the rustic Americans had to cope with the most accomplished and cultured of Europe's diplomatists. This home-spun man must impress the cleverness of the most brilliant court in Europe. How he did we can never know. We can but say, he did it.[51]

Interestingly enough, despite skepticism about Franklin's personal life, the discovery of his own relics stimulated warmth and sympathy. The return and exhibition of a Franklin press was a case in point. When Franklin was a lad in the early 1720s, he went to England and worked at Watt's Printing Office in London. Almost one hundred and twenty years later an American named John B. Murray found that press and brought it back to the United States in 1842. Since then the press had been exhibited in the Patent Office Building in Washington, D. C. It was also on display during the Centennial Exposition in Philadelphia for several months in 1876.[52]

Many people who saw it were deeply impressed, including those whose personal views of Franklin were not necessarily friendly. Mark Twain spent four hours in the Patent Office when he visited the capital. He looked at the heavy wooden brown press, and was able to imagine the toil that Franklin had experienced. After Twain further witnessed a much more advanced modern press working in the same building, he recorded his impression of the Franklin press:

The bed is of wood and is not unlike a very shallow box. The platen is only half the size of the bed, thus requiring two pulls of the lever to each full-size sheet. What vast progress has been made in the art of printing! This press is capable of printing about 125 sheets per hour; and after seeing it, I

---

51. *Prize Medal Essay Contest* (Kansas City, Mo., 1896), 10, 14, 8.

52. Hugh M'Neile, *A Lecture on the Life of Dr. Franklin* (Liverpool, [England] 1841), 1–46; *New York Times*, 15 December 1875, p. 10; 14 November 1876, p. 4; "The Franklin Press at Watt's Printing Works, London," *The Numismatist* 69 (December 1956): 1377–79; Stephen O. Saxe, "'Franklin'[s] Common Press," *Printing History* 12 (1990): 34–35.

have watched Hoe's great machine throwing off its 20,000 sheets in the same space of time, with an interest I never before felt.[53]

Memories did change in different context. Poor Richard's didactic aphorisms disgusted Mark Twain when he was a young apprentice. But long after he established his reputation as a man of letters, Twain continued to keep a manual press in his elegant Connecticut house as a habit to amuse himself in leisure.

V

For Franklin's admirers, few things could be more highly treasured than his literary legacies. When in 1881 a collection of Franklin papers, previously owned by William Temple Franklin, was offered for sale by Henry Stevens, the *New York Tribune* published a series of articles and reports, urging that the federal government take action to buy the papers. One of its editorials announced that, compared with the historical significance of the Franklin collection, the price of $35,000 for those papers was "certainly trivial." "Whatever Dr. Franklin himself thought worthy of preservation must be valuable. . . . Hardly anything from the pen of Franklin could be devoid of interest and value," the editorial concluded.[54]

This manuscript collection comprised nearly 3,000 pieces and several hundred printed books. It included such rare copies as the *Dissertation on Liberty and Necessity*, which Stevens sought vigilantly over the years. When advised that his tag of £ 7,000 or $ 35,000 might be too high, he insisted that he would not accept a cent less. That was a lot of money for the collection, he admitted to Bancroft Davis. "But there is a great deal of Uncle Sam's history and glory in it," the Vermont bookman added.[55]

Two years later in 1883 when the collection finally arrived in Washington, the *New York Tribune* rejoiced that "papers of the greatest

---

53. Quoted from Edgar Marquess Branch, *The Literary Apprenticeship of Mark Twain* (New York, 1966), 35.

54. *New York Tribune*, 30 January 1881, p. 6; 22 December 1881, p. 4; 1 March 1882, p. 4; 6 January 1883, p. 1; 12 February 1883, p. 6. See also *New York Times*, 20 January 1881, p. 1; 21 December 1881, p. 1; 23 February 1882, p. 1; and *47th Congress, 1st Session. Senate. Miscellaneous Documents, No. 21*, 1–99.

55. Whitfield J. Bell, Jr., "Henry Stevens, his Uncle Samuel, and the Franklin Papers," *Proceedings of the Massachusetts Historical Society* 72 (October 1957-December 1960): 147–48, 153.

historical and patriotic importance" now belonged to the National Archives.[56] Well–informed people soon realized, however, that the newly-obtained Stevens collection in the State Department contained several papers by Franklin that could prove damaging to his reputation, such as his essay on "Perfumes" and another on "The Choice of a Mistress." Surprisingly, few scholars took adverse advantage of those pieces, although Stevens's collection had stimulated considerable new research on Franklin, as seen in Edward Everett Hale and Edward Everett Hale, Jr.'s *Franklin in France* (1887–88).

Some observers openly lamented that the essays "On Perfume" and "The Choice of a Mistress" were "too indecent to print," and a number of them used the two pieces to criticize Franklin's morality. In his article, "The Ideal versus the Real Benjamin Franklin," the doctor of divinity Edward D. Neill of St. Paul, Minnesota, tried his best to be delicate about his wording. Without mentioning either the title or the substance of "The Choice of a Mistress," he revealed that "editors more than once rejected" that essay, in which Franklin advised a young man on how to select a proper person "to sustain a relation of neither maid nor wife."[57] Providing no detail from the two essays by Franklin, John Bach McMaster also commented in 1895:

> Morality he never taught, and he was not fit to teach it. Nothing in his whole career is more to be lamented than that a man of parts so great should, long after he had passed middle life, continue to write pieces so filthy that no editor has ever had the hardihood to print them.[58]

Concerned about the public sentiment on morality, the State Department carefully concealed those two pieces and prevented them from publication. When John Bigelow was preparing his edition of Franklin's works in the 1880s, he asked for permission from that department to use "The Choice of a Mistress" in his new selection. Thomas F. Bayard, secretary of state, politely rejected the request and declined to provide that documentation.

Behind the scenes, however, a different situation developed. Paul Leicester Ford revealed that the secretary of state provided a copy of

---

56. *New York Tribune*, 12 February 1883, p. 6.
57. Edward D. Neill, "The Ideal versus the Real Benjamin Franklin," *Macalester College Contributions*, 2nd ser., no. 4 (1892): 98.
58. McMaster, *Franklin as a Man of Letters*, 278, 266.

"The Choice of a Mistress" to one of his close political friends,[59] who in turn had the piece read aloud at a dinner party in New York City after the ladies had withdrawn. Several gentlemen at the party immediately asked for copies, and it was suggested the essay might be privately printed. In 1887 Paul Leicester Ford, through his personal press, produced twenty-five copies under the title of "A Philosopher in Undress." Ford, however, did not further exploit "The Choice of a Mistress" in his published works to defame Franklin, not because he was concerned about protecting Franklin's reputation, but because he thought that the essay would "shock modern taste."[60]

It is clear that toward the end of the nineteenth century, only a handful of privileged people were able to peek into some of Franklin's innermost sentiments about women through reading his "Choice of a Mistress." In a personal letter to Senator George F. Hoar of Massachusetts, Edward A. Kelly asked his friend's opinion about a list of persons he proposed for the Hall of Fame, including Washington, Franklin, Jefferson, Webster, and Lincoln. In his reply, the senator struck out Franklin's name "without any hesitation whatever" and explained:

> With all his services as a Diplomatist and Counsel, Dr. Franklin's conduct of life was that of a man on a low plane. He was without idealism, without lofty principle, and on one side of his character gross and immoral. I have read the original of his letter to a friend on the question of keeping a mistress which, making all allowance for the manners of the time, and all allowance for the fact that he might have been partly in jest, is an abominable and wicked letter; and all his relation to women, and to the family life were of that character.[61]

Whatever his disgust at Franklin's writing, Hoar emphasized that his letter should be kept in confidence. That both the senator and Paul

---

59. Before Stevens sold the Franklin papers, he had withdrawn the original manuscript of "The Choice of a Mistress," which was later acquired by the Chicago collector Charles Frederick Gunther (Whitfield J. Bell, Jr., editorial note, *The Old Mistresses' Apologue by Benjamin Franklin* [Philadelphia, 1956], n.p.; *Papers* 3: 28).

60. Goodspeed's Book Shop, Inc., *Rare Americana, Catalogue 268* (Boston, n.d. [1936?]), item 74; Paul Z. Dubois, *Paul Leicester Ford: An American Man of Letters, 1865–1902* (New York, 1977), 107–08; Ford, *Many-Sided Franklin*, 410.

61. George F. Hoar to Edward A. Kelly, the Hoar Papers, Massachusetts Historical Society.

L. Ford did not publicly exploit the piece indicated their hesitance to break the prevailing standards of decency, or to criticize the deceased person openly. It was not until the 1930s that this moral restraint became loosened and Franklin's naughty essays finally appeared in print.[62]

VI

In a codicil of his last will Franklin prescribed that one thousand pounds sterling should be donated to Boston and to Philadelphia. He predicted that if the money was loaned annually to apprentices at 5 percent interest, the total would become 131,000 pounds one hundred years later. "I hope, however," Franklin wrote in his will, "that if the two cities should not think fit to undertake the execution, they will at least accept the offer of these donations, as a mark of my good-will, a token of my gratitude, and testimony of my earnest desire to be useful to them even after my departure."

Yet realities in 1890, were not exactly as Franklin had anticipated: First, the apprenticeship system had long disappeared; and second, many people argued passionately about what to do with the fund. Some of Franklin's descendants contended that they were entitled to the bequest after one hundred years, and sued the two cities. In the end, although they lost the law suits, the funds were tied up for several years. Furthermore, the managers of the Boston funds decided not to give out loans to apprentices as early as in 1825, and began to invest the money in the stock market. By the end of the first one hundred years, the Franklin fund in Boston totaled $390,000, which was much larger than the sum of $172,000 in Philadelphia. Boston, therefore, proposed to build a park in Roxbury, to be named Franklin Park. A court ruling declared, however, that such a purpose was not what the donor intended. Finally, after much public discussion, Boston decided to allocate $400,000 to establish a new institute. Philadelphia, on the other hand, provided $133,000 from its fund to the Franklin Institute, to build a science museum. Both cities seemed to

---

62. The original manuscript of "The Choice of a Mistress" passed through several hands in the nation, and was finally bought by the Philadelphia book collector, Abraham Simon Wolf Rosenbach, for the price of $3,500 in 1926. Rosenbach's interest in the manuscript was such that he could find it in dark from his huge collection. He enjoyed sharing the rare piece with his friends, reading it himself with a "twinkle in his eyes" and "overlong pauses for emphasis" (Edwin Wolf 2nd, *Rosenbach: A Biography* [Cleveland, (1960)], 255, 317–18).

be convinced that any improvement of the education of the young would always satisfy the good intentions of the deceased benefactor.

The money to the Franklin Institute of Philadelphia proved to be insufficient to begin the project, which would not reappear on the public agenda until the 1930s. In Boston, Henry Pritchett, president of the Massachusetts Institute of Technology, was head of the Franklin Fund. He approached Andrew Carnegie, who promised to match Franklin's money on two conditions: one, Boston should provide a piece of land for the new project; and two, the new institute should be founded along the principles of the Cooper Union and the Mechanics' and Tradesmen School of New York. When both conditions were met, the Franklin Union was formally opened in 1908 (and remains a technical school today).

The beginning of the twentieth century was marked by widespread celebrations of the two hundredth anniversary of Franklin's birth in 1906. The Pennsylvania legislature appropriated $20,000 for the occasion. Ceremonies were organized by the American Philosophical Society, which invited prominent guests from more than thirty distinguished universities in the nation and around the world, including Oxford, Cambridge, St. Andrews, Glasgow, Edinburgh, Harvard, Yale, and William and Mary.

The grand celebration in Philadelphia attracted much public attention, but similar ceremonies were held in other places; the small town of Franklin, Massachusetts was an example. Located twenty-seven miles south of Boston, the community was proud that it had been the first in the union to be named for Franklin in 1778.[63] As early as November 1905 community leaders in Franklin began to organize their own celebration; eight special committees were formed, which had more than fifty members. A major local newspaper, the *Franklin Sentinel*, claimed that the Franklin birthday celebration on January 17, 1906, was "one of the most memorable" events in the community's history. The *Sentinel*'s issue for January 19, which carried extensive reports of the event, was reprinted several times to satisfy heavy demand from townspeople who wanted to keep it as a souvenir[64] (Fig. 26).

---

63. Franklin was pleased with the compliment, and he sent to that town a gift of more than one hundred books for a new library. I[saac] Minis Hays, ed., *Calendar of the Papers of Benjamin Franklin in the Library of the American Philosophical Society* (Philadelphia, 1908), 3: 260, 264, 311, 318; 4: 140.

64. *Franklin Sentinel*, 19 January 1906, pp. 1–3; also 9 January, p. 1; 12 January, pp. 1, 2; 16 January, p. 1; 23 January, pp. 2, 3; and 26 January, p. 2.

26. *The Franklin Sentinel* of Franklin, Massachusetts. Commemorating the bicentennial of Franklin's birth in 1906, this issue for January 19 was reprinted several times to meet the demand of those townspeople who wished to keep the newspaper as a souvenir.

The small town was overwhelmed in the celebration, which featured sermons, a parade, a concert, and a Frankliniana exhibition. The main ceremony took place at the Morse Opera House, where four formal addresses were delivered by the lieutenant governor, Eben S. Draper, ex-governor John L. Bates, Professor Arthur W. Peirce, and Professor Leon H. Vincent. A member of a prominent local family, Miss Maude L. Ray, read a poem that she had written for the occasion. In it she called Franklin "the great humanitarian," and praised his wisdom, serene manner, unsurpassed courage, and generous service to the country.[65]

Despite the ceremonial atmosphere, Franklin's birthday also prompted skeptics to question his reputation. An editorial that appeared in the *New York Times* said: "He seems to have been quite without definite ambition, his attitude toward life was mildly cynical, and by inclination he was a manager rather than a leader of men."[66] Some realized that one of the most intriguing aspects of Franklin's life lay not only in his achievements, but also in the way he had accomplished them.

For instance, no matter how many admirers praised Franklin as a man of letters, others insisted that even though Franklin wrote voluminously, his jottings were an avocation rather than a vocation. Most of his writings were produced for immediate and practical purposes when he was a printer, newspaperman, natural observer, politician, and correspondent of his family members and friends. Even talented students of Franklin, including John Bach McMaster and Paul Leicester Ford, believed that it was almost impossible to pinpoint the exact position that Franklin had in American literature.[67] Because literary pursuits had hardly been Franklin's profession, Paul Elmer More, when asked in 1906 to write an article about Franklin's literary achievements, complained: "There is a certain embarrassment in

---

65. *Two Hundredth Anniversary of the Birth of Benjamin Franklin, 1706–1906* (Franklin, Mass., [1906]), 57.

66. *New York Times*, 17 January 1906, p. 10.

67. McMaster, *Franklin As a Man of Letters*, 272; Ford, *Many-Sided Franklin*, 389, 261. For different views of Franklin's role in American literature during this period see Theodore Parker, *Historic Americans* (Boston, 1870), 63; Moses Coit Tyler, *A History of American Literature* (New York, 1878), 2: 251; Charles F. Richardson, *American Literature* (New York, 1887), 1: 168; Mildred Cabell Watkins, *American Literature* (New York, 1894), 18; Brander Matthews, *An Introduction to the Study of American Literature* (New York, 1896), 38; Katharine Lee Bates, *American Literature* (New York, 1898), 58; and William P. Trent, *A History of American Literature* (New York, 1903), 127–28.

dealing with Franklin as a man of letters, for the simple reason that he was never, in the strict sense of the word, concerned with letters at all."[68]

Take his scientific achievement as another example. Symbolized by a dramatic kite experiment, the household notion of Franklin the scientist was always that of Prometheus incarnate, stealing from heaven the vital spark that had given light to man and life to electrical science.[69] At the same time, John Trowbridge, a professor of applied science at Harvard University for forty years, remarked that Franklin could have been killed because of the unsafe design of his kite, and that the success of his experiment should be regarded as "one of the most convincing examples of luck on record."[70] Furthermore, as far as his invention of the lightning rod was concerned, an anonymous author suggested that many ancient peoples, including the Tuscans, Romans, Celts, Persians, and Jews, had already had the idea of using metal as a lightning conductor.[71]

Even at formal ceremonies in honor of Franklin, like the one hosted by the American Philosophical Society at Philadelphia in 1906, a speaker as eminent as Professor Ernest Rutherford, Fellow of the Royal Society of London, warned his audience not to idealize Franklin's accomplishment. Acknowledging that Franklin did contribute to electrical theory "at a time when the knowledge of electricity was of the scantiest character," Rutherford continued:

We must not, in consequence of this fact, unduly exaggerate the importance of the contributions of Franklin to electrical knowledge nor underestimate the fundamental importance and magnitude of the advances made in electricity since Franklin's time.

We recognize that Franklin possessed unusual clearness of physical insight, but we must not refrain for that reason from endowing him with the uncanny gift of prophetic vision.[72]

---

68. More, "Franklin in Literature," *Independent* 60 (11 January 1906): 98.

69. Talcott Williams, *Proceedings of the American Philosophical Society* 28 (17 April 1890): 198.

70. Trowbridge, "Benjamin Franklin and Electricity," *Nation* 82 (1 February 1906): 93.

71. Anon., "Was Benjamin Franklin the First Inventor of the Lightning Conductor?" *Scientific American* 105 (16 December 1911): 554.

72. Rutherford, "The Modern Theories of Electricity and Their Relations to the Franklinian Theory," *The Record of the Celebration of the Two Hundredth Anniversary of the Birth of Benjamin Franklin, Under the Auspices of the American Philosophical Society* (Philadelphia, 1906), 1: 156–57.

The bicentennial ceremonies in 1906 stood out as a high mark among all the Franklin celebrations. Along with abundant praise, his shortcomings were frequently discussed. When Americans became more familiar with his personal life, their skepticism grew as well, even though that skepticism did not always lead to public criticism. As Americans moved into the twentieth century, Franklin's image had been considerably humanized.

Chapter 6

"The Many-Sided Genius"

From the early 1900s Americans began to focus their attention on Franklin's versatility, often characterized as "many-sidedness." An inspiration for an age of rapid development in new science and technology, Franklin symbolized the future and modernity. His broad experiences in American and European cities made him a prominent metropolitan figure rather than a provincial one. His bourgeois values of life, success, wealth, and leisure continued to be accepted by modern Americans. His wit and humor delighted the old as well as the young, and his charisma captivated those who were concerned about personality.

The public's interest in this hero seemed to decline, however. Franklin's domestic life was under a growing attack and his simple virtues appeared obsolete in an increasingly pluralized and stratified society. Moreover, when the Puritan tradition came under fire and the sexual revolution began to spread during the 1920s, people's perceptions of Franklin became further fragmented. Stuart P. Sherman, for example, saw Franklin's life as a departure from the past, stating that his experience "was the revolt of a living Puritanism from a Puritanism that was dead."[1] After various aspects of his career, especially his relations with women, became frequent objects of amusement and public satire, some journalists, public speakers, novelists, and dramatists went as far as to vulgarize Franklin as a womanizer.

The end of this period was marked in 1938 by the establishment of a magnificent memorial in his honor in Philadelphia, and by the completion of Carl Van Doren's comprehensive biography of Franklin.

---

1. Sherman, "What Is a Puritan?" *The Atlantic Monthly* 128 (September 1921): 354. See also Jan C. Dawson, *The Unusable Past: America's Puritan Tradition, 1830 to 1930* (Chico, Calif., 1984), esp. chaps. 4, 5.

I

It was well known that during his eighty-four years, Franklin had been involved in a wide range of activity. As early as 1856 Robert C. Winthrop used the phrase "myriad-minded" to describe Franklin. But for a long time this characterization failed to catch the public's imagination. Americans' interest in his versatility was doubtless boosted when Paul Leicester Ford published his *Many-Sided Franklin*, which first appeared as a serial for the *Century Magazine*, beginning in 1898, and then was printed in book form the following year.

Before long newspaper reporters, public speakers, and contributors to journals and magazines readily adopted the phrase "many-sidedness," and a good many Franklin biographers praised its acuteness. William Cabell Bruce claimed that Ford's title "is a felicitous touch of description." Bernard Faÿ said that Ford's work was "incomparably precise." Carl Becker acknowledged that "Franklin was indeed 'many-sided.'" Carl Van Doren believed that Ford's book was an "excellent survey of Franklin under the heads of his different activities."[2] Almost overwhelmed by Franklin's versatility, some felt that a better way to approach his career was not to study his life as a whole but to learn about it bit by bit, because as James Madison Stifler insisted, "Franklin was so entirely human, which means so many-sided, that the best one can do is to observe him piecemeal."[3]

Piecemeal indeed. The result was an extraordinary output of work concerning the details of Franklin's life.[4] While people like Sydney George Fisher, Phillips Russell, and Bernard Faÿ continued to write full–length biographies of Franklin, others began to concentrate on particular aspects of his career. William Cabell Bruce's *Benjamin Franklin, Self-Revealed*, printed in 1917, was essentially a cluster of studies on Franklin's life and thought, and on his relationships with friends. James Madison Stifler's *The Religion of Benjamin Franklin* appeared in 1925 and *"My Dear Girl"* in 1927. In addition, four works were

---

2. Bruce, *Benjamin Franklin, Self-Revealed* (New York, 1917), 1: 2; Faÿ, *Franklin, The Apostle of Modern Times* (Boston, 1929), v; Becker, *Benjamin Franklin* (Ithaca, N.Y., 1946), 36; Van Doren, *Benjamin Franklin* (New York, 1938), 787. For a dissenting view see Francis Newton Thorpe's review essay in *American Historical Review* 5 (April 1900): 579–82.

3. Stifler, *"My Dear Girl," The Correspondence of Benjamin Franklin with Polly Stevenson, Georgiana and Catherine Shipley* (New York, 1927), v.

4. The best approach to this literature is Melvin H. Buxbaum's exhaustive bibliography, *Benjamin Franklin, 1721–1983: A Reference Guide*, 2 vols. (Boston, 1983–88).

published in 1928: Lewis J. Carey's *Franklin's Economic Views*, Malcolm R. Eiselen's *Franklin's Political Theories*, Willis Steell's *Benjamin Franklin of Paris, 1776–1785*, and Lois Margaret MacLaurin's *Franklin's Vocabulary*.

These monographs by well–informed observers comprised but a fraction of the new literature about Franklin, because different journals, magazines, and newspapers were bombarded with ever-growing discussions of his life. Those who were interested in Franklin's contact with foreign countries found such titles as "Franklin in France," "Franklin in Germany," "Franklin in Canada," "Franklin in Italy," "Franklin and Russia," "Franklin in Scotland and Ireland," or "Franklin as an Internationalist."[5]

Those who wanted to know more about his domestic experiences could easily find numerous works such as: "Franklin as a Printer," "Franklin as an Editor," "Franklin as a Journalist," "Franklin as a Scientist," "Franklin as an Inventor," "Franklin as a Businessman," "Franklin as an Advertiser," "Franklin as an Educator," "Franklin as a Man of Letters," "Franklin as a Humorist," "Franklin as a Freemason," "Franklin as a Soldier," "Franklin as a Philanthropist," and "Franklin as an Agricultural Leader."[6]

Within those specific areas, close studies were carefully conducted. For instance, many, who praised him as a scientist and inventor, also described his kite experiment, invention of the lightning rod, obser-

---

5. John Jay, "Franklin in France," *Century Magazine* 71 (January 1906): 447–58; Phillips Russell, "Franklin in Paris," *McNaught's Monthly* 6 (September 1926): 75–77; Beatrice Marguerite Victory, *Benjamin Franklin and Germany* ([Philadelphia], 1915); William Renwick Riddell, "Benjamin Franklin and Canada"; "Benjamin Franklin's Mission to Canada and the Causes of Its Failure," *Pennsylvania Magazine of History and Biography* 48 (1924): 97–110, 111–58; Emilio Goggio, "Benjamin Franklin and Italy," *Romanic Review* 19 (1928): 302–08; William Guggenheim, "Franklin and Our Relations with Russia," *Benjamin Franklin Gazette* (The International Benjamin Franklin Society), January 1929, 1; J[ames] Bennett Nolan, *Benjamin Franklin in Scotland and Ireland, 1759 and 1771* (Philadelphia, 1938).

6. William Perrine, "Franklin As an Editor," *Saturday Evening Post* 171 (14 January 1899): 460–61; A. E. Upham, "Franklin As an Inventor," *Outline* 44 (1899): 1–4; Julius Friedrich Sachse, *Benjamin Franklin As a Free Mason* (Philadelphia, 1906); Asa Don Dickinson, "Benjamin Franklin, Bookman," *Bookman* 53 (May 1921): 197–205; John Clyde Oswald, "Benjamin Franklin As a Business Man," *American Printer* 80 (5 January 1925): 24–27; Howard Hovde, "B. Franklin—Advertiser," *Pennsylvania Gazette* 25 (21 January 1927): 341–42; Earle D. Ross, "Benjamin Franklin As an Eighteenth-Century Agricultural Leader," *Journal of Political Economy* 37 (February 1929): 52–72.

vations of the gulf stream, hot air balloons, and daylight saving sched-ule.[7] Enthusiastically exploring Franklin's essays, familiar letters, vo-cabularies, ballads, bagatelles, fables, and epitaph,[8] people who admired Franklin for his literary accomplishments considered him as an essayist and humorist.

Those who were anxious to promote Franklin's fame did not lack inspiration. In a single volume prepared under the auspices of the Philadelphia chapter of the Sons of the American Revolution in 1929, one could find Franklin crowned with more than thirty titles of dis-tinction. He was portrayed as "the greatest diplomat of all time," "the advocate of peace," and "the father of American union." He was believed to be "America's first great cartoonist," "the first American English spelling reformer," "the father of the U.S. postal service," and "the friend and founder of public libraries."

Because of his advocacy of work and thrift, both bankers and organized labor leaders considered him their spiritual friend. He was praised as "the athlete," "the father of daylight saving," "the inventor of bifocal lenses," and "the patron saint of the music industries,"[9] for his interest in swimming, in natural observations, in invention of useful gadgets, and in the glass harmonica.

Nevertheless, it did not necessarily follow from these specialized studies that Franklin's identity would be better revealed. In fact, his versatility obscured his deeper characteristics. For his less charitable critics, Franklin's diverse interests and scattered energy only showed how superficial and inconsistent his mind and talent must have been. Still, some might simply have agreed with Herman Melville, who had

---

7. Cleveland Abbe, "Benjamin Franklin as Meteorologist," *Proceedings of the American Philosophical Society* 45 (1906): 117–28; M. I. Wilbert, "Benjamin Franklin, His Influence on the Progress of the Science of Medicine in America," *American Journal of Pharmacy* 78 (May 1906): 214–21; Anon., "Franklin Originated Plan of Daylight Saving," *Pennsylvania Gazette* 16 (29 March 1918): 682; Archibald Sparke, "Dr. Franklin's Air Bath," *Notes and Queries* 150 (17 April 1926): 286; The Garden Club of America, *Benjamin Franklin and Botany* (New York, 1937).

8. Edward E. Hale, "Ben Franklin's Ballads," *New England Magazine,* new ser., 18 (June 1898): 505–07; J[oseph] G. Rosengarten, "Franklin's Bagatelles," *Pro-ceedings of the American Philosophical Society* 40 (1901): 87–135; Cyril Cle-mens, "The Father of American Humor," *Overland Monthly* 88 (April 1930): 124; James Seton-Anderson, "Satirical Epitaphs," *Notes and Queries* 171 (11 July 1936): 25; Cedric Larson, "The Drinker's Dictionary," *American Speech* 12 (April 1937): 87–88.

9. J. Henry Smyth, Jr., ed., *The Amazing Benjamin Franklin* (New York, 1929).

bitterly noted that Franklin was jack-of-all-trades, a master of each and yet the master of none.[10]

Despite some reservations, admiration prevailed among his supporters. Harry Lyman Koopman declared that unlike Washington or Lincoln, whose accomplishments lay primarily in politics, Franklin "united in a single personality more kinds of greatness than any other man known to history."[11] Furthermore, when James M. Beck, one of the most articulate defenders of Franklin's reputation, spoke before the House of Representatives in 1932, his statement summarized what many enthusiastic advocates believed:

> In my judgment, [Franklin] was not only the greatest intellectual genius of the eighteenth century, but shares with Plato, Leonardo Da Vinci, Michel Angelo, Francis Bacon, and William Shakespeare the supreme glory of being one of the few myriad-minded men of all time.[12]

II

Kaleidoscopic as Franklin's career might seem, few aspects of his life were more tempting than his relations with women. Throughout most of the nineteenth century, this dimension of his life had been marginally discussed by knowledgeable observers from Jared Sparks and Charles Sumner to James Parton and John Bigelow. This limited exposure was due to historical circumstances rather than lack of information.

Franklin's intriguing attitudes toward women and his close relations with a number of them had for a long time invited speculation in well–informed circles, even though most preferred not to talk about the subject publicly. For example, Franklin's repeated flirtations embarrassed those who firmly upheld puritanical standards of social behavior. John Adams disapprovingly commented that his colleague "at the age of seventy odd had neither lost his love of beauty nor his taste for it."[13]

After Mrs. Abigail Adams joined her husband in Paris, she was utterly shocked when she first met one of Franklin's female friends,

---

10. Melville, *His Fifty Years of Exile (Israel Potter)* (New York, 1957), 66.

11. Koopman, *Franklin's Claims to Greatness* ([Providence] 1923), 5.

12. Beck, *The Memory of Franklin* (Washington, 1932), 6.

13. Charles Francis Adams, ed., *The Works of John Adams* (Boston, 1850–56), 3: 134. See also Anon., "Franklin's 'Our Lady of Auteuil,'" *Atlantic Monthly* 74 (December 1894): 858–60.

Madame Helvétius. Apparently, the latter's unwashed face, double kiss on Franklin's cheeks and forehead, arm thrown carelessly on his neck, and use of her chemise to wipe her dog fell far short of Mrs. Adams's standard of gentility and decency.[14] Her recollections became public when her grandson, Charles Francis Adams, edited and published the *Letters of Mrs. Adams* in 1841. Since then, particularly during the 1880s and 1890s, few Franklin biographers could resist quoting her description at length, including John Bach McMaster, Sydney George Fisher, Paul Leicester Ford, William Cabell Bruce, Phillips Russell, and Willis Steell.

Around the turn of the present century, more racy details of Franklin's entanglements with women were gradually released to the general public. Perhaps more than anyone else, Paul L. Ford provided the most vivid description of relations between Franklin and his favorite females. In the chapter "Franklin and the Fair Sex" in *The Many-Sided Franklin*, Ford managed to unfold the complicated story in such a way that the brief account contains an enormous amount of information about Franklin's "gallantry."

In addition to his common-law wife, Deborah (Read) Franklin, Ford specifically counted Franklin's most cherished friendships with six women in three countries—there occurring over a period of several decades. These women were: first, in America, Catherine Ray, who later became the wife of William Greene of Rhode Island; second, in England, Mary (Polly) Stevenson, of London, later Mrs. Mary Hewson; and Georgiana Shipley, daughter of Jonathan Shipley, the Bishop of St. Asaph; and third, in France, Comtesse Sophie de la Live de Bellegarde d'Houdetot; Madame Brillon de Jouy (Anne-Louise d'Hardancourt), of Passy; and Madame Anne-Catherine Helvétius, of Auteuil, the widow of Claude-Adrien Helvétius.

Despite Franklin's cordial relations with so many women, Ford cautioned readers not to exaggerate his gallantry. Ford emphasized that Franklin's generation, "both men and women, deemed him a moral man, whose friendship was an honor; and it is unfair to judge him by standards that did not exist at the time he lived, or to hold his other virtues in disrespect because he lacked this one [—restraint]."[15]

Similarly, other sympathetic biographers did not want to focus their attention on Franklin's flirtations, and some tried to provide background information that might explain Franklin's behavior. Bernard Faÿ indicated that the elegant style and conversation of the salon

---

14. Charles Francis Adams, ed., *Letters of Mrs. Adams* (Boston, 1841), 2: 55–56.
15. Ford, *Many-Sided Franklin*, 267.

provided an ideal environment for the display of Franklin's true personality. "France had roused all of Franklin's ardor, it had developed tastes in him that he had never known he possessed," the French historian stated. He also observed that Franklin's disposition embraced fascinating characteristics that appeared both serious and ironic, rustic and exquisite, reserved and audacious. For many French ladies, therefore, the novelty of his personality was "unbelievably delightful."[16]

If sympathetic observers, such as Ford and Faÿ, did not believe that Franklin was guilty of scandalous lust, neither were they able to present a coherent explanation of his romantic relations. It is clear, however, that as they unfolded Franklin's jolly relations with the women, readers would realize that Franklin, the ardent preacher of industry, frugality, and hard work, embraced a great deal of gaiety, pleasure, amusement, and gallantry. At the same time, some observers who regarded Franklin's behavior to be immoral considered him to be "a lively lecher."[17]

After the 1920s stories about Franklin's private life became so widespread that his detractors recognized his sexuality as a vulnerable spot. D. H. Lawrence picked up Franklin's fondness for the word "venery," and missed no chance to satirize him: "I always thought books of Venery were about hunting deer."[18] Skeptical as they were, few Americans used the same kind of language as Lawrence to attack Franklin. Henry Seidel Canby, a writer and editor who was associated with the Book-of-the-Month Club for more than twenty years, privately admitted that "Ben Franklin's injunction to practice venery only for health would have shocked us."[19] As William E. Leuchtenburg has observed, Americans in the 1920s were "obsessed with the subject of sex" and "taboos about sex were lifted." Even women were no longer

---

16. Faÿ, *Franklin*, 462, 460–61.
17. Van Doren, *Franklin*, 639.
18. Lawrence, *Studies in Classic American Literature* (Garden City, N.Y., 1951), 23. But Lawrence himself was an enthusiastic advocate of candid sexuality. He believed that whenever human beings fell in love, their passion should not be controlled. "Sex is a very powerful, beneficial and necessary stimulus in human life, and we are all grateful when we feel its warm, natural flow through us, like a form of sunshine." He continued: "So we can dismiss the idea that sex appeal in art is pornography. It may be so to the grey Puritan, but the grey Puritan is a sick man, soul and body sick, so why do we bother about his hallucinations?" (*Pornography and Obscenity* [London, 1929], 11).
19. Canby, *American Memoir* (Boston, 1947), 80.

shocked by the topic.[20] Most Americans were amused by Franklin's attitude toward sex, not offended by it. Franklin was often portrayed as a "lover," a term not entirely a compliment, nor a severe criticism.[21]

Biographer Willis Steell's first impression was that Franklin's relations with French women had to do with love. But after he completed his study, he realized that Franklin's attitudes toward the women were too complicated to be categorized as love. He acknowledged that he had used the word *love* in his book only because there was no better alternative. Steell finally recognized the ambiguities in Franklin's relations with women, which he characterized as being "rather more than friendship, a little less than love."[22]

Those dramatists and novelists who were aware of the popular curiosity about Franklin's gallantry did not hesitate to take advantage of the opportunity. Noting that Franklin wore a pair of double spectacles, a playwright added: "So that he can look at two such pretty ladies at once!"[23] Adopting William Temple Franklin as the protagonist in a novel called *The Gentleman from America*, Polan Banks used the grandson to present his grandfather's views about women and marriage in the following way:

> Women are books, and men the readers be,
> Who sometimes in those books erratas [sic] see;
> Yet oft the reader's raptured with each line,
> Fair print and paper, fraught with sense divine;
> Tho' some, neglectful, seldom care to read,
> And faithful wives no more than bibles heed.
> Are women books? says Hodge, then would mine were
> An Almanack, to change her every year![24]

Other authors and playwrights made similar attempts to portray Franklin in more than a dozen novels and plays in the first several decades of the century. Yet their efforts failed to make an enduring

20. Leuchtenburg, *The Perils of Prosperity, 1914–32* (Chicago, 1958), 167–70.
21. Anon., "Franklin and Love," *The Art Digest* 7 (1 February 1933): 22; M. M. Hughes, "Benjamin Franklin—Lover," *Cornhill Magazine* 149 (January 1934): 101–06.
22. Steell, *Franklin of Paris*, 169, 202–03.
23. Frederick J. Pohl, *Made in Paris: A Play of Humor and History* ([Brooklyn, N.Y.], 1921), 10.
24. Banks, *The Gentleman from America* (New York, 1930), 252.

impact on the public's imagination. The reasons were manifold. For one thing, the prototype of a vigorous, energetic, and humorous Franklin was so deeply rooted in many people's minds that most authors were unable to provide an alternative image of him. They repeated familiar stories; rarely could they grasp the historical depth of Franklin's career or reveal new insights about him.

For another, Franklin's maxims and proverbs had been so popular over the years that many authors seemed to believe that once they could put Poor Richard's sayings back into Franklin's mouth, they would recreate a lively new Franklin. In fact, relying heavily on Franklin's own words, most writers failed to characterize him in a refreshing and artistic fashion. Furthermore, compared with Franklin's spontaneous humor, their imitations were inadequate to recapture the essence of eighteenth-century wit.

In spite of his familiar image at first glance, Franklin was a difficult figure to depict. The combined demands of deep historical understanding and unusual literary skill proved to be too great for most American writers, who were unable to create an impressive Franklin either on stage or in fiction. Not impressed by second-rate dramatization, many continued to look into Franklin's own writings. For example, after many years of obscurity, his essay on "The Choice of a Mistress" was finally released in Phillips Russell's popular account, *Benjamin Franklin: The First Civilized American*, which was reprinted twelve times between 1926 and 1930.

In 1938 Abraham Simon Wolf Rosenbach exhibited in the Free Library of Philadelphia his most treasured Frankliniana collection on the theme of "The All Embracing Doctor Franklin." In this exhibit the original draft of "On the Choice of a Mistress" was for the first time on public display, and what each visitor could read under the document was such a caption: "The most famous and the wittiest essay ever written by Franklin."[25]

---

25. Rosenbach, *The All-Embracing Doctor Franklin* (Philadelphia, 1938), 4, 6. Within two years Max Lincoln Schuster included the piece in his *Treasury of the World's Great Letters* (New York, 1940), and his selection was delivered as a dividend by the Book-of-the-Month Club to its quarter-million members. Charles Lee, *The Hidden Public: The Story of the Book-of-the-Month Club* (Garden City, New York, 1958), 174; *Papers* 3: 29. Several years later Franklin's essay, "On Perfumes," became available to the general public in Nathan G. Goodman, ed., *A Benjamin Franklin Reader* (New York, 1945), 739–41.

III

Versatility and gallantry aside, Franklin's champions considered him as a symbol of fundamental Americanness. This assumption became especially important when, in 1904–05, the German sociologist Max Weber published *The Protestant Ethic and the Spirit of Capitalism.* In this work he declared that some of Franklin's homespun maxims embodied the quintessential elements of capitalism, like "time is money" and "credit is money." Or in his phrase, Franklin's beliefs expressed the spirit of capitalism with "classical purity."[26]

Ironically, Weber's theme was raised at a time when the real economic situation gravely undermined Franklin's premise. The industrial world of the early twentieth century was known for its increasing demand for productivity and efficiency.[27] Frederick Winslow Taylor, the best-known supporter of this doctrine, published *The Principles of Scientific Management* in 1911. His pioneer study of time and motion was designed to take away the self-control and self-reliance on which individual craftsmen in the past had thrived. Modern manufactures, Taylor emphasized, should be based on scientific management in order to prevent underwork and to increase productivity. A modern industry did not need rule-of-thumb experience, which would lead only to ignorance, waste, and idleness. Contrary to Franklin's confidence in individual autonomy, Taylor plainly told contemporary manufacturers that his principle meant "cooperation, not individualism," and that "in the past the man has been first; in the future the system must be first."[28]

In the long run, however, Weber's observation was to have a profound impact on the way American scholars would examine the nation's character. In the subsequent search for the origins of American civilization many students were convinced that Protestant ideas, especially the Protestant ethic based on calling, contributed a great deal to the birth of modern capitalism.[29] Furthermore, long before Weber's

---

26. Weber, *The Protestant Ethic and the Spirit of Capitalism* (Charles Scribner's Sons ed.: New York, 1958), 48.

27. "The Gospel of Efficiency: A New Science of Business Management," *American Magazine* 71 (March 1911): 562–81; (April 1911): 785–93; 72 (May 1911): 101–13.

28. Quoted in Taylor, *The Principles of Scientific Management* (Norton Library ed.: New York, 1967), 140, 7.

29. For example, A. Whitney Griswold, "Three Puritans on Prosperity," *New England Quarterly* 7 (September 1934): 475–88; Moses Rischin, ed., *The American Gospel of Success* (Chicago, 1965).

book was translated into English in 1930, some Americans had already realized that Franklin's life style could be regarded as a crucial
link tying America's past to its present. As early as 1876 an article in
Harper's Monthly Magazine stated that if American civilization was to
be represented by two men, they ought to be Benjamin Franklin and
Jonathan Edwards. Franklin's career epitomized Americans' obsession with materialistic success and interest in this world, while Edwards's life and writings expressed Americans' concerns with spiritual
pursuits and the next world.[30]

In this century, Van Wyck Brooks went further, saying that
"Jonathan Edwards displayed the infinite inflexibility of the upper
levels of the American mind, nor any more typically than Franklin the
infinite flexibility of its lower levels." Both men with their distinctive
philosophies "determined the American character," which, as Brooks
described, embraced both "highbrow" and "lowbrow" elements.[31]
Some modern authors and writers concurred, such as F. Scott Fitzgerald's cynically portrayed businessman in *The Great Gatsby* (1925),
and William Carlos Williams's explicitly expressed dislike of Franklin
in his *In the American Grain* (1925).

Admirers of Franklin, of course, disagreed. In an introduction to a
new edition of Franklin's autobiography, Ainsworth R. Spofford wrote
that "the impress of a sincere and honest personality pervades the
entire narrative."[32] In 1914 when James M. Beck discussed the reason
for Franklin's enduring popularity, he insisted that

both his virtues and his failings were characteristic of the American character
as it has since developed. His shrewdness, utilitarianism, philosophic good
humor, poise of judgment, tolerant spirit, democratic temperament, inven-

---

30. "The First Century of the Republic," *Harper's New Monthly Magazine* 52 (February 1876): 401–04. David Levin believed that this sort of comparison could
be traced back to George Bancroft as early as the 1840s, "Reason, Rhythm, and
Style," in Barbara B. Oberg and Harry S. Stout, eds., *Benjamin Franklin,
Jonathan Edwards, and the Representation of American Culture* (New York,
1993), 171.

31. Brooks, *America's Coming-of-Age* (New York, 1915). Also Carl Van Doren, ed.,
Benjamin Franklin and Jonathan Edwards: Selections from Their Writings
(New York, 1920); and David Levin, ed., *The Puritan in the Enlightenment:
Franklin and Edwards* (Chicago, 1963).

32. Benjamin Franklin, *Autobiography. Poor Richard. Letters*, ed. Spofford (Aldine
ed.: New York, 1900), iii.

tive genius, intellectual inquisitiveness, love of industry and pride in achievement are all characteristically American qualities.[33]

A decade later Beck maintained that in recent years, revived interest in Franklin's life and personal characteristics had been remarkable.[34] Those who were concerned about the nation's spirituality believed that Franklin's popularity presented "a colossal misfortune to the United States." In the word of Charles Angoff:

Thrift, industry, and determination were essential virtues in the building of the nation, but they were not, then or at any other time in history, of sufficient human dignity to build a life philosophy on. Franklin did precisely that for his private life, and by the force of his personality did more than any other man in his day to graft it upon the American people. The vulgarity he spread is still with us.[35]

Interestingly enough, one of the most rigorous critics of Franklin during this period was the English writer D. H. Lawrence. He visited the United States from the end of the 1910s until the early 1920s, and published *Studies in Classic American Literature* in 1923. His acid comments would long be remembered by many Americans.[36] This gifted but controversial novelist wrote that "middle-sized, sturdy, snuff-coloured Doctor Franklin" was "the first dummy American" and "the most complete citizen that ever 'used venery.'"[37]

That Lawrence did not like Franklin was obvious. He believed that "when genuine passion moves you, say what you've got to say, and say it hot," which he did. Lawrence's criticism was aimed at who Franklin was as much as what he represented, because the critic wrote at the outset: "The Perfectibility of Man! Ah heaven, what a dreary theme! The perfectibility of the Ford Car!" Charles L. Sanford

---

33. Beck, *The Youthful Franklin* (Philadelphia, 1914), 10.
34. Beck, *The Memory of Benjamin Franklin* (New York, 1924), 5.
35. Angoff, *A Literary History of the American People* (New York, 1931), 2: 296, 310.
36. H. I. Brock, "D. H. Lawrence Strings Some American Literary Pearls," *New York Times Book Review*, 16 September 1923, p. 9.
37. All statements here by Lawrence are quoted from the chapter, "Benjamin Franklin," *Studies in Classic American Literature* (Doubleday Anchor Books ed.: Garden City, N.Y., 1951), 19–31. For an earlier version of the essay and background information see *The Symbolic Meaning: The Uncollected Versions of Studies in Classic American Literature*, ed. Armin Arnold (New York, 1961), ix–xi, 1–11, 33–47.

pointed out that Lawrence was challenging Franklin's "narrow prudential morality with a wholesale attack on America."[38] In fact, Lawrence's sweeping criticism was so assertive and his style so sketchy that for quite some time few Americans knew how to respond to his charges.[39]

Perhaps both the critic and his object represented the same individualism much more than what Lawrence would like to admit. The difference, however, is that the buoyant Franklin symbolized the emerging bourgeois confidence in self-determination and self-control, whereas the skeptical Lawrence challenged the *status quo*. Material acquisition was the driving force for progress and industrialization. But if mechanical perfection could be achieved only at the expense of individual souls, this trend would lead to Lawrence's "blind passion of rejection."[40]

Lawrence believed that "the *wholeness* of a man is his soul," and that "the soul of man is a dark vast forest," where no restrictions of any kind should be placed. He called the wholeness of man "it," which suggested the inseparability of man's qualities as indicated in his formula "that I am I." He also insisted:

> We are only the actors, we are never wholly the authors of our own deeds or works. *It* is the author, the unknown inside us or outside us. The best we can do is to try to hold ourselves in unison with the deeps which are inside us. And the worst we can do is to try to have things our own way, when we run counter to *IT.*

Franklin, however, attempted to control and reform what Lawrence saw as the sacred "it" or self. Franklin tried to apply moralistic rules to formulate a person's soul, or to set up a "barbed wire of shalt-not ideals and shalt-not moralism" in order to control a person's behavior. Such an intention was distasteful because Franklin claimed that ev-

---

38. Charles L. Sanford, ed., *Benjamin Franklin and the American Character* (Boston, 1955), vii; most recently Kenneth Silverman noted that under Lawrence's pen neither America nor Franklin had a soul (Benjamin Franklin, *The Autobiography and Other Writings*, ed. Silverman [Penguin Books ed.: New York, 1986], xiii).

39. After several years Herbert Wallace Schneider was one of the few who responded to the critic and defended Franklin (*The Puritan Mind* [New York, 1930], 237–56).

40. Raymond Williams's chapter on Lawrence remains one of the most relevant analyses, *Culture and Society, 1780–1950* (New York, 1960), 199–215.

erything he did was for the sake of virtue, and, what was worse, he did it with great self-consciousness.

While many Americans admired Franklin's unusual ability to examine and project himself, Lawrence saw the same trend as a threat to his belief in an indivisible self. Lawrence declared that Franklin's mode was self-conceit, and that Franklin's moral codes were like thorns in his flesh. "Anyhow I defy you," the critic wrote, "I defy you, oh society, to educate me or suppress me, according to your dummy standards." Lawrence concluded that "I, at least, know why I can't stand Benjamin," for "he tries to take away my wholeness and my dark forest, my freedom."

What Lawrence criticized was exactly what fascinated many Americans. Franklin was the self-made man in the purest sense. Claiming that he believed in one God, he imitated Jesus and Socrates and set up his own standards of conscience. He not only made his way in education, business, and politics, but also analyzed his own rise in his autobiography. His career validated modern psychological thinking: the self could split itself into two parts, and one part could examine the other. "The ego can take itself as object," as Freud said, "it can treat itself like any other object, observe itself, criticise itself, and do Heaven knows what besides with itself."[41]

Lawrence, however, did not recognize Franklin's complex inner life. Since he did not believe that human instinct should be controlled in any way, he ridiculed Franklin as a hypocrite who tried to master his own destiny. Thus Lawrence also failed to analyze why more than a century and thirty years after his death, Franklin continued to captivate Americans' imaginations not as a moralist, but as a characteristic man.

IV

For those who were concerned about the education of the younger generation or about the Americanization of newly-arrived immigrants, Franklin was an ideal lesson of patriotism and a prime illustration of American values and traditions.

For more than fifty years, "character-building" organizations proliferated in America: the Young Men's Christian Association (1851), the Young Women's Christian Association (1866), and the Boy Scouts

---

41. Sigmund Freud, *New Introductory Lectures on Psycho-analysis* (New York, 1933), 84.

and Girl Scouts of America around the turn of this century. These organizations stressed traditional Christian values such as piety and honesty, and paid considerable attention to their members' mental and physical well-being. In addition to vocational and recreational activities, repeated emphases on loyalty to gender, age, or ethnic groups became an integral part of their institutional functions.[42]

Patriotism and citizenship continued to be more important than group loyalty. Nevertheless, understanding the importance of one's duty to the nation was no longer sufficient to meet a person's diverse obligations in a highly pluralistic society. The education of character, therefore, would be very difficult if it were left to individuals. In fact, group affiliation was as important as self-control in modern America, and discipline, obedience, and loyalty continued to be regarded as laudable individual characteristics.

Samuel Smiles, the popular English author and a well-known authority on the topic, declared that "character is human nature in its best form." Character "is moral order embodied in individual," he said. "Men of character are not only the conscience of society, but in every well-governed State they are its best motive power. . . . The strength, the industry, and the civilization of nations—all depend upon individual character."

Good morals and manners test the strength of character, such as courtesy, kindness, benevolence, civility, gentleness, and humanity. Individual character begins with self-culture, self-discipline, and self-control. Integrity and honesty, loyalty to veracity, truthfulness in action as well as words, shape one's character. Above all, "Character is power," Smiles said:

> The crown and glory of life is character. It is the noblest possession of a man, constituting a rank in itself, and estate, and exalting every position in society. It exercises a greater power than wealth, and secures all the honor without the jealousies of fame. It carries with it an influence which always tells; for it is the result of proved honor, rectitude, and consistency—qualities which, perhaps more than any other, command the general confidence and respect of mankind.[43]

Character education, therefore, reemerged as a means to reinforce loyalty, order, law, manners, discipline, and uniformity. When Frederick Winslow Taylor discussed the modern concept of success, he stressed:

---

42. Kenneth E. Reid, *From Character Building to Social Treatment: The History of the Use of Groups in Social Work* (Westport, Conn., 1981), 62–73.

43. Smiles, *Self-Help* (revised ed.: New York, 1884), xi, 416–42.

Character is the ability to control yourself, body and mind; the ability to do those things which your common-sense tells you you ought to do; the ability above all to do things which are disagreeable, which you do not like. It takes but little character to do difficult things if you like them. It takes a lot of character to do things which are tiresome, monotonous and unpleasant.[44]

Shortly before Franklin's centennial in 1906, Edwards Brooks, the superintendent of public schools in Philadelphia, sent a circular letter to local schools that gave many concrete suggestions. "Principals and teachers," he began, "repeat for your pupils the story of [Franklin's] early struggles and successes; draw the picture of the hungry youth and his penny rolls; explain the incident of the bottling of the flash of the thunder-cloud; narrate the wise deeds by which he helped to secure our liberties and establish our great republic." In 1910 a special committee of eight, headed by James Alton James, submitted to the American Historical Association a report entitled *The Study of History in the Elementary Schools*. It recommended that children should begin to learn about Franklin's life as early as the fourth grade, with strong emphasis on his struggling boyhood and great service to the American Revolution.[45]

About the same time, Ernest Cobb, an English teacher at Chelsea High School in Massachusetts, wrote to the *Journal of Education*, pointing out that Franklin's *Autobiography* should be recommended on almost every school reading list. He remarked, however, that the *Autobiography* was hardly a classic if judged by literary criteria, for "it lacks utterly in high lights, contrasts, delicate shades and nuances, fine sense of structure." But he conceded that, as material to improve both the students' moral sensitivity and their plain and direct English, the *Autobiography* could be beneficial. He further suggested that students should stop at each incident relating to virtue, and let them discuss the event and its implications before they went on to the next episode.[46]

Another school teacher, Mary C. Quinton of Providence, Rhode

---

44. Taylor, "Success, A Lecture to Young Men Entering Business," *Bulletin of the Taylor Society* 11 (April 1926): 68.

45. A letter from the Department of Superintendence signed by Edwards Brooks, Philadelphia, 4 January 1906 (*Frankliniana*, 1906, the Historical Society of Pennsylvania). The Committee of Eight, *The Study of History in the Elementary Schools: Report to the American Historical Association* (New York, 1910), 15, 17.

46. Cobb, "Suggestions for the Use of Franklin's Autobiography," *Journal of Education* (Boston), 75 (22 February 1912): 207.

Island, found out that many of her pupils were of foreign origin, with slight knowledge of American traditions and the English language. In order to promote their interest in the American heritage and to improve their skill at reading English, she told them stories of Benjamin Franklin.[47] To instill Franklin's creeds and example into young people's minds, creative methods were adopted. Like many adults, high school students might go to Franklin's grave or his statue to pay tribute on his birthday,[48] as often happened in Philadelphia, New York, and Boston (Fig. 27). Dramatization and story telling were found particularly useful for elementary school children, whose mental and reading abilities were not yet fully developed.[49] Attempts were even made to establish a new holiday. At a meeting of the International Association of Printing House Craftsmen in May 1937, Howard A. Lukens of Philadelphia called for Franklin's birthday to be observed nationwide, but this suggestion came to nothing.[50]

When the country began to witness a constitutional revival during the 1920s and 1930s, the artist Howard Chandler Christy painted Franklin at the center of his widely-circulated picture, "We, the People." Some staunch advocates of the Constitution, such as James M. Beck, John Huston Finley, and George Wharton Pepper, were the most enthusiastic defenders of Franklin's reputation.[51] All of them belonged to an organization called the International Benjamin Franklin Society. Founded in 1923 with the sole purpose of perpetuating the fame of Franklin (Fig. 28), the society included many business-

---

47. Quinton, "Franklin—The Wisest American of His Time," *Normal Instructor and Primary Plans* (Dansville, N.Y.), 32 (January 1923): 59.

48. The Poor Richard Club in Philadelphia, for example, began their annual pilgrimage to Franklin's grave in 1907. The practice was later followed by the Franklin Institute, the American Philosophical Society, the Pennsylvania Hospital, the Post Office, and military and naval groups. Jack Lutz, *The Poor Richard Club* (Philadelphia, 1953), 10.

49. Hattie Rainey, "A Type-Study of Benjamin Franklin," *Normal Instructor and Primary Plans* 34 (January 1925): 32, 33, 85; Mary P. Davis, "A Life of Usefulness," *Popular Educator* (Boston), 42 (January 1925): 275, 294, 296; Fannie Sadik, "Benjamin Franklin: A Fifth Grade Project," *Primary Education* (Boston), 34 (March 1926): 190–91. Detailed suggestions and plans also came from John Clyde Oswald, president of the International Benjamin Franklin Society, and J. Robert Stout, president of Educational Thrift Services. Both wanted the younger generation to observe Franklin's virtues as well his birthday, *Normal Instructor and Primary Plans* 32 (January 1923): 58.

50. *New York Times*, 30 May 1937, section 2, p. 2.

51. Michael Kammen, *A Machine That Would Go of Itself: The Constitution in American Culture* (Vintage Books ed.: New York, 1987), 220, 303, and figure 25.

A PILGRIMAGE TO THE GRAVE OF FRANKLIN

The Benjamin Franklin High School of Philadelphia pays tribute to
Franklin on the 150th Anniversary of his Death.

IT WAS especially fitting that on April 17th, 1940 the 1900 young men students of the Benjamin Franklin High School at Broad and Green Streets in Philadelphia should have held Memorial services for Benjamin Franklin on the 150th Anniversary of his death. Benjamin Franklin would have been proud of the tribute from these young Americans who are, economically, from one of the least favored groups of his Philadelphia. There are among these youths, according to their principal, Mr. A. O. Michener, many fine boys of promise. More than half of the students are negro and about one-third of the total number are of foreign-born parents. Mr. Michener and his loyal and devoted faculty of sixty-five men are therefore especially zealous about presenting Franklin to these young citizens as a model and a guiding spirit.

The Memorial services began at the school at nine o'clock; following this the program planned for the ceremony at Franklin's grave was presented for the entire student body, after which a delegation of 100 students went by bus to the grave at 5th and Arch Streets. Buglers played taps at the simple impressive ceremony, which consisted of the following addresses and prayer:

FRANKLIN'S FUNERAL DESCRIBED

Address by Mr. Joseph Cottler of the Faculty in the School Auditorium preceding the Pilgrimage.

This morning we sons of Franklin are bringing up the rear of a procession that began also on a Wednesday morning 150 years ago to pay a last token of respect to him who was called at that time the most famous private citizen of the world. We read that the procession assembled at the State House, where Franklin had been a familiar figure for 50 years.

Now, here is the order of that procession as they trooped to the cemetery: In the front rank were the clergy of the city; then came a group of citizens carrying the body; the pall supported by the Governor of the State (Franklin's successor in office), Chief Justice, President of the Bank (also Franklin's successor), and other high civil officers and leading citizens among whom it is worth mentioning David Rittenhouse, the astronomer and Franklin's fellow scientist. Next came the family and special mourners; the members of the General Assembly among whom Franklin had often sat; the Supreme Court Justices; the Mayor; the various societies in which Franklin had held membership and most of which he had founded.

(Among them were the printers, the fire company, the College of Physicians, the Faculty of the College of Philadelphia, the Philosophical Society), and, finally, the general public.

Altogether some 20,000 people, the greatest assembly up to that time. The bells of the city were muffled and tolled; the flags on ships in the harbor were flown at half mast. As the corpse was lowered into the grave the militia fired the funeral guns.

I am not sure that Ben Franklin would have cared much for his funeral. It would have seemed to him too showy and sumptuous, too pompous. He had written in his will, "I wish to be buried by the side of my wife, and that a marble stone be made, plain, with only a small moulding around the upper edge, and this inscription—'Benjamin and Deborah Franklin,' and the date." Only that. Had someone suggested to him a grand turnout with all its attendant ceremonies, he would probably have prevented it, even if he had to keep alive to do it. Or he might have wanted to invent another kind of lightning rod to ground such public display. The old man in homespun would certainly have thought it ludicrous that a college president would orate over him in Latin, considering that he himself had founded the Academy which became the University of Pennsylvania to exclude Latin and base its curriculum on English, a revolutionary step in education at that time.

But he would have liked to know, I think, that his old friends in France were in mourning for him. The French Leader, Mirabeau, suggested in the National Assembly that nations ought to wear mourning, not for kings and the like, but for benefactors and heroes of humanity like Mr. Franklin, who, he said, had tamed both lightning and tyrants. Lafayette seconded the motion, which was carried by acclamation, and for three days the French lawmakers wore black. The British and French scientific societies made speeches about him in their formal proceedings, but Ben Franklin would have been more pleased to hear the speakers in the streets and cafes of Paris, who coupled his name with that of Liberty and Humanity. And he would likewise have been pleased and touched, I think, at the thought of a group of high school boys arranging a testimonial to his memory.

Witnesses tell of the last year of his life, during which he was confined to his bed, on the second floor of his house on Market Street. They tell us that despite the great physical pain which hardly ever left him, he was cheerful and gay. He spent his days playing with his grandchildren, the youngest

of which was five months old. Every day he heard the lessons of the nine-year-old Deborah. About the 14th of April an abscess developed in his chest, and his temperature shot up. He got out of bed and requested his daughter "to make it up" so that he might die decently. His daughter was shocked. He had many more years ahead of him, she assured him. "I hope not," he said, and there was no bitterness in his tone. He was 84 years old. He had lived a full and active life. He had known kings and common people, had helped to discover truth, from electricity to the rights of man. He had served his community and nation most responsibly, offering them his inventive genius, his fortune, and his life. We could sum up his account in a remark he made at a meeting of his old fire company shortly before: "I am keeping my bucket in good order." And now the scientist was interested in one last crucial experiment: to determine the truth about life *after death* and that he was soon to find out. On Saturday, the 17th of April, 1790, the abscess in his chest burst, and at about eleven o'clock that night his son and daughter drew the sheet forever over him.

27. *The Benjamin Franklin Gazette* (publication of the International Benjamin Franklin Society) often promoted events that commemorated Franklin, such as this report in May 1940: "A Pilgrimage to the Grave of Franklin: The Benjamin Franklin High School of Philadelphia Pays Tribute to Franklin on the 150th Anniversary of His Death."

men, scientists, editors, and publishers, like William Guggenheim, John Clyde Oswald, Francis X. Dercum, George Bruce Cortelyou, William Smith Mason, Henry Butler Allen, Henry Norris Russell, James Wright Brown, and Arthur Willis Goodspeed.

Early in 1920, the Young Men's Christian Association in New York proposed a thrift week beginning on Franklin's birthday of the next year. The scheme met little support until such people as J. Robert Stout, John Clyde Oswald, and William Guggenheim promised sup-

THE FRANKLIN REBUS

We are indebted to the Franklin Society for Savings, of which our First Vice-President, Mr. Charles O'Connor Hennessy is President, for the plate of the Rebus, or puzzle reproduced here. It was composed by Franklin probably in 1780.

At *this* time when *the* general complaint is *that* money eyes *so* scarce, *it* eyes must bee *an act of kindness* toe inform *the* pennyless how *they* can reinforce *their* pockets. Eye *weyell* acquaint yew *with the* true *secret of* money. Ca*tching the certain way* toe fill empty purses *and how* toe keep them aw*ltways* full. Two simple rules well obser*ved* *weyell* do *the* bus*eyeness*. 1*st.* Let honesty *and* industry bee thy constant compan*ions*. 2*nd.* Spend one penny *every* day *less than* thy clear *gains.* Then *shawl* thy pockets soon *thrive* *begin* *to threvene.* Thy *credevetors* *will* n*Ever* insult *thee* nor want oppress *nor* hunger bite *nor* nakedness *freeze* *hee.* The whole hemisphere *will* *sheyene* *brighter and* pleasure *spring up* in *every corner of thy* heart. Now, there*fore, embrace these rules and* bee *Happy.*

28. Franklin Rebus: "The Art of Making Money Plenty in Every Man's Pocket: By Doctor Franklin," a souvenir that has become popular since the beginning of the twentieth century. This one was printed in the *Benjamin Franklin Gazette*, (publication of the International Benjamin Franklin Society), October 1929, p. 9.

port. All of them later became important figures in the International Benjamin Franklin Society. Guggenheim was invited by the YMCA to act as chairman of their "Benjamin Franklin Memorial Committee" (Fig. 29). He wrote to Governor Nathan Lewis Miller of New York, and suggested that the latter issue a proclamation for thrift week, which the governor gladly did.[52]

Encouraged by the first successful Thrift Week in 1921, the YMCA decided to continue observing the ceremony in New York City and other parts of the nation.[53] The observance of Thrift Week attracted

---

52. Gatenby Williams [pseud.], *William Guggenheim* (New York, 1934), 204–05, 207.

53. A typical Thrift Week began on Franklin's birthday, with the six following days designated as: National Thrift Day, National Budget Day, Make-a-Will Day, Life Insurance Day, Own Your Own Home Day, and Safe Insurance Day. *New York Times*, 1 December 1931, p. 50.

A MESSAGE

from

WILLIAM GUGGENHEIM

Honorary President of the International Benjamin Franklin Society

MY DEAR MR. STOUT:

It is with infinite pleasure that I respond to your kind request to send a message to our members and their guests, at the event of our Fifteenth Annual Meeting and luncheon. Nothing would give me greater pleasure than to be with you, but my health required that I again leave our great city to seek the warmer clime, which I find here in Beverly Hills, California.

Although the new year opens auspiciously for the activities of our Society, I regret exceedingly that I cannot say as much for the economic conditions that for the moment confront our beloved country. We have made our usual efforts during the past year to keep alive the memory of Franklin, and to spread his teachings. Little heed, however, has been paid by responsible authorities to warnings that we and many others found it advisable to proclaim. The very fears that we entertained for the uneconomic policies that were prevailing, continue to disturb us. As a result of those policies we now find ourselves confronted with what may prove to be a major business depression. Only the greatest financial skill furthered by patriotic endeavor on the part of Congress can help us out of this unfortunate situation.

Useless attacks on our business community from every quarter should cease. The few supposed "rats," as one might say, have, I hope, been smoked out; but the magnificent edifice that finance and industry have been building for years, is partly destroyed and it must be restored. Further pandering to the public through legislative appeals would seem like a smoke-screen set up for political effect only. It would prove of no avail. "Big" business, as it has been frequently styled, has become part and parcel of us. We must not for a moment imagine that we can readily dismiss it or undermine it in the least, unless we are willing permanently to injure our prosperity and welfare. Our industrial pioneers have devoted their lives to the building up of our great industries, which now have reached every corner of the earth. Big business alone is capable of carrying on our foreign trade which is so essential to us.

On October 5, 1937, I made a suggestion through certain channels for the formation of a non-partisan league, to be founded on the common sense and wisdom of Benjamin Franklin, the father of our liberty. Such a league was to conform in purpose to the following:

"As the country's welfare is best served by the election to office of those who are in every sense best qualified by learning, integrity and ability to interpret and enforce its laws, and as the country's peace and happiness can only come from competent and efficient business administration of our government, we, therefore, agree to indorse nominations to office accordingly; and furthermore agree that those indorsed, if elected, shall abide by the following creed:

"I believe in the United States of America as a government of the people, by the people, for the people; whose just powers are derived from the consent of the governed; a democracy and a republic; a sovereign nation of many sovereign states; a perfect union, one and inseparable, established upon those principles of freedom, equality, justice and humanity for which American patriots sacrificed their lives and fortunes.

"I therefore believe it is my duty to my country to support its Constitution, to compel obedience to its laws, respect for its flag, and a united defense against all enemies."

With this suggestion as a conclusion to my views herein expressed, may I further state that capitalism is essential for progress and civilization as well as good government, and that civilization cannot continue unless a happy and fair spirit is shown on all sides. We must remember that we do not want tyranny of government, of capital, of labor, or of any set, for it is in tyranny we would find our downfall. The industrial chaos caused by our uneconomic thinkers and false philosophers, that exists today, is not new; we have had the same conditions before and we survived. Though I entertain some fear of the future, I feel history will repeat itself, and that we will continue to remain a free and unfettered people. But, Oh Lord, how we do love to take punishment!

I extend to you all my heartiest greetings and best wishes for the Society's continued success. GOD BLESS YOU ONE AND ALL.

Sincerely yours,

(Signed) WILLIAM GUGGENHEIM

BEVERLY HILLS, CALIFORNIA
JANUARY 17, 1938

29. William Guggenheim's letter of January 17, 1938 to the International Benjamin Franklin Society, published as frontispiece in *The Benjamin Franklin Gazette* (May 1938).

attention from prominent politicians ranging from Calvin Coolidge to Herbert Hoover. Thereafter as many as fifty national organizations began to cooperate with the YMCA, and sponsors included economists, bankers, insurance agents, businessmen, social workers, and religious leaders.[54] Spreading the gospel of frugality, the joint effort by different organizations and individuals made it possible for the observance of Thrift Week to continue for nearly two decades.

Toward the end of the 1920s the Great Depression set in and many felt that there was little to save. Yet Franklin's mold of rugged individualism was used again as inspiration for average men and women. Herbert Hoover declared at a public ceremony that Franklin's career not only represented self-reliance, but also reflected the traditional laissez-faire policy of the federal government. Hoover was apparently denouncing Franklin D. Roosevelt's New Deal philosophy when he said: "The ideal today has shifted from the self-made man toward the government-coddled man." Convinced that self-help, not government intervention, should be the foundation of a healthy national economy, Hoover paraphrased Joseph Choate and warned: "When the spirit of Franklin decays the sun of America will have begun to set."[55]

V

Franklin's many-sidedness was also exploited by people from unexpected quarters. On February 3, 1934 a journal called *Liberation* (Asheville, North Carolina) carried an article, which contained an excerpt purporting to be from the "Private Diary" of Charles Pinckney of South Carolina. Here Franklin was quoted as denouncing Jews at the Constitutional Convention of 1787. Although the diary was later proved to be a forgery, the publication of that passage began a long battle concerning Franklin's reputation.

At first the so-called statement by Franklin, or "Franklin's Prophecy," did not draw much public attention. For one thing, William Dudley Pelley, the publisher of *Liberation*, was head of a pro-Nazi organization named the Silver Legion of America and was known as a professional publicist of anti-Semitism. For another, well–informed

---

54. *New York Times*, 1 December 1931, p. 50; 18 January 1932, p. 17; 18 January 1935, p. 11.

55. *New York Times*, 22 May 1938, p. 2; Herbert Hoover, *Addresses upon the American Road* (New York, 1938), 1: 366, 368. He repeated the same theme two decades later: "Franklin was an individualist. He held no belief in people's leaning on government. He contended they must have a sterner fare if the nation was to go forward. He insisted that they must possess qualities and strength of character which would give them calmness and poise in prosperity and courage and vision in adversity. They must be guided not only by patriotism of the tribe, but by morality and religious faith which belong alone to the individual spirit" (*Wisdom* 1 [March 1956], 76).

people realized that if there had ever existed a private diary by Pinckney, it would have been discovered long before.

Nevertheless, in August the "prophecy" reappeared in Nazi Germany in three languages—German, French, and English. Thereafter Nazi leaders and their organs repeatedly used the alleged document to promulgate anti-Semitic sentiment.[56] Some time in late September 1934 Charles A. Beard received a pamphlet containing a similar allegation by Robert Edward Edmondson, who had the reputation of being a Nazi agent in the United States. As a noted historian and critic of the framers of the Constitution, Beard had studied all delegates to the Constitutional Convention, including Franklin and Pinckney,[57] but was never aware of such a statement by Franklin. He immediately contacted Edmondson, asking his source for the original document. The latter referred to Madison Grant, who was a nativist and Anglo-Saxon supremacist in New York City. Beard wrote to Grant and received a reply stating that although Grant had seen a copy of Franklin's remarks some years earlier, he had "no information, whatever as to the authenticity of the paper."[58]

At that point Beard was almost certain that the "prophecy" was a pure fabrication, but he proceeded cautiously and sent an inquiry to John Franklin Jameson, chief of the Manuscripts Division of the Library of Congress. Jameson told Beard that to the best of his knowledge Pinckney did not keep a diary of Convention proceedings in 1787, nor was it conceivable that Franklin could have made the alleged speech.

Meanwhile, Beard reexamined Franklin's writings and, with assistance from others, searched through the vast Franklin collections in Philadelphia. Nothing of that nature was uncovered. What Beard found was that the phraseology of the alleged paper was not that of the eighteenth century. Jews of that century did not use the word "homeland," and the idea of returning to Palestine, or Zionism, was not a popular movement in Franklin's time. Beard thus concluded:

---

56. A Swiss Nazi organ reprinted the "prophecy" in August 1934. So did Robert Edward Edmondson in the United States on 25 September of the same year. For continuous exploitations of this forgery on both sides of the Atlantic see *Pelley's the Silver Shirt Weekly*, 3 October 1934, p. 1; *Pelley's Weekly*, 5 August 1936, p. 7; [Julian P. Boyd, an editor's note], *Pennsylvania Magazine of History and Biography* 61 (April 1937): 233–34; *New York Times*, 1 December 1938, p. 1.

57. Beard, *An Economic Interpretation of the Constitution of the United States* (New York, 1913).

58. Beard, "Charles A. Beard Exposes Anti-Semitic Forgery about Benjamin Franklin," reprint of *Jewish Frontier* (New York), 2 (March 1935): 4–8.

All these searches have produced negative results. I cannot find a single original source that gives the slightest justification for believing that the "Prophecy" is anything more than a bare-faced forgery. Not a word have I discovered in Franklin's letters and papers expressing any such sentiments against the Jews as are ascribed to him by the Nazis—American and German. His well-known liberality in matters of religious opinions would, in fact, have precluded the kind of utterances put in his mouth by this palpable forgery[59] (Fig. 30).

Despite Beard's tireless investigation, the issue did not die away. It resurfaced in the New York gubernatorial campaign of 1938, between the Republican candidate, Thomas E. Dewey, and the Democratic incumbent, Herbert H. Lehman. Some members in the Republican camp thought that the so-called statement by Franklin might be used as ammunition against their Democratic opponent. Soon voters in the state got the "prophecy" in pamphlets and handbills at all sorts of public places, such as trains, buses, public waiting rooms and lavatories, and even through the United States mail, which was against the law. As the propaganda frenzy spread, an indignant citizen in Syracuse reported that one morning in Onondaga County the printed accusation was found "under every windshield wiper in every car." A man named Arthur Butler Graham was equally outraged, and he wrote an open letter to the editor of the *New York Times* in protest against "the vicious act": "I am writing in order that in every group in which the subject comes up for discussion there may be one person present who will nail the calumny, and further that the source of the propaganda may be discovered and exposed."[60]

Meanwhile, someone alleged that the original Pinckney diary was in the Franklin Institute in Philadelphia. The director of the institute, Henry Butler Allen, promptly denied it: "We *do not* possess the notorious diary."[61] At the same time, Alfred Rigling, librarian of the Institute, added that no such diary by Pinckney existed in his institute, the Library of Congress, the New York Public Library, or the Historical Society of Pennsylvania. Distinguished scholars and celebrated Franklin experts from J. Henry Smyth, Jr., Carl Van Doren, and Julian P. Boyd to John Clyde Oswald all publicly and unequivocally stated that

---

59. Ibid., 8.
60. Allan Nevins, *Herbert H. Lehman and His Era* (New York, 1963), 196; *New York Times*, 18 September 1938, section 4, p. 9.
61. Franklin Institute, *The Institute News* 3 (August 1938): 1.

BENJAMIN FRANKLIN AND THE JEWS

"In whatever country Jews have settled in any great numbers, they have lowered its moral tone, depreciated its commercial integrity, have segregated themselves and have not been assimilated, have sneered at. and tried to undermine the Christian religion, have built up a state within a state, and have, when opposed, tried to strangle that countr to death financially.

"If you do not exclude them from the United States in the Constitution, in less than 200 years they will have swarmed in such great numbers that they will dominate and devour the land and change our form of government.

"If you do not exclude them, in less than 200 years our descendants will be working in the fields to furnish the substance while they will be in the counting house rubbing their hands. I warn you, gentlemen. if you do not exclude the Jews for all time, your children will curse you in your graves. Jews, gentlemen, are Asiatics; they will never be otherwise".

30a. Reprint of the forged statement Franklin supposedly made about Jews.

30b. Reprint of Charles Beard's defense of Franklin's attitudes toward the Jews, New York (ca. 1935). (Courtesy of The Papers of Benjamin Franklin, Yale University Library)

Franklin had never had anything to do with the speech, which was a malicious forgery[62] (Figs. 31 and 32).

The majority of voters in New York seemed to understand that peeking into Franklin's private life was one thing, slandering his uni-

---

62. International Benjamin Franklin Society, *Benjamin Franklin Vindicated* (New York, [1938]), 11–15.

EXPLANATION BY JULIAN P. BOYD

Mr. Julian Boyd is the Librarian of the Historical Society of Pennsylvania.

WITHIN the past month Franklin's mythical speech full of animadversions against the Jews, which he is supposed to have delivered before the Constitutional Convention, has reappeared in the daily press. According to the published account, this speech warned the people of the United States against the "vampire" race, and concluded: "I warn you, gentlemen, if you do not exclude the Jews forever, your children and your children's children will curse you in their graves."

The prevalence of these statements has been traced to the February 3, 1934, issue of *Liberation*, the publication of a Fascist organization which appeared in Asheville, N. C. in 1933. "Franklin's Prophecy," so-called, was immediately reprinted by papers in Germany and Switzerland and from thence, recrossing the Atlantic, it turned up in the United States in September 25, 1934, in a pamphlet circulated from New York by Robert Edward Edmondson.

The "Prophecy," characterized by Professor Charles A. Beard, in the *Jewish Frontier* for March, 1935, as a "barefaced forgery", was supposed to be found in a diary kept by Charles Pinckney of South Carolina. No such diary is known to exist nor can anything resembling it be found among any of the extant Pinckney papers. Furthermore, neither Professor Beard's examination of Franklin's writings nor careful searches in the available records "including the vast collections of Frankliniana in Philadelphia" have produced anything that "gives the slightest justification for believing that the 'Prophecy' is . . . more than a barefaced forgery. Not a word," wrote Professor Beard, "have I discovered in Franklin's letters and papers expressing such sentiments against the Jews as are ascribed to him by the Nazis—American and German." There is, moreover, positive evidence that Franklin held Jews in high esteem, and when the Hebrew Society of Philadelphia was trying to raise money for a "religious house",

Franklin not only signed the petition appealing for contributions to "Citizens of every religious denomination", but he also contributed £5 to the fund. Finally, it should be remarked that the language of the "Prophecy" is neither of the eighteenth century nor in the usual vein of Franklin.

The history of this document, falsely ascribed to one whose liberal opinions are so well known as to be almost axiomatic, is typical of the course of similar pieces of propagandist literature. Originating in some obscure corner, the story travels and gains credence as it goes. Exposure follows in due time, but often not until a wrong impression, difficult to eradicate, has been created. In this case, it is to be hoped that Professor Beard's statement will be more than sufficient to prevent any further misunderstanding of Franklin's attitude towards the Jews.

From "Society News and Accessions," *Pennsylvania Magazine of History and Biography*, Vol. 61, April, 1937, pages 233-234.

31. Julian Boyd's response to the charge of anti-Semitism against Franklin in the *Pennsylvania Magazine of History and Biography*, 61 (April 1937): 233–34.

STATEMENT BY CARL VAN DOREN

> CARL VAN DOREN, well-known writer and lecturer, is the author of *Benjamin Franklin*, New York, 1938

THE speech against the Jews which Benjamin Franklin is alleged to have made at the Constitutional Convention of 1787 is a forgery, produced within the past five years. The forger, whoever he was, claims that the speech was taken down by Charles Pinckney of South Carolina and preserved in his Journal. The forger presumably knew that, in a letter to John Quincy Adams dated December 30, 1818, Pinckney said he had kept a Journal of the proceedings at the Convention. But this Journal, if it ever existed, has never been found. The forger claims that Pinckney "published" the Journal "for private distribution among his friends" with the title *Chit-Chat Around the Table During Intermissions.* No copy of any such printed Journal has come to light. Not content with these two claims, the forger has further asserted that the original manuscript of Franklin's speech, apparently from Pinckney's Journal, is in the Franklin Institute, Philadelphia. The Franklin Institute does not possess the manuscript.

The forger's authority for his document is nearly as mythical as could be imagined. He cites a manuscript which does not exist, a printed book or pamphlet which nobody has seen, a Journal which has been lost for more than a hundred years. There is no evidence of the slightest value that Franklin ever made the alleged speech or ever said or thought anything of the kind about the Jews.

> Most of this material is reprinted from the November, 1938, issue of the CONTEMPORARY JEWISH RECORD.

32. Carl Van Doren's response to the charge of anti-Semitism against Franklin in the *Contemporary Jewish Record*, November 1938.

versally acknowledged belief in toleration was quite another. The Republican candidate did not win the election in New York. When Frederick Lewis summarized the whole event, he believed that the base attempt to use Franklin "as a mouthpiece of racial and religious hatred" ended like "A Lie Smashed."[63]

VI

As Franklin's image was exploited and in some cases vulgarized and distorted, his supporters tried to preserve his legacy. As early as the late 1920s Van Doren, one of the nation's leading literary critics, was convinced that the increasing piecemeal study had grossly distorted Franklin's life and reputation. Disdaining provincial and fragmentary interpretations of Franklin, Van Doren was particularly disturbed that some "dry, prim people" further reduced him to a symbol of prudence and frugality. A Franklin admirer for twenty years, he was determined to write a new Franklin biography "in his grand dimensions."[64]

Franklin supporters considered it a shame that one hundred and forty years after his death there was no national shrine to him. One significant move was initiated by the Philadelphia Poor Richard Club, which was always mindful of the future progress of the city.[65] On January 17, 1927, its president, Morton Gibbons-Neff, suggested that a national memorial should be built in Franklin's honor, which might attract "mass acclamation." His proposal was accepted "with thundering applause," and a campaign under the vigorous leadership of Cyrus H. K. Curtis was soon under way. Two years later in 1930, five million dollars was raised for the construction of the new memorial, which was to be a part of the Franklin Institute in Philadelphia[66] (Figs. 33 and 34).

Designed by John T. Windrim, the memorial building was completed and opened to the public in 1933. For the next five years two million people visited the new memorial. In 1937 the Philadelphia city authorities decided to rename the boulevard in front of the memorial "the Benjamin Franklin Parkway."[67] Mayor S. Davis Wilson

---

63. A reprint from *Liberty*, 29 July 1939, n.p., Lewis's commentary, "Benjamin Franklin and the Jews—A Lie Smashed!" was also broadcast on radio stations.

64. Van Doren, *Franklin*, vi–vii.

65. Founded in May 1906, it was an exclusive society for publishers and advertisers. See Jack Lutz, *The Poor Richard Club: Its Birth, Growth and Activities; and Its Influence on Advertising, the City, State and Nation* (Philadelphia, 1953), 1–4, 87.

66. Ibid., 88–90, 114–15, 128, 131, 148–50.

67. A full description of the historical and architectural development of the Ben-

33. One initial design of the exterior of the Franklin Memorial and Franklin Institute, from the fundraising promotional portfolio *A Living Memorial* of the late 1920s, n. p. (Courtesy of the Benjamin Franklin National Memorial, Philadelphia)

called Franklin "that amazing and almost universal genius," and declared that Franklin "stands beside Washington as one of the greatest Americans of all time."[68] But the final official dedication was yet to come a year later in May 1938, when a huge marble statue of Franklin was unveiled inside the grand building.[69]

The sculptor was James Earle Fraser. He seemed to have peculiar difficulty in characterizing the versatile genius of Franklin. The artist acknowledged that "probably no one in history was so great in diverse ways as Franklin, with the exception of Leonardo da Vinci." Finally, Fraser explained that because Franklin had "an all-pervading curiosity," he decided to model the statue in the following way:

[It was] a massive figure, tranquil in body, with latent power in his hands, but with an inquisitive expression in the movement of his head and the alertness of his eyes, ready to turn the full force of his keen mind on any problem that concerned life.[70]

jamin Franklin Parkway is David B. Brownlee, *Building the City Beautiful: The Benjamin Franklin Parkway and the Philadelphia Museum of Art* (Philadelphia, 1989).

68. *New York Times*, 11 September 1937, p. 3.

69. [Franklin Institute], *Dedication of the Benjamin Franklin Memorial* [Philadelphia, 1938], 21, 69.

70. Fraser, "Franklin's All-Pervading Curiosity," *Dedication of the Benjamin Franklin Memorial*, 31.

34. Drawing of the proposed Franklin Memorial Hall and Franklin statue, from *A Living Memorial.* (Courtesy of the Benjamin Franklin National Memorial, Philadelphia)

The final dedication ceremony was on a grand scale (Fig. 35). Never before had Franklin been so honored.[71] From May 19 to 21 distinguished speakers praised him. They included the French am-

---

71. By a congressional act in the early 1970s, this Benjamin Franklin Memorial Hall at the Franklin Institute in Philadelphia was rededicated as a national memorial. *New York Times*, 24 June 1972, p. 63.

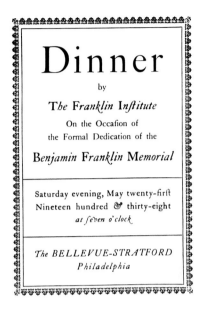

Dinner
by
The Franklin Inſtitute
On the Occaſion of
the Formal Dedication of the
Benjamin Franklin Memorial

Saturday evening, May twenty-firſt
Nineteen hundred & thirty-eight
at ſeven o'clock

*The BELLEVUE-STRATFORD
Philadelphia*

35. Program of a dinner party to celebrate the official dedication of the Franklin Memorial in 1938. (Courtesy of the Benjamin Franklin National Memorial, Philadelphia)

bassador to the United States, Count René Doynel de Saint Quentin; former president Herbert Hoover; Secretary of Commerce Daniel C. Roper; and Roland S. Morris, president of the American Philosophical Society.[72]

As early as January President Franklin D. Roosevelt, who expressed his intention to attend the celebration, was invited. Although the president changed his plans, he sent a letter to Philip C. Staples, president of the Franklin Institute and chief official of the dedication ceremony, saying that "Franklin touched the life of his time at so many angles and his character showed so many and such diversified facets" that he should be considered as "one of the greatest and most useful public men."[73]

Only five months after the Franklin memorial was dedicated, Van Doren's new biography appeared. He successfully incorporated many of Franklin's own words, indicating that all the biographer had attempted to do was to present Franklin's true thought and deed. Van Doren believed that Franklin's life embraced numerous contradictions, including a particular discrepancy between what he preached and what he did. Van Doren thus interpreted Franklin in the following way:

---

72. *Nature* 142 (2 July 1938): 9.
73. Roosevelt to Staples, 12 April 1938, *The Public Papers and Addresses of Franklin D. Roosevelt* (New York, 1941), 7: 213–14.

They [the dry, prim people] praise his thrift. But he himself admitted that he could never learn frugality, and he practised it no longer than his poverty forced him to. They praise his prudence. But at seventy he became a leader of a revolution, and throughout his life he ran bold risks. They praise him for being a plain man. Hardly another man of affairs has ever been more devoted than Franklin to the pleasant graces.[74]

Because of the depth of Van Doren's research, lucid style, and balanced presentation, his book was warmly hailed by the public and critics alike. Some reviewers declared the new biography to be thus far "the most fully informed, the most readable and the most illuminating." Julian P. Boyd, then director of the Historical Society of Pennsylvania, said that Van Doren's success was what "only the artist in the scholar can achieve."[75] Regarding Van Doren's work as the fullest life of Franklin since James Parton's, Carl Becker pointed out that mastery of sources alone would never produce such a biography had there not been "a sympathetic understanding of the mind and personality of the subject." Van Doren understood his subject thoroughly and did not need to eulogize or defend Franklin. He presented Franklin as what he was without exaggerating his virtues or concealing his defects.[76]

The Book-of-the-Month Club selected the biography as its unanimous choice for October 1938, and issued a promotional release recommending the selection to thousands of its members. It read in part:

---

74. Van Doren, *Franklin*, vi–vii.

75. Boyd, [review of Van Doren's *Franklin*], *American Historical Review* 46 (October 1940): 160.

76. Becker, "The Salty Sense of Benjamin Franklin, His Fantastic Life Story Told in a Masterly Biography," *New York Herald Tribune*, 9 October 1938, section 9, p. 1. For example, the biographer never avoided the issue of Franklin's intrigue with women from the period of his youth till his advanced years. William Allen White remarked: "Mr. Van Doren presents the romantic episodes in his life with no attempt to gloss them over but equally without a leer or chuckle." While praising Van Doren's book, Henry Steele Commager also observed that Franklin was a philosopher without a philosophy, for he was primarily a pragmatist. He was a scientist, but his science was utilitarian. He was a literary figure, yet his medium was journalism. He was noted in politics, and his contribution was mainly compromise. He preached morality but his emphasis was laid on work rather than faith (Commager, "Franklin, The True American; Carl Van Doren's Biography Unfolds His Many-Sided Genius," *New York Times Book Review*, 9 October 1938, p. 1).

The profound scholarship that informs it, the wide, patient, and intelligent research on which it rests, are craftily concealed by a forthright if rather easy-going style. Even the footnotes [there are nearly thirteen hundred of them] do not scare the reader into the consciousness that he is reading a book of exceptional academic quality.[77]

What is more, from the first day of its publication in early October, several critics declared that the book should be awarded a Pulitzer Prize. Later the publisher complacently reported that this biography had been more widely distributed than any other American biography since Mason L. Weems's life of Washington.[78] Van Doren's book was awarded the Pulitzer Prize for biography in 1938. Thus, until the eve of World War II, biographies of Franklin were the only ones to win the Pulitzer twice within twenty years.[79]

---

77. A review written by William Allen White in *Book-of-the-Month Club News* (New York), September 1938, n.p.

78. Lewis Gannett, *New York Herald Tribune*, 7 October 1938, p. 17; Charles Poore, *New York Times*, 7 October 1938, p. 19; Clifton Fadiman, "Poor Richard Indeed!" *New Yorker* 14 (8 October 1938), 67–68; Malcolm Cowley, "Tribute to Ben Franklin," *New Republic*, 26 October 1938, 338–39; Boyd, *American Historical Review*, 160.

79. William Cabell Bruce's *Benjamin Franklin, Self-Revealed* (New York, 1917) won the same prize in 1918. [Columbia University], *The Pulitzer Prizes, 1917–1983* [New York, 1983], 56–57.

Part III:
Character and
Personality
1945–1990

Chapter 7

"Who Was Benjamin Franklin?"

In concluding his landmark biography of Franklin, Carl Van Doren predicted that "the death of a great man begins another history, of his continuing influence, his changing renown, the legend which takes the place of fact."[1] A prolific writer and discerning critic, Van Doren was keenly aware of Franklin's posthumous reputation. While his biography delineated facts in order to clarify some popular misunderstandings of Franklin, he knew that no biographer could prevent others from forming their opinions according to their own needs and circumstances.

Legend or fact, considering the rapidly changing social and cultural conditions in the nation and around the world during the post-World War II period, Van Doren's warning proved to be correct. The re-shaped images of Franklin for the last several decades do reflect people's varied interests in him. What is surprising, however, is that many Americans' attitudes toward Franklin have changed so much that even some of the most gifted Franklin scholars seem to be unable to answer the question who he really was.

I

The ordeal of the Second World War had a profound impact on the way people perceived Franklin. After the German Jewish playwright and novelist Lion Feuchtwanger fled from Europe to the United States late in 1940, his long-conceived ideas for a new historical novel began to crystallize. As he put it:

For decades I have been concerned with the strange fact that such different people as Beaumarchais, Benjamin Franklin, Lafayette, Voltaire, Louis

---

1. Van Doren, *Benjamin Franklin* (New York, 1938), 781.

XVI and Marie Antoinette, each for his own reasons, had to collaborate in bringing the American Revolution to a successful conclusion, and through it the French Revolution as well. When Roosevelt's America intervened in the war against the European Fascists and supported the Soviet Union's battle against Hitler, the events in France of the 18th century became transparent to me and made the events of my own time radiantly clear.[2]

Several years later he finished a novel called *Proud Destiny*, in which he portrayed the war for American independence as a turning point in human history and Franklin as the architect of the new nation's successful diplomacy[3] (Figs. 36 and 37). Unlike some students of this period, Feuchtwanger did not simplify the tasks before Franklin when he was minister to France. The novelist showed that although the American Revolution was a noble cause, it did not receive immediate financial support from Louis XVI. Besides his own financial constraints, the ambivalent king was reluctant to sponsor a rebellion against another monarchy. The author demonstrated how Franklin, largely because of his tremendous personal skill and patience, succeeded in securing an alliance with the French. Feuchtwanger's deep understanding of European culture and history, warm support for the American cause, and extensive research on Franklin's experience in France made his novel one of the most sophisticated and intelligent portrayals of Franklin[4] (Fig. 38).

Feuchtwanger's deep admiration for Franklin from an international perspective in the 1940s, and his strong belief in America as the land of liberty only heralded a new outburst of enthusiasm that culminated a decade later. The victory over Nazism at the end of World War II and the subsequent confrontation with Communism confirmed the belief that the American system was the last refuge on earth for freedom. When Americans and people of many countries celebrated the

---

2. Quoted from Hilde Waldo, "Lion Feuchtwanger: A Biography (July 7, 1884-December 21, 1958)," in John M. Spalek, ed., *Lion Feuchtwanger: The Man, His Ideas, His Work* (Los Angeles, 1972), 16.

3. Because of the author's praise for the American Revolution, the media in the Soviet Union began to portray him as an advocate of American militarism and imperialism. Lothar Kahn, *Insight and Action: The Life and Work of Lion Feuchtwanger* (Rutherford, [N.J.] 1975), 282–85.

4. The German edition titled *Waffen für Amerika* (*Arms for America*) was published in Amsterdam in 1947. Renamed as *Proud Destiny: A Novel*, its English version first appeared in September the same year and quickly became the Literary Guild's selection for October. It was on the best-seller list of the *New York Times* for several months. Sometimes under the title *Die Füchse im Weinberg* (*Foxes in Weinberg*), the novel has been translated into several European languages and is still in print.

CHAPTER II
Franklin

The old man stood at the railing, tightly wrapped in his fur coat since it was very cold these early December days; his large, heavy head was also well covered by a fur cap. Beneath this cap, his white hair fell in long locks *s/hands* over the coat collar.

A very strong wind was blowing, and even here in the quiet bay of Quiberon the ship danced wildly up and down. The old man fastened himself instinctively with both hands to the rails while he looked through large, iron-framed spectacles toward the coast.

The voyage had not been long. This crossing to Europe had taken hardly five weeks, but it had not been pleasant. It was not ~~~~~~ the constantly strong wind which had caused him discomfort; for old Benjamin Franklin never suffered from seasickness. But already when starting on this trip, he had felt tired and exhausted owing to the long session with the Congress and to lack of exercise, and the unwholesome food on board had further reduced his health. Since fresh fowl was too hard for his teeth, he had been compelled to sustain himself, on the whole, by eating salt meat and ship-biscuit, which had caused him a slight attack of scurvy; dandruff inconvenienced him on his ▮▮▮▮ head, which was *getting bald,*

36. Draft page from the English translation of Lion Feuchtwanger's *Waffen für Amerika* (*Arms for America*). (By permission of the Feuchtwanger Memorial Library, Department of Special Collections, University of Southern California)

Lion Feuchtwanger

PROUD DESTINY

A Novel

THE VIKING PRESS
New York · 1947

37. Title page from *Proud Destiny* by Lion Feuchtwanger, translated by William Rose, translation copyright 1947, renewed 1974 by The Viking Press, Inc. (By permission of Viking Penguin, a division of Penguin Books USA Inc.)

2. *Kapitel*
Franklin

38. Volker Pfüller's illustration of Franklin, in Lion Feucht-wanger's *Die Füchse im Wein-berg* (*Foxes in Weinberg*, a different title for *Waffen für Amerika*), 1976. (© Verlag Neues Leben, Berlin)

250th anniversary of Franklin's birth in 1956, his name became a synonym for democracy and freedom, an embodiment of the American experience, and a symbol of hope and peace for mankind.

The prevailing mood of Franklin's birthday celebrations in 1956 was one of jubilation, confidence, pride, and optimism.[5] *Life* magazine published a special issue that included some forty treasures of Frankliniana lent by the Metropolitan Museum of Art, the American Philosophical Society, the Historical Society of Pennsylvania, and other institutions. An exhibition of more than a hundred and sixty imprints and autograph documents of Franklin was held at the Library of Congress in his honor. As many as fifty museums nationwide put

---

5. A list of no less than four hundred such pieces from the 1956 commemorations can be found in Melvin H. Buxbaum, ed., *Benjamin Franklin: A Reference Guide* (Boston, 1983–88), 2: 454–525.

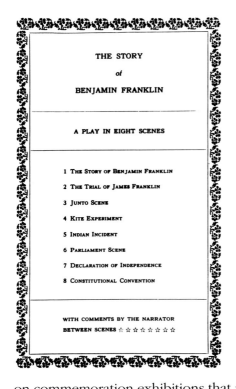

39. Title page of *The Story of Benjamin Franklin*, a short play promoted by the International Benjamin Franklin Society during the 1956 celebrations of the 250th anniversary of Franklin's birth.

on commemoration exhibitions that promoted the public's interest in science and technology[6] (Fig. 39).

"Franklin still speaks to us," the noted historian Henry Steele Commager began his long article in the *New York Times Magazine*. He asserted that "America was to be many things, and Franklin represented most of them."[7] Franklin's ingenuity and competence exemplified American know-how. His common sense and practicality

---

6. *Life* 40 (9 January 1956): 72–96. American Philosophical Society, *Benjamin Franklin, The Two Hundred and Fiftieth Anniversary of His Birth, 1706–1956: An Exhibition in the Library of Congress, Washington, D. C.* (Philadelphia, 1956). Franklin Institute, *Program for the International Celebration of the 250th Anniversary of the Birth of Benjamin Franklin, 1706–1956* ([Philadelphia], 1955), 27–28. See also The *Philadelphia Inquirer Magazine*, 15 January 1956, pp. 2, 10–13. Franklin National Bank, *An Exhibition of Benjamin Franklin* (New York, 1953). *The Numismatists* 69 (December 1956) is a special Franklin issue, with more than a dozen articles about medals, coins, portraits, and medallions relating to him.

7. Commager, "Franklin Still Speaks to Us," *New York Times Magazine* (15 January 1956), 19, 74A, 74B, 76A, 76B. See also I. Bernard Cohen, ed., *Benjamin Franklin: His Contribution to the American Tradition* (Indianapolis, 1953), 27–67. For both supporting and opposing views on this issue, see Charles L. Sanford, ed., *Benjamin Franklin and the American Character* (Boston, 1955).

indicated the embryonic stage of American pragmatism. His ever-present wit contributed to the development of American humor and his energy and entrepreneurship demonstrated the dynamics of the middle class. Franklin's constant thirst for knowledge and natural inclination for science represented his countrymen's persistent drive for progress. While his overt pursuit of personal wealth and happiness was representative of American individualism, his philanthropy manifested many Americans' commitment to civic duty and social improvement. If his widely acknowledged toleration and benevolence highlighted America's democratic tradition, his life-long efforts to defend and preserve his independent mind and free spirit reflected one of the cornerstones of American self-government.

The famous French sociologist Émile Durkheim once said that "personality is the individual socialized."[8] In a fantastic twist, the frenzy of celebrating Franklin's birth suggested a reverse pattern, in which the fundamental characteristics of a nation might be personified by a single individual: Franklin's career epitomized the American character. What was more striking at that moment, however, was the implication that Franklin's experience spoke not only to Americans but also to the rest of the world.

Dramatic as it sounds, the claim for universality of an American was not simply chauvinism. It is true that if he was viewed primarily as an emblem of the nation's struggle for progress, modernity, and cosmopolitanism, praise of Franklin sometimes implied that what proved to be good for America should be a model for the world. It is also true that the 250th anniversary was celebrated worldwide, and that the United States Information Agency, through its two hundred offices in eighty countries, sponsored numerous lectures, broadcasts, motion pictures, and exhibitions to promote the occasion.

People in many foreign countries genuinely appreciated Franklin, who was a world citizen in his own time. One of the most traveled and most cosmopolitan persons of his generation, Franklin's experience was never provincial. The primary organizer behind all the activities was the Franklin Institute in Philadelphia. Its Anniversary Committee sent out information and programs and invited hundreds of domestic and foreign organizations to join the celebration. The response was overwhelming; an estimate suggested that in the end five hundred million people in seventy-two countries participated.[9]

---

8. Quoted from Christopher Lasch, *The Culture of Narcissism: American Life in an Age of Diminishing Expectations* (New York, 1979), 76.

9. Helen and Clarence Jordan, eds., *Benjamin Franklin's Unfinished Business* (Philadelphia, [1956/57?]), vii, viii, 19, 21, 41, 257, 259.

人民日报 1956年12月14日 第七版

△ 威廉·杜波依斯的贺信

40. Chinese translation of William E. B. DuBois's long letter of November 19, 1956, published in the *People's Daily*, December 14, 1956, p. 7. His letter congratulated China on the official celebration in the People's Republic of China at the 250th anniversary of Franklin's birth. This letter also summarized Franklin's life and discussed the struggle for racial equality in the United States.

In addition to several major western countries, such as England, France, West Germany, Canada, and Italy, official agencies in the Soviet Union and the People's Republic of China also held ceremonies to commemorate Franklin's birth (Fig. 40). Above all, nations that

joined the celebrations were from all kinds of political and geograph-
ical regions in Europe, Latin America, Asia, and Africa.[10]

In South America, native patriots had viewed Franklin's rise as an
inspiration in their struggles for social justice and economic reform.
Franklin influenced several prominent figures in nineteenth-century
South American history, such as Simon Bolívar, José de San Martín,
Francisco de Miranda, Domingo Faustino Sarmiento, Eugenio Espejo,
Manuel Lorenzo de Vidaurre, Nicolás Piérola, and Don Pedro. The
statesman and scholar Sarmiento of Argentina, who used to call him-
self "a little Franklin," stated:

> The Life of Franklin was for me the same as Plutarch was for him. I felt
> myself to be a Franklin. And why not? I was very poor, as he was, and by
> contriving to follow in his steps, I could some day succeed in forming myself
> in his image, to be like him, an honorary doctor and to make a place for
> myself in American letters and political life.[11]

Dr. Tatsuo Morito, president of Hiroshima University in Japan, delivered an address on "Benjamin Franklin as a Well-Rounded Personality" on January 17, 1956. He emphasized that Franklin came from
Philadelphia, the "City of Brotherly Love" and "the home of the
Quaker faith, a religion of pacifism." He believed that Franklin was "a
balanced and complete man" who should be adopted as a model for
young Japanese students. He told his audience that "it is our greatest
honor to commemorate here on this day the 250th Anniversary of the
Birth of Benjamin Franklin in the auditorium of Hiroshima University,
a sanctuary of learning in the City of Peace, the great American and

---

10. It is estimated that more than one thousand organizations and five thousand
agencies of the news media around the world helped to promote the celebrations. The Soviet Union issued a special postage stamp to honor Franklin, a first
for that country to pay tribute to an American. A state-supported general meet-
ing to commemorate Franklin was held in Beijing, China, in December 1956.
Other countries and regions involved were Scotland, Ireland, Austria, Denmark,
Luxembourg, Belgium, Netherlands, Switzerland, Sweden, Finland, Norway,
Iceland, Greece, Spain, Yugoslavia, Rumania, Bulgaria, Australia, New Zealand,
India, Pakistan, Iran, Turkey, Israel, Lebanon, Syria, Japan, Korea, Indonesia,
Malaya, Philippines, Ceylon (Sri Lanka), Hong Kong, Mexico, Barbados, Cuba,
Panama, Puerto Rico, Argentina, Brazil, Chile, Peru, Colombia, Costa Rica,
Paraguay, Dominican Republic, Ecuador, Guatemala, Haiti, Nicaragua, Vene-
zuela, Egypt, Morocco, Ethiopia, Gold Coast, Kenya, and Tunisia. Ibid., 19, 21,
33, 52.
11. Ibid., 112.

prominent international figure who loved peace and learning and was a distinguished champion of human rights, freedom, independence and happiness."[12] F. Correia-Afonso, professor at Megji Mathradas College of Arts in Bombay, India, wrote that Franklin was one of the greatest benefactors of mankind, one of the greatest citizens of the world, and an ambassador of peace. Convinced that Franklin's strong commitment to liberty and equality was closely related to his belief in fraternity and brotherhood, the scholar said, "I can hail Benjamin Franklin as a Brother."[13]

The year 1956 was a milestone in Franklin's posthumous renown. The success of these celebrations was so impressive that two of the chief organizers, Helen and Clarence Jordan of the Franklin Institute, appropriately quoted what Franklin had wished more than one and a half centuries earlier: "God grant that not only Love of Liberty but a thorough Knowledge of the Rights of Man may pervade all the Nations of the Earth, so that a Philosopher may set his foot anywhere and say 'This is My Country.'"[14]

II

More substantive than those ceremonial events was the undertaking of a monumental project, *The Papers of Benjamin Franklin.* James H. Hutson participated in the project during the 1960s and later became chief of the Manuscripts Division of the Library of Congress. Commenting on the papers' inception at Yale University in the early 1950s, he wrote that when Chester Kerr, director of the Yale University Press, brought the Franklin project to New Haven, "the Yale bulldog now marched with the Princeton tiger into the fray against the Russian bear."[15] This comment overstates the linkage between the initiation of the Franklin project and the hostile political atmosphere

---

12. Ibid., 103, 105, 109.

13. Ibid., 69, 71.

14. Ibid., 5. Their quote is from Franklin's letter to his English friend David Hartley on 4 December 1789. See Albert H. Smyth, ed., *The Writings of Benjamin Franklin* (New York, 1905–07), 10: 72–73.

15. Hutson, "Franklin at Twenty-Five: A Review of Volumes 1–25 of *The Papers of Benjamin Franklin*," *The Pennsylvania Magazine of History and Biography* 111 (October 1987): 556.

of the Cold War. In spite of his exaggerated analogy, Hutson's assessment does draw attention to some of the basic elements in the commencement of the Papers.

Like several similar projects of the same period, such as the papers of John Adams and his family, the project of a new edition of Franklin documents was inspired by and modeled after *The Papers of Thomas Jefferson*. Initiated during the Jefferson bicentennial celebration in 1943 and blessed with President Franklin D. Roosevelt's support, the Jefferson papers were edited under the masterful leadership of Julian P. Boyd, then librarian and later professor of history at Princeton University.[16] When the first volume was published in 1950, its remarkable editorship, ambitious scope of documentation, and authentic annotation achieved an instant national acclaim. After President Harry Truman, who was a professed lover of history,[17] received a copy of that volume on May 17, he praised the work highly and directed the National Historical Publications Commission to study the means to "make available to our people" the writings of not only famous politicians but also those industrialists, labor leaders, artists, and scientists "who have made major contributions to our democracy."[18]

Subsequently, the commission completed a preliminary report on May 21, 1951, called "A National Program for the Publication of the Papers of American Leaders." Truman "immediately and vigorously" endorsed the report.[19] "I am convinced," he said, "that the better we understand the history of our democracy, the better we shall appreciate our rights as free men and the more determined we shall be to keep our ideals alive. Publications such as the commission recommends will greatly help to further this understanding." Believing that "Franklin did as much as any man in our history to shape the kind of country we live in today," the president further pointed out that "I

16. For an account of the inception of *The Thomas Jefferson Papers* see Merrill D. Peterson, *The Jefferson Image in the American Mind* (New York, 1960): 439–42.

17. Truman, *Memoirs*, 2 vols. (New York, 1955–56), 1: 119–21. For a critique of Truman's interest in history see Michael Kammen, "Changing Presidential Perspectives on the American Past," *Prologue: Quarterly of the National Archives* (Spring 1993): 55–56.

18. "Address delivered by the President at the Library of Congress on the occasion of publication of Volume One of The Papers of Thomas Jefferson, May 17, 1950," news release, Harry S. Truman Library.

19. *Philadelphia Inquirer*, 17 June 1951, p. A1.

would also like to see plans made soon for the publication of Benjamin Franklin's papers."[20]

Three years later the commission made a second report. Titled "A National Program for the Publication of Historical Documents," this 1954 report indicates that the commission received suggestions from all parts of the nation, recommending as many as 361 persons whose papers deserved publication. Based on these recommendations, the commission and its staff selected a short list of 112 names and called attention to 5 persons for special consideration in both its 1951 and 1954 reports: John Adams, John Quincy Adams, Benjamin Franklin, Alexander Hamilton, and James Madison, whose papers later became known in the documentary editing community as the "Five Priority Projects."[21] According to the commission:

> The first of these [five persons] is Benjamin Franklin—scientist, philosopher, and statesman—perhaps the greatest of all Americans who lived wholly in the eighteenth century. His papers are those that the scholars who have been consulted regarding the proposed program recommended most frequently and most highly above all others as deserving publication equal in all respects to the current publication of Jefferson's papers.[22]

Important as they might be, the commission always recommended that the projects should be conducted under both public (federal, state, and local governments) and private auspices. The commission was particularly pleased to point out that the American Philosophical Society and Yale University had agreed to launch a project of jointly collecting, editing, and publishing Franklin's papers.

At the time when the proposal of a new and comprehensive edition of Franklin's works was raised at the national level, a group of alumni gathered at the William Smith Mason Collection in the Sterling Memorial Library of Yale University. A graduate of the Sheffield Scientific School of Yale in 1888, Mason later became a successful businessman. He was an ardent admirer of Franklin and spent a lifetime collecting a marvelous library of more than fifteen thousand books, manuscripts, and pamphlets. He bequeathed his collections to his

---

20. Truman's letter to Jess Larson on 16 June 1951, Truman Library.
21. See Hutson, "Franklin at Twenty-Five," 556.
22. The National Historical Publications Commission, *A National Program for the Publication of Historical Documents: A Report to the President* (Washington, 1954), 18; *A National Program for the Publication of the Papers of American Leaders* (Washington, 1951), 11.

alma mater in the 1930s, and such scholars and writers as Carl Van Doren, Chester E. Jorgenson, and James Madison Stifler benefited from this extraordinary library when they were preparing their books on Franklin (Fig. 41). Invited by Yale University as a honorary fellow in the early 1950s, President Truman had a brief chance to visit the collection and expressed his appreciation. Equally impressed by the magnificent Mason-Franklin collection, the group of Yale alumni decided to seek financial endowment and lure the Franklin project to Yale University.[23]

In the name of *Life* magazine Henry R. Luce donated $475,000 for that purpose to Yale in 1954. But the proposed project did not become a reality until the American Philosophical Society agreed to sponsor the proposal with a cash contribution of $175,000, and to provide access to its Franklin manuscript collection, the single largest and most important repository of this kind in the nation. Aimed at publishing all extant Franklin papers, this ambitious undertaking made headline news when it was announced by the president of the American Philosophical Society, Owen J. Roberts, and the president of Yale University, A. Whitney Griswold. The former Supreme Court justice Roberts held that "the publication of the papers of Benjamin Franklin will enable our people to understand his ideas of what our country should be, [and] at no time would this have been more appropriate than today." Dr. Griswold echoed this, saying that "few Americans epitomized in their own lives so much of the life and talents and interest of their countrymen as Franklin; few have so much to teach us about ourselves today," and that "[the publication] will take us deep into the origins of our country and our culture and the first principles of our form of government."[24]

Leonard W. Labaree, professor of history at Yale University, assumed the first editorship. He and his associates spent the first four years making copies and transcripts in order to assess the scope of their planned publications. More than 29,000 pieces of original

---

23. Mr. Mason, it is said, was a very modest man and little was written about him. Nevertheless, anyone who has visited his library would certainly appreciate his great contribution to the preservation of Franklin's legacy. George Simpson Eddy, "A Ramble through the Mason-Franklin Collection," *Yale University Library Gazette* 10 (April 1936): 65–90; D[orothy] W. B[ridgwater], "The Mason-Franklin Collection," *Yale University Library Gazette* 15 (July 1940): 16–19; "The Benjamin Franklin Collection," *Yale University Library Gazette* 38 (April 1964): 165–66.

24. Quoted in News Release #351 for 17 January 1954, Yale University News Bureau.

My dear Mr. Mason: —

Here is the first copy of the little book that you inspired me to complete. The days of our investigation and writing in your hospitable library are among my most delightful memories. St. Paul recommends among the virtues "in honor preferring one another". It is because of your practice of the virtue that your name does not stand with mine on the title page. You are equally responsible with me for the work. I hope that the years will prove that our labors have added a little to our country's appreciation of Franklin.

Faithfully yours,

James M. Stifler

41. James Stifler's thank-you note to William Mason, whose "unimaginable wealth" of Franklin material helped the former to prepare his *Religion of Benjamin Franklin*, 1925. The author then sent Mason a gift copy of the book and his note was written on that copy. (Courtesy of The Papers of Benjamin Franklin, Yale University Library)

manuscripts and documents were assembled, plus 2,200 photo-copies. Since publication of the first volume in 1959, the new edition has superseded all previous editions of Franklin's writings, including those edited by William Temple Franklin, William Duane, Jared Sparks, and John Bigelow in the nineteenth century, and Albert H. Smyth early in this century. Because of the persistent efforts of the successive chief editors—Labaree, William B. Willcox, Claude-Anne Lopez, and Barbara Oberg—and their assistants, this edition has been widely recognized as a permanent monument to Franklin's legacy.[25]

The *Pennsylvania Magazine of History and Biography* described the new edition as "a tour de force of editorial enterprise." The *William and Mary Quarterly* called the new volumes "magnificent." William S. Hanna commented that the project was "a prodigious, monumental, thorough, and scholarly effort to put everything that can be found written by and to Franklin before us in beautifully prepared chronologically arranged editions." "To read any one of these volumes," Edmund S. Morgan said, "is to be thrust into a part of the past that still bears heavily on the present." Even some foreign observers admitted that "once more American scholarship dazzles us."[26]

In 1963 Labaree and other editors of the "Priority Projects" were invited to the White House to have lunch with President John F. Kennedy. The president thanked his guests for their painstaking commitment, and hoped that the more the American people could learn from those new publications, the more confidence they would have in the future.[27] The continuous publication of Franklin papers over the last thirty years has become a part of what Professors Bernard Bailyn and Esmond Wright called the great movement of documen-

---

25. Labaree led his team for ten years and fourteen volumes were published between 1959 and 1969. When he retired, William B. Willcox became editor. After eleven new volumes were issued, Willcox died in 1986. Claude-Anne Lopez supervised two volumes, and the project is now led by Dr. Barbara Oberg. Those who have assisted the editors are Whitfield J. Bell, Jr., Helen C. Boatfield, Helene H. Fineman, Ralph L. Ketcham, James H. Hutson, Dorothy W. Bridgwater, Mary L. Hart, Catherine M. Prelinger, G. B. Warden, C. A. Myrans, Douglas M. Arnold, Jonathan R. Dull, Ellen R. Cohn, and Marilyn A. Morris. Whitfield J. Bell, Jr., "Franklin's Papers and the Papers of Benjamin Franklin," *Pennsylvania History* 22 (January 1955): 1–17; Claude-Anne Lopez, "A Brief History of the Franklin Papers," *Franklin Gazette* (publication of the Friends of Franklin, Philadelphia), 1 (Summer 1989), n. p.

26. *The Papers of Benjamin Franklin* (pamphlet compiled by the Friends of Franklin, 1991), n. p.

27. "President Kennedy's Remarks at a Luncheon for Sponsors and Editors of Historical Publications, June 17, 1963," *New York History* 45 (April 1964): 153.

tary history.[28] This remarkable project represents a new phase of Franklin studies, and the invaluable information contained in the edition will enrich people's understanding of Franklin for generations to come.[29]

III

Although public adulation of Franklin reached new heights in the mid-1950s, it was also a time when his personality underwent intensified scrutiny. A host of historians and literary critics of the post-World War II period renewed their interest in Franklin. The deeper these scholars searched, however, the less they could agree on who Franklin really was. Indeed, the range of differences in their findings was such that, as early as 1963, John William Ward began to suggest that because "Franklin could mean so many things to so many men" and because "he was so many-sided . . . in other words, so many different characters," the important matter was not to expect any consensus but to insist on asking the question who he was.[30]

Students in the past seldom viewed all of the episodes and anecdotes in Franklin's autobiography as historical facts. Since the 1950s many scholars, using literary and psychological techniques, concluded that the *Autobiography* was a mask carefully designed to shield its author's true identity. They suggested that there were in essence two different Franklins, one public and the other hidden or

---

28. See the National Historical Publications Commission, *A Report to the President* (Washington, 1963), 11, 13.

29. Combining their exceptional knowledge of the Franklin manuscripts with their expertise in eighteenth-century American and European history, the editors were able to shed new light on a broad range of topics concerning Franklin's domestic and public life. Some of their most noticeable publications include "In Search of 'B. Franklin'" (1959) by Leonard W. Labaree; "Benjamin Franklin as an American Hero" (1957) and "Henry Stevens, His Uncle Samuel, and the Franklin Papers" (1959) by Whitfield J. Bell, Jr.; *Benjamin Franklin* (1965) by Ralph L. Ketcham; *Mon Cher Papa: Franklin and the Ladies of Paris* (1966) by Claude-Anne Lopez; *The Private Franklin: The Man and His Family* (1975) by Lopez and Eugenia W. Herbert; "Benjamin Franklin and the American Prisoners of War in England during the American Revolution" (1975) by Catherine M. Prelinger; and *Franklin the Diplomat: The French Mission* (1982) by Jonathan R. Dull.

30. Ward, "Who Was Benjamin Franklin?" *American Scholar* 32 (Autumn 1963): 542. This essay is reprinted as "Benjamin Franklin: The Making of an American Character" in the author's *Red, White, and Blue: Men, Books, and Ideas in American Culture* (New York, 1969): 125–40.

private. The familiar picture of a hard-working, frugal, candid, and modest Franklin was all but an invention by the author himself in the *Autobiography*. Despite its enormous popularity, the self-portrait in the book did not reveal the real Franklin, who was hiding behind his self-created images. The public's general assumptions about Franklin, therefore, were not altogether reliable because they were based on an uncritical acceptance of his self-presentation. Only persistent efforts and penetrating analyses might recapture him.

Verner W. Crane believed that Franklin's frank and appealing *Autobiography* did not settle the issue of his true personality. Franklin was friendly, humorous, and gay, but frequently silent and reserved; ambitious but never avid for power; often amazingly candid, but secretive when it served his turn. "These traits," Crane observed, "added up to a charm which few could resist, the charm that beguiles us still in all that he said and wrote." Charles L. Sanford thought that Franklin was morally committed to promote "a new man and a new society in the world of nations." The *Autobiography* was a description of his "moral regeneration" "in the new heaven on earth," and hence could be regarded as "a great moral fable pursuing on a secular level the theme of John Bunyan's *Pilgrim's Progress*."[31]

David Levin was convinced that sometimes people tended to underestimate Franklin because he deliberately appeared "to be more simple than he is." Although Levin did not describe the *Autobiography* as fiction, he reminded readers that Franklin was a writer with a habit of creating characters. The first part of the *Autobiography*, he agreed with Sanford, illustrates Franklin's early experience in a perilous world, resembling many stories in *The Pilgrim's Progress*. But Franklin also inherited a Puritan custom, which was to "improve every opportunity to find moral instruction and signs of universal meaning in particular experience." Franklin's indulgence in moralistic self-examination and didactic anecdotes indicated that he was unable to separate himself completely from the Puritan tradition. Franklin also lived in an age of reason and experiments. His persistent self-improvement, his adherence to the doctrine of enlightened self-interest, and especially his ability to proceed in life with a prudent choice between good and evil were definite signs of wisdom, balance, and virtue. It was lamentable that the romantic English novelist D. H. Lawrence failed to recognize those profound philosophical undercur-

31. Crane, *Benjamin Franklin and a Rising People* (Boston, 1954), 205; Sanford, "An American Pilgrim's Progress," quoted in Sanford, ed., *Benjamin Franklin and the American Character* (Boston, 1955), 71.

rents of Franklin's time and therefore treated him as "a symbol of acquisitive smugness."[32]

Because Franklin's famous memoirs began with the salutation "My Dear Son," J. A. Leo Lemay contended that "the son as well as the father is a deliberate literary creation." Such an arrangement enabled Franklin to address the reader directly as if they were engaging in an intimate conversation. This "brilliant literary ploy" was "a supreme achievement." Disarming as it may seem, Lemay insisted, the ploy was a highly intelligent device by which Franklin could dictate the tone and contents of the conversation and persuade his audience, while creating little resentment.[33]

Many literary experts concurred, including James A. Sappenfield, Melvin H. Buxbaum, John Griffith, and Ormond Seavey. All of them insisted in one way or another that Franklin's *Autobiography* was indeed a literary creation, that the protagonist in the piece was more a fictional *persona* than a historical figure, and that the narrator intended not to confess, but to deceive. Sappenfield agreed that Franklin's *Autobiography* was "an artifact," and pointed out that the success of the book lay in its dramatic structure. Franklin understood that the essence of drama is conflict. He therefore presented a series of contrasting characters in his *Autobiography* and thoughtfully placed "the story of his success into a context of failure." When readers responded to this kind of depiction, as its author predicted they would, they had to choose between good and bad, success and failure, and thus were "insensibly led to Franklin's position."[34]

Buxbaum insisted that "the *Autobiography* constitutes Franklin's most significant attempt to create the personal image of himself that he wanted to leave behind." Griffith believed that "there is at the heart of Franklin's works a mystery," because reading his writings was "to have one's imagination stirred by the sense of something unique and not wholly explicable going on between and behind the lines." Convinced that the mysterious force came from Franklin's complete control over his language, reasoning, audience, and himself, Griffith claimed that "the true, natural Franklin disappeared behind a variety

---

32. Levin, "The Autobiography of Benjamin Franklin: The Puritan Experimenter in Life and Art," quoted in Brian M. Barbour, ed., *Benjamin Franklin: A Collection of Critical Essays* (Englewood Cliffs, N.J., 1979), 76, 79, 80, 87, 91.

33. Lemay, "Franklin and the *Autobiography:* An Essay on Recent Scholarship," *Eighteenth-Century Studies* 1 (December 1967), 199, 200.

34. Sappenfield, *A Sweet Instruction: Franklin's Journalism as a Literary Apprenticeship* (Carbondale, Ill., 1973), 202, 203, 204, 211.

of thoughtfully constructed masks." Franklin, therefore, "had to be understood as a complex of identities . . . behind which lurked the real Franklin, a cautious, secretive, perhaps . . . even a sinister inner man, who controlled the actions of the visible Franklin like a puppeteer or a Madison Avenue advertising expert intent on selling his product by creating a pleasing image of it."[35]

Seavey believed that Franklin's *Autobiography* was an obstacle, not an instrument for understanding the real person, and stressed that Franklin's greatest achievement was the creation of himself. He further stated that "he was at work on the creation all his life, not only in living that life but also in projecting models by which he and his imitators might live it." In a slight variation the English biographer Esmond Wright reiterated that "Franklin himself is his own creation. He made books, and he made news—and his books and news 'made' Franklin. Here is a man who talks to us apparently so frankly about himself while increasingly obscuring himself behind the public images, that at intervals we do not know what is fact and what is fiction."[36]

Perhaps the writer John Updike's imaginative analogy best illustrated many observers' reservations about Franklin. In 1988 he contributed an article to the *New Yorker*, which was appropriately entitled "Many Bens." He said that like those brightly painted Russian dolls, Franklin seemed to possess several intriguing personalities, one hiding behind another.[37] Updike's characterization signified a critical departure from Paul L. Ford's insistence on Franklin's "many-sidedness." Around the turn of the present century Ford and a generation of Franklinists believed that Franklin's whole life would automatically emerge once all aspects of his career were assembled. For most of them, Franklin was a simple, straightforward, and innocent man, whose extraordinary career was difficult to understand only because of the broad range of his varied genius and diverse activities. Updike and a number of modern critics disagreed. They emphasized the complex, secretive, and intricate nature within Franklin, who was

---

35. Buxbaum, *Benjamin Franklin and the Zealous Presbyterians* (University Park, [Penn.] 1975), 10, 225n. Griffith, "Franklin's Sanity and the Man behind the Masks," in J. A. Leo Lemay, ed., *The Oldest Revolutionary: Essays on Benjamin Franklin* ([Philadelphia], 1976), 124, 127.

36. Seavey, *Becoming Benjamin Franklin: The Autobiography and the Life* (University Park, [Penn.] 1988), 7, 99. Esmond Wright, *Franklin of Philadelphia* (Cambridge, Mass., 1986), 9.

37. Updike, "Many Bens," *New Yorker*, 22 February 1988, 106.

indeed a man with many masks. His inner life was highly elusive to grasp and his calculated self-portrayal fooled many readers over the last two centuries.

The strong claim that Franklin wrote his *Autobiography* to conceal rather than to reveal his true identity was not unchallenged. Alfred Owen Aldridge doubted whether Franklin was as self-conscious as many modern scholars tended to think he was. Unable to accept the premise that "there is any kind of conscious act in Franklin's over-all structure," Aldridge suspected: "It is more likely that Franklin was writing for his own amusement and gratification than for any particular external audience." Aldridge's assessment resembled that of John W. Ward. Both reminded the reader that Franklin's memoirs were made of four parts written over a long time and under very different circumstances.

When Franklin began to draft the first part of the memoirs in 1771, he was clearly writing for his own family. Franklin changed his mind, however, after he received letters from Abel James and Benjamin Vaughan in the early 1780s. When he resumed his writings in 1784 while in France, and later in 1785 back in America, "he did so in full self-consciousness" that he was writing for the general public as well.[38] Ironically, readers were most attracted to the intimate and spontaneous style of the first part, whereas subsequent portions of the memoirs became evidently tedious and didactic.

Believing that "the existence of a secret man can neither be demonstrated nor argued with any hope of progress," Mitchell Breitwieser perceived the self in the *Autobiography* as a broad treatment of human nature in general rather than a single individual in particular. Claiming that Americans generally cared not who you were but what you could do, Franklin depicted in his *Autobiography* what he had been able to accomplish, with very little thought about who he was. The historian Edmund S. Morgan suggested that modern scholars have perhaps overestimated the complexity of Franklin. Like John Adams, he was less able to conceal his true feelings than some of his distinguished colleagues, such as George Washington and Thomas Jefferson. More often than not his writings did reveal what he thought and who he was. The problem, therefore, was not whether or not modern readers should trust his words. What made reading Franklin problematic was the size of his writings. His voluminous works were

---

38. Aldridge, "Form and Substance in Franklin's Autobiography," in Clarence Gohdes, ed., *Essays on American Literature in Honor of Jay B. Hubbell* (Durham, N.C., 1967), 48; Ward, "Who Was Franklin?" 544.

produced at different times, dealt with different issues, and covered
an extraordinarily long career. These documents could easily confuse
anyone who attempted to find a consistent personality but was not
fully aware of the changing historical context of Franklin's writings.
"Does the real Franklin lie hidden behind a mask or masks?" The
question is worth asking, but it would scarcely be worth the trouble
if little of Franklin was hidden at all, Morgan said.[39]

IV

In an essay written in 1976 Professor P. M. Zall pointed out that
"the manuscript of Franklin's *Autobiography* lies open to public view
twenty-seven hours a week, eleven months of the year, at the center
of the magnificent treasures in the Huntington Library."[40] Certainly
visitors from all parts of the nation often swarmed around the *Autobiography*—the most precious possession of the Huntington collection, as Professor Zall described it. Before or after "these happy le-
gions" saw the manuscripts that were safely placed behind a huge
glass showcase, they could go to the library's bookstore and purchase
a copy of *Ben Franklin's Wit & Wisdom* or *On the Choice of a Mistress*, each for under five dollars (Fig. 42). What visitors saw might be
quite different from what they actually relished.

The contrast between the locked and heavily guarded treasure on
the one hand, and the inexpensive and readily available publications
for amusement on the other, is a telling example of divergent interests
gravitating toward opposite ends. For a long time many scholars have
tried to expose the hidden Franklin who, after years of scrutiny, appeared sophisticated, elusive, secretive, mysterious, and intriguing.
For the general public, however, he seemed, more than ever before,
simple, direct, personal, and earthy. What gave the average citizen a
feeling of friendliness and intimacy toward the historical man was a
development that occurred over the last several decades, particularly
during the 1960s and 1970s.

The highly successful children's book, *Ben and Me*, was one of the
early indicators of the popular trend (Fig. 43). After his big hit *Mr.
Revere and I*, the gifted artist Robert Lawson turned his attention to

---

39. Breitwieser, *Cotton Mather and Benjamin Franklin: The Price of Representative
Personality* (New York, 1984), 3–5, 7, 177, 233–34; Morgan, "Secrets of Benjamin Franklin," *The New York Review of Books*, 31 January 1990, 41–46.
40. Zall, "A Portrait of the Autobiographer as an Old Artificer," in Lemay, ed., *The
Oldest Revolutionary*, 53.

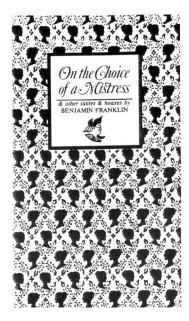

42. Jacket design by J. O'Neill for a collection of Franklin's light-hearted essays, 1976. (By permission of Peter Pauper Press, Inc., New York)

Franklin and found in him fantastic material for amusement. In hilarious black and white illustrations, Lawson portrayed Franklin as a splendid, although at times stupid, fellow who had a fictional encounter with a mouse. "For many years," the mouse named Amos said, "I was his closest friend and adviser and, if I do say it, was in great part responsible for his success and fame."[41] Lawson's light-hearted story did not pretend to relate historical truth, and his dramatization made its protagonist funny and laughable, not heroic. First published in 1939, Lawson's book was reprinted more than twenty times within a decade and forty times by the end of the 1970s. It should be pointed out that even though Franklin was ridiculed throughout, Lawson's aesthetic taste, bold imagination, good humor, and excellent execution of the illustrations made his book a work of art (Fig. 44).

Beginning in the early 1950s, an increasing number of exhibitions of Franklin's manuscripts and relics brought him to thousands of viewers. The students, faculty, and staff of the University of Pennsylvania and Harvard University were some of the first to benefit because of the extensive collections of Frankliniana at the two institu-

---

41. Lawson, *Ben and Me: A New and Astonishing Life of Benjamin Franklin As Written by His Good Mouse Amos* (1939; Boston, 1951), 4. Lawson's story was adapted as a Disney World cartoon movie in the early 1980s, and his book is still in print today.

BEN and ME

A New and Astonishing *LIFE* of
BENJAMIN FRANKLIN
As written by his Good Mouse
AMOS
Lately Discovered. Edited
& Illustrated by
ROBERT LAWSON

LITTLE, BROWN
AND COMPANY
BOSTON 1951

ERIPUIT·CŒLO·FULMEN·SCEPTRUMQUE·TIRANNIS

43. Frontispiece and title page of Robert Lawson's highly successful book, *Ben and Me*. Copyright 1939 by Robert Lawson; © 1967 by John W. Boyd. (By permission of Little, Brown and Company, Boston)

Then, for some unknown reason, I thought of Ben Franklin and that messy looking old fur cap of his. It always looked to me as though it must be inhabited by something and why not a mouse?

44. Robert Lawson cheerfully recalls how he created *Ben and Me*. (By permission of Little, Brown and Company, Boston)

tions.[42] Most of these exhibitions, including the ones during the 1956 celebrations of Franklin's birth, relied on old paintings, documents, and relics. New artifacts were exceedingly rare. In fact, with the exceptions of the colorful sketch on the cover of L. Jesse Lemisch's selection of Franklin's writings, and of Norman Rockwell's beautiful illustrations for the 1964 edition of Poor Richard's almanacs[43] (Figs. 45 and 46), few American artists painted any portrait of Franklin that offered a significant new interpretation. But why should they? When the 1950s quickly gave way to a turbulent new decade, not only did the glory of the Founding Fathers seem to fade, but even the significance of the Revolution itself began to appear irrelevant.[44]

The prolonged war in Vietnam during the 1960s led to widespread protest against the political leadership of the nation, and the Watergate scandal in the early 1970s added another severe blow to public confidence in government. As an era of civil rights movements "from the bottom up," the late 1960s and early 1970s also witnessed a steady decline in the public's view of politicians, a tendency that the historian Arthur Schlesinger, Jr. lamented in "The Decline of Greatness" (1968) and the sociologist Richard Sennett investigated in *The*

---

42. [University of Pennsylvania], *Benjamin Franklin, Winston Churchill: An Exhibition Celebrating the Bicentennial of the University of Pennsylvania Library* (Philadelphia, 1951). I. Bernard Cohen, introduction, in Louise Todd Ambler, ed., *Benjamin Franklin: A Perspective* (Cambridge, Mass., 1975), 15.

43. L. Jesse Lemisch, ed., *Benjamin Franklin: The Autobiography and Other Writings* (Signet Classics ed.: New York, 1961); *Benjamin Franklin: Poor Richard's Almanacks* (Heritage Club ed.: New York, 1964), introd. by Van Wyck Brooks.

44. Michael Zuckerman, "The Irrelevant Revolution: 1776 and Since," *American Quarterly* 30 (Summer 1978): 224–42.

45. Cover of L. Jesse Lemisch's selection, *Benjamin Franklin: the Autobiography and Other Writings* (1961), depicts a witty and sly Franklin. (By permission of Dutton/Signet, a division of Penguin Books USA Inc.)

Fall of Public Man (1977). Non-conformity, defiance, and revolt became fashionable, pragmatism and diplomacy out of date. Rejecting a number of traditional heroes as hypocrites, including Washington and Jefferson, the militant black activist Eldridge Cleaver blatantly stated that "[I] look with roving eyes for a new John Brown, Eugene Debs, a blacker-meaner-keener Malcolm X, a Robert Franklin Williams with less rabbit in his blood, an American Lenin, Fidel, a Mao-Mao, A MAO MAO, A MAO MAO, A MAO MAO. . . ."[45]

Under these circumstances, there should be little surprise that some people began to read Franklin differently. Carol Ohmann found certain similarities between Franklin and Malcolm X, not only because both wrote their autobiographies but also because they had been rebellious youths. Both men offered in their memoirs "spectacular contrast between then and now," and both told stories of obscurity turned to eminence.[46] The similarities between the two men struck Philip Abbott so much that he declared that both Franklin and Mal-

45. Cleaver, *Soul on Ice* (1968; Ramparts Book ed.: New York, 1971), 31, 69–84. Ronald Berman, *America in the Sixties: An Intellectual History* (New York, 1968), 281–82. Kathleen Rout, *Eldridge Cleaver* (Boston, 1991), 12–41.
46. Carol Ohmann, "The Autobiography of Malcolm X: A Revolutionary Use of the Franklin Tradition," *American Quarterly* 22 (Summer 1970): 133. This sort of "romantic comparison" is criticized in Archie Epps, ed., *Malcolm X: Speeches at Harvard* (New York, 1991), 105–06.

46. "Franklin with French court ladies," an illustration for *Benjamin Franklin: Poor Richard's Almanacks*, New York, 1964, facing p. 272. Unlike many of his paintings that were based on life models, the artist Norman Rockwell said: "This is completely from my imagination." (© Heritage Press, New York)

colm X went from street hustlers to revolutionaries.[47] Cecil B. Curry, on the other hand, emphasized Franklin's political experience from a revisionist perspective. He believed that Franklin remained loyal to the British and was very interested in the expansion of the empire until the eve of the Revolution.[48] Reviving allegations from Franklin's old political detractors, Curry insisted that "he made himself a party to treason toward his own country while serving as its representative abroad."[49] The attempt to reinterpret his secretive nature was not limited to his public life. Believing that Franklin's attitudes toward women and his ways of conducting business were the forerunners of Hugh Hefner, Morton L. Ross went so far as to say that Poor Richard and "Playboy" were brothers under the skin.[50]

It is doubtful that any of these radical assertions has been generally accepted. What really agonized Franklin's admirers was a widespread apathy toward the Revolutionary generation. Printers, who used to be mindful of Franklin anniversaries, no longer held regular celebrations of his birth. Some of them continued to print annual keepsakes on January 17, yet their publications revealed great interest in the art of fine printing rather than in the person[51] (Fig. 47).

In the highly successful Broadway musical "1776," critics noted that the solemn moment of debating and signing a declaration of independence became a piece of amusement. Those who achieved American independence were not great men, but individuals with grave frailties, such as John Adams's "obnoxiousness," Thomas Jefferson's sexual urges, and Benjamin Franklin's indolence. From 1969 to 1972, the award-winning play was performed more than 1,200 times and was soon adapted into a Hollywood movie. The reviewer,

---

47. Abbott, chap. 2, "Hustling: Benjamin Franklin, Malcolm X, Abbie Hoffman," *States of Perfect Freedom* (Amherst, Mass., 1987), 27–57.

48. Currey, *Road to Revolution: Benjamin Franklin in England, 1765–1775* (Garden City, N.Y., 1968).

49. Currey, *Code Number 72/Ben Franklin: Patriot or Spy?* (Englewood Cliffs, N.J., 1972), 12.

50. Ross, "Poor Richard and 'Playboy': Brothers under the Flesh," *Colorado Quarterly* 15 (Spring 1967): 355–60.

51. *The Printing Week Library of Benjamin Franklin Keepsakes published in connection with the Celebration of Printing Week in New York commemorating the birthday of Benjamin Franklin, Printer.* Numerous issues (1953–78) can be found in Green Library, Stanford University and Bancroft Library, University of California, Berkeley. Most of these publications were in limited edition, and their fine and sometimes elegant prints are samples that demonstrate how to achieve high standards of design, typesetting, and engraving.

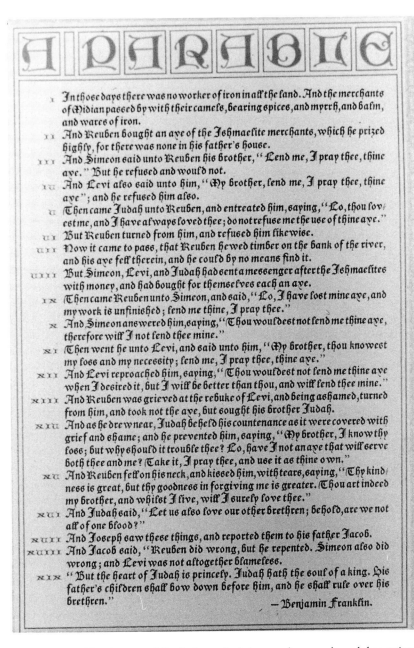

A PARABLE

i. In those days there was no worker of iron in all the land. And the merchants of Midian passed by with their camels, bearing spices, and myrrh, and balm, and wares of iron.

ii. And Reuben bought an axe of the Ishmaelite merchants, which he prized highly, for there was none in his father's house.

iii. And Simeon said unto Reuben his brother, "Lend me, I pray thee, thine axe." But he refused and would not.

iv. And Levi also said unto him, "My brother, lend me, I pray thee, thine axe"; and he refused him also.

v. Then came Judah unto Reuben, and entreated him, saying, "Lo, thou lovest me, and I have always loved thee; do not refuse me the use of thine axe."

vi. But Reuben turned from him, and refused him likewise.

vii. Now it came to pass, that Reuben hewed timber on the bank of the river, and his axe fell therein, and he could by no means find it.

viii. But Simeon, Levi, and Judah had sent a messenger after the Ishmaelites with money, and had bought for themselves each an axe.

ix. Then came Reuben unto Simeon, and said, "Lo, I have lost mine axe, and my work is unfinished; lend me thine, I pray thee."

x. And Simeon answered him, saying, "Thou wouldest not lend me thine axe, therefore will I not lend thee mine."

xi. Then went he unto Levi, and said unto him, "My brother, thou knowest my loss and my necessity; lend me, I pray thee, thine axe."

xii. And Levi reproached him, saying, "Thou wouldest not lend me thine axe when I desired it, but I will be better than thou, and will lend thee mine."

xiii. And Reuben was grieved at the rebuke of Levi, and being ashamed, turned from him, and took not the axe, but sought his brother Judah.

xiv. And as he drew near, Judah beheld his countenance as it were covered with grief and shame; and he prevented him, saying, "My brother, I know thy loss; but why should it trouble thee? Lo, have I not an axe that will serve both thee and me? Take it, I pray thee, and use it as thine own."

xv. And Reuben fell on his neck, and kissed him, with tears, saying, "Thy kindness is great, but thy goodness in forgiving me is greater. Thou art indeed my brother, and whilst I live, will I surely love thee."

xvi. And Judah said, "Let us also love our other brethren; behold, are we not all of one blood?"

xvii. And Joseph saw these things, and reported them to his father Jacob.

xviii. And Jacob said, "Reuben did wrong, but he repented. Simeon also did wrong; and Levi was not altogether blameless.

xix. "But the heart of Judah is princely. Judah hath the soul of a king. His father's children shall bow down before him, and he shall rule over his brethren."

— Benjamin Franklin.

47. "'A Parable' by Franklin." A typical keepsake produced by printers in the 1970s, with emphasis more on fine printing than on Franklin. (By permission of the Department of Special Collections, Stanford University Libraries)

Clive Barnes, predicted that "it might even run until the celebration of the bicentenary in 1976." It did not.[52]

When the bicentennial of independence was approaching, the popular science-fiction writer Isaac Asimov was invited to contribute an article about Franklin to the *Saturday Evening Post*. Asimov finally agreed to write a fantasized dream in which he would meet with Dr. Franklin. In his piece the fictional Franklin was deeply concerned about whether or not the United States was still independent and whether or not the union could last. To inject some upbeat spirit, Asimov's Franklin finally suggested a worldwide celebration of peace and harmony—a dream that the bicentennial should become a celebration of the union of humanity. Asimov's fiction generated considerable response from readers. A woman from Chicago wrote to the *Post*: "I am awakened to the discouraging thing that America seems careless of how we celebrate our birthday, if we do it at all." Another reader, Richard Henson of Brandon, Mississippi, responded:

I found Isaac Asimov's story entitled "The Dream" to express an ideal which should be coming to all men. The urgent need for all nations to unite against their real enemies (ignorance, hunger, disease, hatred) was beautifully brought to light through the person of Benjamin Franklin in this moving article. It is about time mankind worked toward the common goals of all sane beings. Let's hope that this dream materializes before we all disintegrate.[53]

Unfortunately, despite these wishful hopes, the dream did not materialize. Asimov's scheme was a little too idealistic for the 1970s (Fig. 48), and his fiction ended at the fourth installment after he had a disagreement with the *Post*. He recalled that "one of the editors did a fifth dream, I know, but I don't know if anything happened thereafter."[54] Even worse, few historical sites, including Boston and Philadelphia, were able to attract large groups of visitors. Many vacationers

---

52. Peter Stone and Sherman Edwards, *1776: A Musical Play* (New York, 1973). *New York Times*, 17 March 1969, p. 46; 3 April 1971, p. 17; 10 November 1972, p. 44.

53. *Saturday Evening Post*, January/February 1974: 45, 47; April 1974: 8; June/July 1974: 50–51.

54. Asimov, *In Joy Still Felt: The Autobiography of Isaac Asimov, 1954–1978* (New York, 1980), 656–57.

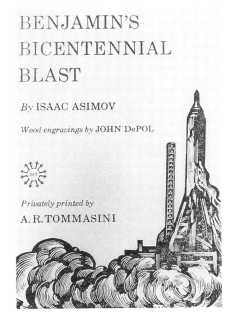

BENJAMIN'S
BICENTENNIAL
BLAST

By ISAAC ASIMOV

Wood engravings by JOHN DePOL

Privately printed by
A. R. TOMMASINI

48. *Benjamin's Bicentennial Blast* by Isaac Asimov, with John DePol's wood engravings, was reproduced by A. R. Tommasini in December 1976 as a keepsake for printers. (By permission of the Department of Special Collections, Stanford University Libraries)

ignored bicentennial promotions altogether and went instead to California, the Southwest, and Hawaii to spend their holidays.[55]

V

"Likability" became a fashionable expression in the media during the 1980s when personal charm was frequently discussed in Washington circles. According to one presidential authority, likability "is the ability to disclose a sense of the private self in public." This emphasis suggested that the spell of charisma possessed a unique power that could obscure, if not transcend, disagreements on the substance of political and social issues, and could captivate many people's imaginations regardless of their party affiliations.[56]

---

55. Zuckerman, "The Irrelevant Revolution," 225. For more cynical attitudes toward the Revolutionary generation see Art Ritchie, *Hero[e]s of 76* (South Bound Brook, N.J., 1980).

56. The new obsession with likability, of course, had much to do with Ronald Reagan's presidency. The undue focus on Reagan's personality, Michael Schudson argues, was a product of the elitist members of the media in Washington. Schudson, "Ronald Reagan Mis-remembered," in David Middleton and Derek Edwards, eds., *Collective Remembering* (London, 1990): 108–19. An in-depth examination is Robert Dalleck, *Ronald Reagan: The Politics of Symbolism*

Comparable to this new trend in the nation's political domain, a similar attitude toward Franklin emerged. According to Michael Frisch, professor of history and American studies at the State University of New York at Buffalo, his students throughout the 1980s consistently identified Franklin as one of the most well-known figures in history. Although he never served as president of the country, Franklin's name was, in almost every survey the professor conducted, placed right behind George Washington, Abraham Lincoln, and Thomas Jefferson.[57]

Nevertheless, to interpret the meanings of Franklin's notoriety was not as easy as to put his name in relative ranks, particularly when one recalls that this decade was preceded by the turbulent sixties and seventies. "Why should anyone have heroes?" asked the cultural critic Allan Bloom in his controversial book *The Closing of the American Mind*, published in 1987. Democracy needs no hero, he held, because its principle "denies greatness and wants everyone to feel comfortable in his skin without having to suffer unpleasant comparisons." Of today's young people, the critic observed that "their lack of hero-worship is a sign of maturity."[58]

At first glance, neither Professor Frisch's survey nor Professor Bloom's criticism explains the apparent paradox that Franklin retained his popularity in an era of political apathy. A closer look indicates, however, that the very contradiction between Franklin's sustained popularity on the one hand and the general disdain for great men on the other provides a critical clue to the contemporary mentality. No longer looking for pertinent instructions or for an inspiring model, many people in the 1980s simply ceased to regard Franklin as a hero in the conventional sense.

The name Franklin no longer generated the kind of respect, admiration, or enthusiasm it used to. Many may still be curious about his life, but few would take him seriously as a role model. The reason Franklin continued to satisfy their fantasies was not because he was

(Cambridge, Mass., 1984). For the concern with likability in the 1988 presidential campaigns, see *Time* (24 October 1988): 18–20. The magazine itself asks, "Has the pursuit of the presidency become trivialized by this intense emphasis on likability?"

57. Frisch, "American History and the Structures of Collective Memory: A Modest Exercise in Empirical Iconography," *Journal of American History* 75 (March 1989): 1130–55.

58. Bloom, *The Closing of the American Mind: How Higher Education Has Failed Democracy and Impoverished the Souls of Today's Students* (New York, 1987), 66.

right or wrong in politics, frugal or prodigal in economy, and moral or immoral in ethics. He was perceived primarily as a non-political figure, whose versatile experience and colorful career entertained the public regardless of their age, gender, or ethnic differences. Franklin's likable personality pleased modern Americans like a soothing historical feast, because he, a benign old fellow with bifocal spectacles on his nose and a cunning smile on his lips, was absolutely harmless, funny, and interesting.

Early in the 1980s an extensive selection of anecdotes by and about Franklin revealed his easy-going nature as well as his fondness for small talk and gossip. Social columnists capitalized on his relations with women from time to time, but the topic seemed so worn-out that few perceptive analyses could be found and even fewer sensations were created. Unlike most statues in the past which presented heroes on pedestals, the first full-size bronze of Franklin sitting and reading a newspaper on a bench was modeled by George Lundeen in 1987. Located along a busy sidewalk on the University of Pennsylvania campus, this new sculpture became a convenient spot for any visitor who could spare a few seconds to sit down beside the old man and have a picture taken with him[59] (Fig. 49).

Perhaps one of the most telling examples was the success of the impersonator Ralph Archbold, who has devoted more than a decade to performing as Franklin. In front of hundreds of businessmen, professionals, retired senior citizens, and young students, Archbold brought the eighteenth-century man to life, and delighted his audiences again and again with his remarkable likeness and good humor. Between 1973 and 1988 Archbold gave more than 6,500 performances across the nation. Reports about his enterprise appeared on numerous television programs and in more than 100 news articles nationwide, including *People Magazine, Time,* the *Saturday Evening Post, USA Today,* the *Wall Street Journal,* and the *New York Times.* When asked why Franklin achieved his extraordinary versatility as well as his long-lasting attractiveness, the actor chuckled at the compliments and answered, "I'd say it's being able to adjust." It seems that adaptability might also account for the popularity of his own perfor-

---

59. P. M. Zall, ed., *Ben Franklin Laughing: Anecdotes from Original Sources by and about Benjamin Franklin* (Berkeley, 1980). Elton Duke, "Franklin on Women," *Susquehanna Monthly Magazine* 11 (September 1986): 15–17. For a report of Lundeen's new sculpture see *News Update* (Wharton School of the University of Pennsylvania), September 1987, p. 1.

49. George Lundeen's statue of Franklin sitting on a bench, University of Pennsylvania, 1987.

50. Ralph Archbold poses as Franklin, the printer.

51. Holding an item from his private collections, Ralph Archbold makes his point.

mances, which have been adjusted to the diverse needs and tastes of his modern audiences[60] (Figs. 50 and 51).

The preference for an intimate and entertaining Franklin need not suggest that little progress was made through the 1980s. In fact, after diligent studies of Franklin's writing style and his *Pennsylvania Ga-*

---

60. Author's interviews with Ralph Archbold on 13 and 14 January 1992; Roy Bongartz, "Shaking Hands with Ben Franklin," *Americana* (March/April 1985): 41–43; Promotional Literature, Ralph Archbold/The Franklin Experience, Philadelphia.

zette, Professor J. A. Leo Lemay discovered that as many as fifty-seven unsigned articles in that newspaper could be attributed to Franklin. These new attributions contained many gloomy descriptions of human behavior, and grave doubt about the goodness of human nature.[61]

Lemay's findings revealed a previously little known aspect of Franklin and prompted Professor Ronald A. Bosco to begin a serious investigation into "the dark side of Benjamin Franklin." His reexamination of Franklin's private correspondence and many of those newly-attributed articles indicated that contrary to the conventional portrayal of a "Renaissance man" and optimist, Franklin harbored in his heart a contempt for human beings and a disdain for human nature. As a warning to the reader who would encounter a very unfamiliar type of utterance from a pessimistic Franklin, Bosco wrote:

> Significantly, in the writings discussed below one finds not the postures of amusement, burlesque, bawdiness, or facetiousness typically associated with the satirical Franklin, but a posture, with accompanying literary tone, that deliberately ranges from bitter irony to outright pessimism and disgust with human nature. Significantly, too, these writings date from periods throughout Franklin's life, indicating that he did not come to his opinions as a result of either unreflective, pre-romantic youthful angst or world-weariness born of age. In all, Franklin's treatment of the dark side of human character and his own dark views of man elicit the most savage comments to be found in any of his writings.[62]

The new findings and picture of a pessimistic Franklin immediately caught the media's attention. Before Bosco's article became available to the public, the *New York Times* announced that "partly because of the newly attributed material, the *Pennsylvania Magazine of History and Biography* is devoting its forthcoming issue to a reassessment of Franklin." The report also quoted Randall Miller, then editor of the *Pennsylvania Magazine*, who "cautioned against drawing an unduly harsh picture of Franklin" because "it is still possible that all the new materials attributed to Franklin were not his." The report finally pre-

---

61. Lemay, ed., *The Canon of Benjamin Franklin, 1722–1776: New Attributions and Reconsiderations* (Newark, Del., 1986), 43–46, 52–53, 106–09.

62. Bosco, "'He that best understands the World, least likes it': The Dark Side of Benjamin Franklin," *Pennsylvania Magazine of History and Biography* 111 (October 1987): 528. In this article the author refers to Lemay more than twenty times.

dicted that if the reassessment could withstand "prolonged academic scrutiny," the public might never look upon Franklin the same way as before.[63]

Because Lemay's and Bosco's new interpretations were very different from the old image of a spirited Franklin, their arguments met neither enthusiastic support nor explicit criticism. Most Franklin scholars remained cautious and did not conclude which Franklin they would choose, optimist or pessimist. The choice could be even more difficult if this either/or model was not valid and if somehow Franklin's ideas embraced both trends. Perhaps foreseeing such a possibility, Lemay in fact deviated from Bosco, who seemed to insist on the dark side of Franklin with little qualification. As one of the most informed experts, Lemay knew Franklin too well to draw a simple conclusion about a complex man. In one of his latest remarks on the topic Lemay suggested that "though he deliberately advocated and practiced optimism, I must conclude that, regarding the essential nature of human beings, Franklin was pessimistic—but he knew that pessimism was foolish and self-defeating."[64]

It is clear that although people still paid attention to Franklin during the 1960s and 1970s, they were less interested in his public service than in his private life. Franklin's lasting attractiveness lay in two areas: first, to the general public, he became an entertaining fellow whose life was often viewed with cynicism; second, for the scholarly community, his complex and elusive personality continued to provoke modern scholars, who were always unable to reach definite conclusions. Somewhere between extraordinary prominence and total oblivion, Franklin has remained at the end of the 1980s a well-known national figure for his distinctive personal characteristics.

---

63. Edwin McDowell, "Darker Side to Franklin Is Reported," *New York Times*, 18 August 1987, p. C18.
64. Lemay, *Benjamin Franklin: Optimist or Pessimist?* (University of Delaware, 1990), 25.

Chapter 8

"Ben Is Back"

❦

As this study passes the year 1990, it is useful to pause for a moment to recall some events of the past. Two centuries ago in 1790 most Americans learned about Franklin's death through newspaper reports. They were seldom timely, but people seemed to care less about the timing of the news than about its substance. A surprising number of odes and poems appeared to commemorate the occasion, even though original poets were rare and some newspapers simply reprinted poems from elsewhere.

A stanza in an anonymous poem read that "while hist'y holds a pen/She'll rank our virtuous Sage/Among the first of men."[1] Another exalted him as "the American Sage" and as a "venerable and illustrious citizen and philosopher."[2] Annis Boudinot Stockton, an ardent patriot, praised "his vast unbounded mind."[3] The poet Philip Freneau called him "philosopher" and "matchless FRANKLIN."[4] After his ode was written, Freneau realized that Franklin had never appreciated poetry. Intrigued by this apparent irony, Freneau wrote a humorous epistle, claiming that it was "from DR. Franklin (deceased) to his Poetical Panegyrists, on some of their Absurd Compliments." It read in part:

---

1. Quoted in *Weekly Monitor* (Litchfield, Conn.), 23 May 1790, p. 4. The publisher T. Collier acknowledged that he reprinted the ode from *The Daily Advertiser* (New York).

2. *The Independent Gazetteer, and Agricultural Repository* (Philadelphia), 24 April 1790, p. 3.

3. Stockton, "Lines on hearing the death of Doctor Franklin," "The All-Embracing Dr. Franklin" (Rosenbach Museum and Library, Philadelphia, 1990), no. 30, n.p.

4. Freneau, *Poems of Freneau*, ed. Harry Hayden Clark (1929; New York, 1960), 103–04. Like many pieces of the day, this ode was unsigned but appeared at least in *Middlesex Gazette, or Foedeal Adviser* (Middletown, Conn.), 15 May 1790, p. 2, which could well be a reprint from another newspaper.

Good Poets, who so full of pain
Are you sincere—or do you feign?
Love for your tribe I never had,
Nor Penned three stanzes, good or bad. . . .

Poets, I pray you, say no more,
Or say what Nature said before;
That reason should your pens direct,
Or else you pay me no respect.[5]

Freneau's sentiment revealed that Franklin's elusiveness made it hard for one to decide whether to praise or to censure him. He was such a serious and gay person at the same time that Franklin always seemed to be at a vantage point of judging, or making fun of, his successors.

Two hundred years have elapsed since Freneau expressed his predicament. Did people in the twentieth century share his views at the anniversary in 1990? If they did, in what way? If they did not, why? To put it another way, was the sentiment of commemoration in 1990 as spontaneous as two centuries ago? Or did the occasion prompt a reaction as ironic and insightful as Freneau's epistle?

I

"Ben is back," the City of Philadelphia proclaimed in 1990 when it commemorated the two hundredth anniversary of Franklin's death. The celebration created such a sensation that few visitors to the city would miss the message: 1990 was indeed the year of Benjamin Franklin.[6]

By a happy coincidence, the period from the late 1980s till the early 1990s involved an unusual concentration of important historical events, such as the bicentennial celebrations of the Constitution in 1987, the inauguration of George Washington's administration in 1989, the Bill of Rights in 1991, and the 500th anniversary of Christopher Columbus's discovery of America in 1992. To many Philadel-

---

5. Freneau, *Poems*, 104–05. This poem appeared at least in *The Pennsylvania Mercury, and Universal Advertiser* (Philadelphia), 1 June 1790, p. 2, which was a reprint from *The Daily Advertiser* (New York), 22 May 1790.

6. Philadelphia Convention and Visitors Bureau, *Philadelphia Almanack*, 1. 4 (1990), n.p.; Joseph F. Schuler, Jr., "Ben Is Back," *Mid-Atlantic Country* 11 (May 1990): 28–32, 78.

phians, therefore, the Franklin bicentennial was by no means an isolated event, and 1990 proved to be just another exciting year in the midst of a recent attempt to revitalize the public's interest in the nation's history.

More than one hundred and forty organizations and institutions in the city participated in a year-long carnival of ceremonies. A series of educational and entertaining programs featured lectures, publications, exhibitions, parades, concerts, opera, ballet, parties, jazz, games, tournaments, contests, kite flying, antique shows, arts festivals, fireworks, water events, automobile and hot-air balloon races, and a laser music extravaganza.[7] An observer was impressed, predicting that "no one will ever forget" the way the city celebrated Franklin.[8]

The success did not come easily, however. In fact, the public's renewed interest in Franklin was less a cause for the celebrations than a result of a calculated campaign. Planning for the big events began as early as 1987, and promotional activities intensified as the date approached. The Philadelphia Convention and Visitors Bureau targeted the media. By the end of September 1989, it had contacted more than forty newspapers and magazines nationwide, pitched the various schemes for the Franklin bicentennial, and encouraged them to report the upcoming celebrations. In the first six weeks of 1990 alone, 38.7 million impressions of news announcement appeared in newspapers and magazines.[9]

According to the bureau's estimate, as much as $1.5 million was spent for the promotion. Its vigorous campaign led one observer to ask: "Hey, Isn't This Guy Dead?" and another to wonder whether

---

7. Philadelphia Convention and Visitors Bureau, "Benjamin Franklin 1990 Projects" (13 October 1989), n.p.; *Philadelphia Daily News*, 17 January 1990, special supplement; "The In-Genius Dr. Franklin," 27 February 1990, pp. B1–15; *History Today*, January 1990, pp. 3–4; Alice L. Powers, "Mr. Franklin, We Salute You," *Americana*, April 1990: 63–66; Christopher G. Eckard and David C. G. Dutcher, "Benjamin Franklin of Philadelphia," *American History Illustrated* 25 (July/August 1990): 28–37; William C. Kashatus, III, "Benjamin Franklin, Image Maker," *Pennsylvania Heritage* 16 (Fall 1990): 16–21; and *The Philadelphia Inquirer*, 12 January 1990, p. 1-A; 16 April 1990, pp. 1-E, 9-E; 18 April 1990, pp. 1-A, 12-A, 1-D; 19 April 1990, pp. 1-D, 3-D; 21 June 1990, p. 9-G.

8. Schuler, Jr., "Ben Is Back," 28.

9. Philadelphia Convention and Visitors Bureau, "1990 Advertising Schedule: First Draft, August 22, 1989," n.p.; "Benjamin Franklin 1990: Press Calls," 29 September 1989, n.p.; "Benjamin Franklin 1990: Public Relations Highlights," n.d.

there were too many wingdings.[10] Despite the complaints, the city did catch many travelers' attention. *Time* magazine selected Philadelphia, along with Berlin, Moscow, Cologne, and Singapore, as one of the major tourist destinations worldwide for 1990. In the same year *Travel & Leisure* magazine listed the Philadelphia celebrations as one of the most exciting events for vacationers. As the bureau happily reported, "More than 3.1 million visitors came to Philadelphia in 1990," which showed a 10 percent increase compared with 1989, and "the Travel Industry Association of America (TIA) has awarded its annual Travel Marketing Award to Philadelphia."[11]

Spectacular as they were, the grand celebrations reminded one that "the great man makes history—and is consumed by it." Merrill Peterson's succinct comment on the Jefferson commemorations in the 1940s applies resoundingly to the case of Franklin.[12] No doubt many events in the celebration were informative and educational, such as the exhibitions and conferences held at the American Philosophical Society, the Library Company of Philadelphia, the Historical Society of Pennsylvania, the University of Pennsylvania, the Franklin Institute, and the Free Library of Philadelphia. For some officials, however, this bicentennial was an opportunity to attract business. Commercialization of the events never seemed to bother those who hoped for "economic benefit to the community."[13]

II

In the midst of the festivities the Benjamin Franklin National Memorial of the Franklin Institute of Philadelphia announced the establishment of two distinguished awards in honor of Franklin: the Bower Award and Prize for Advancement in Science and the Bower Award

---

10. Schuler, Jr., "Ben Is Back," 31; Lou Harry, "Hey, Isn't This Guy Dead?" *Philadelphia Magazine*, May 1990, 23; "The Case for Wingdings," *The Philadelphia Inquirer*, 24 February 1990, p. 8-A.

11. Philadelphia Convention and Visitors Bureau, circular letter to 1990 participants, signed by its president Tom Muldoon and vice president Meryl Levitz; idem, "Benjamin Franklin 1990: Public Relations Highlights," n.d.; and idem, "Ben Franklin, Lenny Dykstra and Futurists Lead Philadelphia's 10 Percent Tourism Increase," 4 April 1991, an information sheet from vice president R. C. Staab.

12. Peterson, *The Jefferson Image in the American Mind* (Galaxy Book ed.: New York, 1962), 443.

13. Philadelphia Convention and Visitors Bureau, "Benjamin Franklin 1990: Press Calls," 29 September 1989, n.p.

for Business Leadership. Both awards were made possible by a generous bequest of $7.5 million from Henry Bower (1896–1988), a Philadelphia chemical manufacturer and an admirer of Franklin. Inaugurated during the bicentennial of 1990, the new awards were to be made annually thereafter. The Bower award in science was intended to be an international honor granted without respect to nationality; with a cash prize always in excess of $250,000, it would be the richest science award in the United States.[14]

Aimed at encouraging ingenuity and excellence in the nation and around the world, the two newly-founded awards highlighted Franklin's renown as a scientist and business leader. The idea that Franklin symbolized the future became equally explicit when the Franklin Institute opened its $65 million Futures Center in May 1990. Connected through an atrium with the old Franklin rotunda, the center added several modern facilities to the Institute. A 340-seat omniverse theater was equipped with a domed wrap-around screen. Two galleries, the only ones of their kind in the world, housed futuristic objects for permanent display. Critics of architecture recognized the contrast between the old Franklin Memorial Hall and the Futures Center. With the imposing statue and memorial representing the past, the new center had sleek designs, bright and crayon colors, and collage of playful shapes—cube, cylinder, and pyramid, all of which "complements and completes its venerable predecessor."[15]

Yet the Franklin bicentennial passed quietly elsewhere in the nation. Two conferences of American and foreign scholars were held at Yale University, and in Philadelphia and its neighboring University of Delaware, but little activity took place among the general public. Major newspapers and magazines ignored the occasion. Except for reports about the current status of Franklin's bequest to Boston and Philadelphia, only two brief articles mentioned his name. Neither discussed his achievements. Both alluded to his dubious relations with women, and one was titled "Our Founding Flirt."[16]

---

14. Larry E. Tise, executive director, Benjamin Franklin National Memorial, [invitation letter], 17 January 1990, *The Benjamin Franklin National Memorial Awards* (Philadelphia, [1990]), 4–5.

15. Margaret Gaskie, [Futures Center], *Architectural Record*, 179 (January 1991): 62–67.

16. Franklin became a historical footnote during the heated controversy over Robert Mapplethorp's photographic exhibition in Cincinnati, Ohio in April 1990, see David A. Kaplan, "A Quick Look at the History of Smut," *Newsweek*, 2 July 1990, 48. He wrote that Franklin penned essays on choosing a mistress and combating flatulence during the Constitutional Convention in 1787 (a wrong

Casual references of this sort showed not only an indifference to the past, but also a lack of imagination about the present. Serious observers wondered, however, whether Franklin's bicentennial commemoration was an appropriate occasion for either self-indulgence or shameless contempt. Peter Baida's book *Poor Richard's Legacy*, which indicated that 1990 would be a year of introspection, was particularly pertinent.

A 1979 graduate of the Wharton School of the University of Pennsylvania, Mr. Baida was as familiar with Franklin (one of the most distinguished founders of his *alma mater*) as he was well versed in American literature. After a lively review of many economic changes in history since Franklin's time, he deplored the deterioration of business integrity and the erosion of the work ethic. The 1980s were notorious for scandals such as Michael Milken's "junk bonds." Ironically another Wharton graduate, Milken like similar wheeler-dealers represented the "me-first" ethic.[17] Donald Trump, also a Wharton graduate, boasted of his success in an autobiography. But his vanity, his extravagance, and his reduction of business activity to making telephone calls all day revealed his superficial mentality.[18]

When the simple virtues of Poor Richard became degraded, Baida argued, so did the cutting edge of American manufactures and Yankee know-how. Preoccupied with spending rather than saving, federal debt mounted to $2.58 trillion in 1988, which meant $11,565 for every man, woman, and child in the nation. "We are borrowing from our children to throw a party for ourselves," the critic observed.[19] Perhaps Mr. Baida appeared to be a little too nostalgic for the past and too worried about the present. In either case, he was as observant and critical as he was savvy and witty. Baida recalled a story that needs to be quoted at length:

---

date). Aaron Goldman wrote "Our Founding Flirt, Cuddlesome Ben Franklin, the Randy Rebel with a Cause," *Washington Post*, 15 April 1990, p. D-5. This article was reprinted in a place as remote as Watertown, New York, *Sunday Weekly*, 29 April 1990, p. 8.

17. *The Wall Street Journal* defines the junk-bond market as "a place where highly risky loans to lower quality companies are traded." Quoted in Baida, *Poor Richard's Legacy: American Business Values from Benjamin Franklin to Michael Milken* (New York, 1990), 334.

18. Trump, with Tony Schwarts, *Trump: The Art of the Deal* (New York, 1987), 3–31.

19. Baida, *Poor Richard's Legacy*, 335–36.

John Shad, the chairman of the Securities and Exchange Commission, was so disturbed by "the large number of graduates of leading business schools who have become convicted felons" that in 1987 he made a gift of $20 million to Harvard Business School to establish a program in ethics. In *The New York Times* on July 27, 1987, Shad explained the point that, in his view, business schools were failing to teach: "In sum, ethics pays: It's smart to be ethical." Cynics may wonder why this straightforward utilitarianism needs to be backed by $20 million, but Harvard was happy to accept the gift.[20]

Baida's point was clear: nowadays everything was related to money, including the improvement of ethics. The sophistication of the modern economy has certainly made many traditional values obsolete. Time is not only money, as Poor Richard used to say; time has also changed the concept of money, as modern businessmen and economists insisted.[21] Still, Baida maintained that there must be something barren in the contemporary mentality and something profound in what Poor Richard once believed. He warned that

perhaps we have lost not merely the capacity to work and to save but also the capacity to listen, not merely the discipline to deny ourselves for the future but also the discipline to learn from the past. If we continue to squander our inheritance, our most precious bequest to our grandchildren may well be a copy of *Poor Richard's Almanack*, to show them where we went wrong.[22]

III

For academia, Franklin's bicentennial seemed most appropriate to reassess his life and reevaluate his legacy. When more than three dozen scholars attempted to do so, what they found was more ambiguity. After fifty years of charting Franklin's contributions to science, I. Bernard Cohen pointed out that many modern biographers failed to "treat his science fully and with respect." Far from a profound and theoretical scientist, the predominant image of Franklin's scientific career has remained as a gadgeteer or tinkerer.[23]

Because so many biographies were written about Franklin, any

---

20. Ibid., 339.
21. *American Heritage*, May/June 1989, 6.
22. Baida, *Poor Richard's Legacy*, 341.
23. Cohen, *Benjamin Franklin's Science* (Cambridge, Mass., 1990), ix, 2–3.

new insights demanded enormous ingenuity and expertise.[24] Most
scholars, however, attempted to use existing information to reinterpret who he was. Michael Zuckerman held that though scholars tried
for a long time to distinguish the myth from the man in his *Autobiography*, the truth thus far was murky. It was commonplace to portray
Franklin as a salesman of the self. Nothing could be farther from the
truth, Zuckerman insisted. Franklin was an utterly public man, for he
always believed in the commonweal, benevolence, mutual help, and
collective action. Unfortunately, he gave himself so completely to the
public that "sophisticated commentators have questioned whether he
had any interior existence at all." Franklin's identity continued to
perplex modern scholars, who often had to struggle with his superb
understanding of the role of exterior appearance: he had carefully
managed his public pose and created many masks, while still maintaining playfulness in almost everything he did.[25]

Literary scholars were not intimidated by the challenge.[26] J. A. Leo
Lemay contended that as a writer Franklin miscalculated his strategy
in "Narrative of the Late Massacres in Lancaster Country." The failure
to adopt a fictional character in the piece, and worse, the decision to
reveal his anger at the massacres made him very unpopular among
his fellow colonists. Franklin's unwise literary strategy, Lemay be-

---

24. Thanks to the painstaking effort of Edwin Wolf 2nd, the late librarian of the
    Library Company of Philadelphia, modern readers were able to have a glimpse
    of what books Franklin might have owned. James N. Green's careful analysis
    illuminated the different ramifications of Franklin's career as a publisher and a
    bookseller. The delicate essay by Ellen G. Cohn studied Franklin's musical taste
    and revealed his humanity. Green, comp., *Poor Richard's Books: An Exhibition
    of Books owned by Benjamin Franklin, Now on the Shelves of the Library
    Company of Philadelphia* (Philadelphia, 1990). Wolf 2nd, "Franklin's Library,"
    in J. A. Leo Lemay, ed., *Reappraising Benjamin Franklin: A Bicentennial Per-
    spective* (Newark, Del., 1993), 319–31; Green, "Benjamin Franklin as Publisher
    and Bookseller," ibid., 98–114; Cohn, "Benjamin Franklin and Traditional Mu-
    sic," ibid., 290–318.

25. Zuckerman, "Doing Good While Doing Well: Benevolence and Self-Interest in
    Franklin's *Autobiography*," in Lemay, ed., *Reappraising Franklin*, 441–51.

26. While some American experts examined Franklin's journalistic style in his sar-
    castic descriptions of drinking and drunkards and his gruesome reports of crime
    scenes, a French scholar added that he was a "Founding Father of American
    humor." Robert D. Arner, "Politics and Temperance in Boston and Philadel-
    phia: Benjamin Franklin's Journalistic Writings on Drinking and Drunkenness,"
    in Lemay, ed. *Reappraising Franklin*, 52–77; Ronald A. Bosco, "'Scandal, like
    other Virtues, is in part its own Reward': Franklin Writing the Crime Beat," ibid.,
    78–97; and Daniel Royot, "Benjamin Franklin as Founding Father of American
    Humor," ibid., 388–95.

lieved, eventually caused him to lose the election in 1764—a major setback in his political career.[27] Yet Lemay's and others' new studies on the piece led Carla Mulford to doubt whether her colleagues derived too much from Franklin's writings in light of modern needs. She said: "To credit Franklin personally for having empathy with native Americans because of the 'sympathy' evoked in the Narrative is, in my view, a particularly troubling aspect of the way twentieth-century readers have been trained to read some eighteenth-century texts."[28]

Esmond Wright, on the other hand, kept the debate alive over whether or not the *Autobiography* was fiction. He pointed out that Franklin was not a Rousseau or a Beaumarchais; nor did he intend to write a confession. Instead, he was a secretive man who remained silent about too many important events in his private and public life. Although his memoirs were "written at wide intervals, with different purposes, and in different tones," one sure thing was that the man we knew for two hundred years "is his own creation." In order to expose "the inner man," modern readers should not only look for additional sources but also be aware that "however spontaneous he may seem, he is on stage, like the actor, who likewise has some say in the parts he chooses to play." Wright concluded that the *Autobiography* "is a work of art, or, at least, a work of artifice."[29]

For decades many critics believed that Jonathan Edwards and Benjamin Franklin represented opposite trends in the American consciousness. The theologian Edwards, concerned with salvation of the soul, was the epitome of spirituality. The practical self-made man Franklin, focused on this world, was the archetype of individualistic materialism. It was not until recent years, particularly in the early 1980s when Norman Fiering published his *Jonathan Edwards's Moral Thought and Its British Context*, that a number of scholars began to reexamine the dichotomy and to find significant continuity beneath Edwards's and Franklin's apparent dissimilarities.[30] For ex-

27. Lemay, "Rhetorical Strategies in *Sinners in the Hands of an Angry God* and *Narrative of the Late Massacres in Lancaster County*," in Barbara B. Oberg and Harry S. Stout, eds., *Benjamin Franklin, Jonathan Edwards, and the Representation of American Culture* (New York, 1993), 192–203.

28. Mulford, "*Caritas* and Capital: Franklin's *Narrative of the Late Massacres*," in Lemay, ed., *Reappraising Franklin*, 347, 355, 357n.

29. Wright, "The *Autobiography*: Fact or Fiction?" in Dilys Pegler Winegrad, ed., *The Intellectual World of Benjamin Franklin: An American Encyclopaedist at the University of Pennsylvania* (Philadelphia, 1990), 29–42.

30. Nowhere is this attempt more explicit than Oberg and Stout, eds., introduction, *Franklin, Edwards, and American Culture*, 3–9.

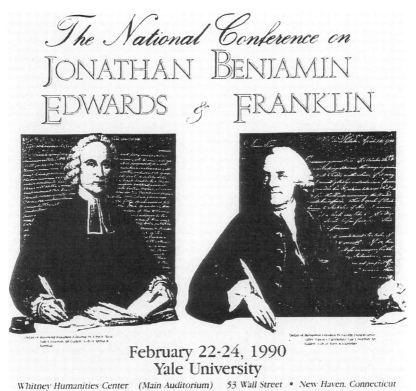

The National Conference on
JONATHAN BENJAMIN
EDWARDS & FRANKLIN

February 22-24, 1990
Yale University

Whitney Humanities Center   (Main Auditorium)   53 Wall Street • New Haven, Connecticut

52. Information sheet of "The National Conference on Jonathan Edwards and Benjamin Franklin, February 22–24, Yale University."

ample, David Levin attributed the disparity of reputation between Edwards and Franklin to the latter's style of "writing self-consciously, cannily, perhaps insincerely." He pointed out that "one major reason why Edwards has enjoyed a much better press in modern scholarship than either Franklin or Mather is the directness, the relentlessly straightforward quality of his prose."[31]

At a national conference held at Yale University in February 1990 (Fig. 52), a number of scholars reported that despite their different ideological orientations, the enlightened Franklin and the New England divine Edwards actually shared more than a few ideas, beliefs, and convictions. Although the intellectual outlooks of the two differed, Edwin S. Gaustad revealed, the immense interest both took in

31. Levin, "Edwards, Franklin, and Cotton Mather: A Meditation on Character and Reputation," in Nathan O. Hatch and Harry S. Stout, eds., *Jonathan Edwards and the American Experience* (New York, 1988), 35.

moral issues indicated that their "worlds moved in a common cosmos." Several participants in the conference expressed a similar impression, and tried to delineate what was characterized as the overlap, mutual concern, and similarities of the two moral philosophers.[32]

An expert in British and American political and intellectual thought, Daniel Walker Howe, pointed out that Franklin and Edwards were very much concerned with such concepts as conscience, prudence, passions, and the will, because these notions were closely related to the debates in the western world on human nature throughout the eighteenth century. Based on frequent references to Richard Steele, Alexander Pope, Thomas Reid, Jonathan Swift, Joseph Butler, as well as Shaftesbury, John Locke, Francis Hutcheson, and David Hume, Howe tried to demonstrate the ideological framework that shaped both Edwards's and Franklin's discourses. He maintained that both men were "observant to" and "informed participants" in trans-Atlantic communication.[33]

No matter how similar their moral and rational ideas may have been, Edwards's theocentricism separated him from Franklin's humanism, as Elizabeth E. Dunn warned. Furthermore, Ruth H. Bloch argued that both men failed to develop a new concept of virtue concerning family and marital love. Both men found no need to redefine the relations between men and women; morality became important only when it was concerned with autonomous males. "Virtue was never for either of them the result of emotional involvement with other people," Bloch stated. "It was instead a quality internal to the individual—for Edwards the product of the gracious awakening of one's spiritual sense, and for Franklin the disciplined quest for worldly happiness." When Franklin proposed his "united party of virtue," he prescribed that the new organization was for "young and single Men only." Finally, William K. Breitenbach observed that because of their intense interest in moralism, both men came to recognize "the unavoidable artificiality of the visible character" and "the need to construct a version of the self in the world." Both had detached, reserved, and elusive personalities and both remained "private public men," Breitenbach concluded.[34]

---

32. Gaustad, "The Nature of True—and Useful—Virtue: From Edwards to Franklin," in Oberg and Stout, eds., *Franklin, Edwards, and American Culture*, 42–57.

33. Howe, "Franklin, Edwards, and the Problem of Human Nature," in Oberg and Stout, eds., *Franklin, Edwards, and American Culture*, 75–97.

34. Dunn, "'A Wall Between Them Up to Heaven': Jonathan Edwards and Ben-

Despite the impressive output of recent investigations, Franklinists might still feel dissatisfied because there were no major break-throughs in several key areas of Franklin studies. Most of this disappointment existed long before 1990; the bicentennial only made it painfully conspicuous. To begin with, after continuous publication of Franklin's papers by the American Philosophical Society and Yale University for more than three decades, few scholars have thoroughly explored those documents, as James Hutson complained.[35]

Exceptions did exist. Quoting extensively from the Franklin papers, Jack P. Greene tried to provide an alternative interpretation of the American Revolution, which might be caused by "pride, prejudice, and jealousy" rather than by what Bernard Bailyn believed to be a fear of "conspiracy."[36] Primarily based on American archives, Esmond Wright's prize-winning biography, *Franklin of Philadelphia*, also highlighted the political side of Franklin. In his portrayal of Franklin as colonial agent in England, Wright emphasized Franklin's interest in expanding the British colonies and delineated his involvement in the Grand Ohio scheme, which was documented in The Papers of Franklin.[37]

Yet it is hard to deny that two hundred years after his death, the reconstruction of Franklin's life remains a formidable task to historians whose training and interest have become even more specialized. In order to comprehend his complex and versatile career, one has to understand eighteenth-century society in its totality, including religion, literature, business, politics and political thought, science, and

---

jamin Franklin," in Oberg and Stout, eds., *Franklin, Edwards, and American Culture*, 59. Bloch, "Women, Love, and Virtue in the Thought of Edwards and Franklin," ibid., 134–151. Breitenbach, "Religious Affections and Religious Affectations: Antinomianism and Hypocrisy in the Writings of Edwards and Franklin," ibid., 13–26.

35. James H. Hutson, "Franklin at Twenty-Five: A Review of The Papers of Benjamin Franklin," *Pennsylvania Magazine of History and Biography* 111 (October 1987): 559–60.

36. Greene, "Pride, Prejudice, and Jealousy: Benjamin Franklin's Explanation for the American Revolution," in Lemay, ed., *Reappraising Franklin*, 119–42. Bailyn, *The Ideological Origins of the American Revolution* (Cambridge, Mass., 1967).

37. Wright, *Franklin of Philadelphia* (Cambridge, Mass., 1986), 211–14. The Grand Ohio or Vandalia scheme has been treated in Cecil B. Currey, *Code Number 72/Ben Franklin: Patriot or Spy* (Englewood Cliffs, N.J., 1972), 23, 37–58. It is a pity that, as an English scholar, Wright did not use the British archives to answer directly Currey's challenge that Franklin might have been a British spy during the American Revolution.

diplomacy. Nevertheless, for the last several decades history has been compartmentalized to such a degree that many historians are unwilling to engage an enterprise that requires varied skills, broad knowledge, and a vision that must penetrate the narrow confines of modern professionalization.

Currently, Franklin research attracts more literary scholars than historians. As Edmund S. Morgan has pointed out, the enormous amount of Franklin documents has certainly provided ample opportunity for critics to analyze and reinterpret his works.[38] Furthermore, using concepts like rhetoric and plot as their basic framework and context, literary scholars have the advantage to choose any writing and focus on its text. Thus, what some of them are apt to do is to reconstruct a microcosm of Franklin's mind without much consideration of other intellectual and social trends. Reminding us that eighteenth-century literature itself had many styles, Richard E. Amacher has correctly observed: "Literature was so closely connected with politics and actual history-in-the-making in Franklin's day that modern investigators, I feel, go wrong in highly specialized studies that tell only part of the truth about a particular Franklin text."[39]

In fact, literary experts have for years scrutinized the style, structure, text, vocabulary, plot, conceit, dramatization, and rhetoric of numerous pieces of Franklin's writings. But one of the major challenges to all Franklinists is to reconstruct him as a conversationalist. His contemporaries, admirers and detractors alike, attested that he was frequently silent in public but congenial with his close friends.[40] The young Franklin valued conversation, declaring that "I had pick'd up some very ingenious Acquaintance whose Conversation was of great Advantage to me." In addition to descriptions of various dia-

---

38. See also Claude-Anne Lopez's revealing and humorous piece, "Some Birthday . . . ," *Franklin Gazette* (publication of the Friends of Franklin, Philadelphia), 4 (Winter 1993), n.p.

39. Amacher to Richard L. Johnson, 27 March 1967. Quoted in Johnson, "Contemporary Trends in Franklin Studies" (M.A. thesis, Claremont Graduate School, 1967), 50.

40. For example, John Adams, James Madison, and William Pierce of Georgia all testified to Franklin's interest in conversation. According to the French Abbé Morellet, Franklin was "invariably good-natured" in conversation (Carl Van Doren, *Benjamin Franklin* [New York, 1938], 649). James M. Beck believed that "he seemed to charm almost all with whom he came in contact. . . . Much of this must have been due to the exquisite charm of his conversation." *Ceremonies Attending the Unveiling of the Statue of Benjamin Franklin, June 14, 1899; Presented to the City of Philadelphia by Mr. Justus C. Strawbridge* (Philadelphia, 1899), 31.

logues, he mentioned "conversation" more than twenty times in his memoirs, which showed his warm reminiscences of intimate conversation.[41] A close investigation of Franklin as a conversationalist in the context of eighteenth-century American life will not only reveal a crucial facet of his personal career, but also make a significant contribution to cultural history.

Meticulous and numerous as they may be, previous biographies have not exhausted every important aspect of Franklin's life. For example, Franklin was known as a self-made man, but he had carefully cultivated patronage, a principal way to get ahead in his time.[42] Franklin's memoirs and some of his widely quoted correspondence remind us of his apparent interest in those powerful people above him, including the deceitful Governor William Keith, who casually promised to sponsor him, and Cotton Mather, whom he did not like particularly but visited eagerly for advice.[43] Few Franklinists have systematically examined the critical functions of friendship, private connections, collective actions, and voluntary associations as means of social advancement in colonial days.[44] In this regard the 1730s might prove to be more crucial in Franklin's life than scholars have thus far believed. It was then that Franklin's behavior pattern apparently changed from a series of individual adventures (from Boston to New York, to Philadelphia, to London, and back to Philadelphia) to a steady cultivation of both new and old institutions, including the *Junto* (1727), his marriage (1730) and family, the Freemasons

---

41. *Autobiography*, 55, 60, 65, 67, 73, 77, 84, 85, 106, 131, 149, 151, 157, 158, 159, 213, 223, 231, 248, 262, 264. Ample reference to conversation can be found in Franklin's other writings, particularly those in dialogue form, such as "Dialogue between Two Presbyterians, April 10, 1735" and "Dialogue between the Gout and Mr. Franklin, October 22, 1780." Last but not least, it may be interesting to note that his most popular *Autobiography* and *The Way to Wealth* began as conversation or speech.

42. See Gordon S. Wood's illuminating chapter on patronage, *The Radicalism of the American Revolution* (Vintage Book ed.: New York, 1993), 57–77.

43. *Autobiography*, 80–83, 86–87, 92–95; Franklin to Samuel Mather, 12 May 1784, *Writings*, 1092–93.

44. Gladys Eleanor Meyer, *Free Trade in Ideas: Aspects of American Liberalism Illustrated in Franklin's Philadelphia Career* (New York, 1941), 11–76. An excerpt from Meyer's book is more easily accessible in Charles L. Sanford, ed., *Benjamin Franklin and the American Character* (Boston, 1955), 48–57. Several scholars have touched on this aspect of Franklin's life, James N. Green, "Benjamin Franklin as Publisher and Bookseller" and Michael Zuckerman, "Doing Good While Doing Well." See also Peter Baida, *Poor Richard's Legacy*, 31–36.

(1731), the proposed Library Company (1731), and his appointments, as the Assembly clerk (1736) and as postmaster of Philadelphia (1737).

Increasingly intrigued by his personal traits and domestic life, few scholars have asked why so many *personae* in his writings were female, such as Silence Dogood, Polly Baker, Bridget Saunders (Poor Richard's wife), and the nameless old mistresses. Even fewer have seriously examined some of the apparently more feminine elements in his personality, such as his tolerance, compromise, benevolence, humanity, and sympathy, as well as his remarkable sensitivity, subtlety, and perception.[45]

Only scant attention has been paid to Franklin's posthumous reputation. Little has been done to trace the long history of his bequest to Boston and Philadelphia, a legacy that has attracted periodic public attention, particularly since the beginning of this century. Few scholars have systematically studied his rich iconography, for example, statues, illustrations, cartoons, likenesses on coins, stamps, furniture, glassware, toys, postcards, and souvenirs.[46] In addition, individuals as well as many counties, towns, streets, schools, and business establishments have adopted Franklin's name. But no one has explored the implications of such a widespread interest.

The link between Franklin's personal traits and the American character deserves further consideration. Perhaps few nations in the world are so preoccupied by the search for their own identity as Americans,[47] and the very premise that the fundamental characteristics of a nation can be detected from those of a single individual is itself

---

45. As Verner W. Crane and others noted, Franklin was ambitious but never avid of power. Crane, *Benjamin Franklin and a Rising People* (Boston, 1954), 205; Carl Becker, "The Salty Sense of Benjamin Franklin, His Fantastic Life Story Told in a Masterly Biography," *New York Herald Tribune*, 9 October 1938, section 9, p. 1; and Henry Steele Commager, "Franklin, The True American; Carl Van Doren's Biography Unfolds His Many-Sided Genius," *New York Times Book Review*, 9 October 1938, p. 1. While George Washington and Andrew Jackson were often praised for their manliness, contemporaries noticed the feminine element in Thomas Jefferson's personality, which was labeled as "pusillanimous character." Merrill D. Peterson, *The Jefferson Image in the American Mind* (New York, 1962), 116–19.

46. A good starting point is Roy Goodman, "A Selective Guide to Printed Material Relating to the Iconography and Artifacts of Benjamin Franklin," *Franklin Gazette* (publication of the Friends of Franklin, Philadelphia), 2 (Fall 1991), n.p.

47. One early example was J. Hector St. John Crèvecoeur's discussion of "what is an American," *Letter from an American Farmer* (1782; New York, 1968), 45–91.

distinctively American. Why *is* there a parallel between the nation's obsession with its identity and the endless discussions of Franklin's personality? To what extent have both quests originated from the deeply-rooted Protestant tradition of self-examination? To what extent could these searches shed light on the nation's historical tendency to scrutinize private virtue in the public arena? And to what extent do these trends reflect Americans' unwillingness to separate the personal integrity of public figures from the soundness of their political judgment and policy?[48]

Finally, a number of monographs have examined Franklin's experience in several western countries, such as England, France, Scotland, Ireland, Canada, Italy, and Germany. But scholars have generally ignored his influence on other parts of the world, such as South America, Russia, China, and Japan. A new generation of scholars must address these areas to do justice to Franklin. He remains a giant in world history because his thirst for knowledge, his keen interest in science and humanity, and his universal renown as a great American have always transcended national boundaries.

---

48. For a renewed interest in the relationship between character and public good see James Q. Wilson, "The Rediscovery of Character: Private Virtue and Public Policy," *The Public Interest* 81 (Fall 1985): 3–16; Thomas C. Reeves, *A Question of Character: A Life of John F. Kennedy* (New York, 1991); and Douglas L. Wilson, "Thomas Jefferson and the Character Issue," *The Atlantic Monthly* (November 1992), 57–74. See also the much publicized confirmation hearings held by the Senate Judiciary Committee on the Supreme Court nomination of Judge Clarence Thomas, especially those from 10 to 12 October 1991 when Professor Anita Hill and others testified before the committee, extensive reports and excerpts in the *Congressional Record* and *The New York Times*, 7–15 October 1991. During these hearings, Thomas described Hill's charge of alleged sexual harassment as "character assassination," Hill's former classmates at Yale University Law School confirmed her impeccable character, and Thomas's defenders contended that Hill had two personalities. George Bush's emphasis on character during his presidential campaign against Bill Clinton in 1992 was another case in point. See Eleanor Clift, Howard Fineman, and Ginny Carroll, "Character Questions," *Newsweek* (10 February 1992), 26–27; Jonathan Alter, "The Real Character Issues," *Newsweek* (30 March 1992): 33; Abigail McCarthy, "The Character Issue: Bill, Franklin, & Pericles," *Commonweal* (8 May 1992): 8–9; J. Bryan Hehir, "Hitting the High Cs: Character, Choice, & Community," *Commonweal* (17 June 1992): 7–9; "The Character Thing," *The New Republic* (2 November 1992): 7; and E. L. Doctorow, "Fate, Hope and Voting: The Character of Presidents," *The Nation* (9 November 1992): 534–36.

Epilogue

The study of Franklin's image for the past two centuries shows that his legacy had a distinctive place in American culture. Few national heroes, including George Washington and Thomas Jefferson, played a more significant posthumous role in shaping the American way of life than Franklin, who personified the ideal of the self-made man, and whose rise from obscurity to eminence exemplified the American dream.

During the early years of the republic, the wide proliferation of his *Autobiography* and of *The Way to Wealth* nurtured numerous generations of Americans, whose obsession with wealth, success, and upward mobility made them particularly interested in Franklin's views of diligence and frugality. The prevailing adulation of his character elevated him to a highly regarded model, especially for hundreds of thousands of young people and artisans. Because the mode of his experience had a profound impact on the daily lives of average Americans, his example of self-help and self-determination would remain an inspiration as long as people continued to believe in the dream of individual success and upward mobility.

The study of Franklin's legacy over the years not only reveals his long-lasting influence on later generations, but also suggests some important changes in American society. Franklin was deeply concerned about his reputation; at the same time he persistently maintained his individual characteristics. Nevertheless, it was only under different historical circumstances that his character and personality began to capture Americans' imaginations. During the first half of the nineteenth century when Americans paid great attention to the righteousness of social behavior, Franklin was generally regarded as a consummate hero. Though they knew some of Franklin's errors and weaknesses from his *Autobiography*, Americans deemphasized his personal failings and portrayed him as a model man, whose successful career could be imitated.

Despite Franklin's individualism, it was not until the second half of

the nineteenth century, when interest in personality gradually overshadowed that of character, that Americans began to pay increasing
attention to his distinctive personal traits. Indeed, few national heroes
in history were as successful as Franklin in capturing the public imagination for so many years after their deaths. Benjamin Franklin has a
unique place in the American pantheon (Fig. 53). Idolized and belit-
tled at once by many, he was nonetheless gentler than some, wiser
than others, and more versatile, delightful, and charismatic than most
national figures. Nathaniel Hawthorne rightly commented that Franklin was fascinating for his common and uncommon qualities.[1] Franklin was one of the few famous Americans whose greatness lay primarily in his personal qualities. The accomplishments of many
distinguished Americans, from Washington and Jefferson to Abraham
Lincoln, were indissolubly linked with a cause, such as the American
Revolution or emancipation and the Civil War. Their reputations were
often promoted by partisan organs and political institutions. There is
a sense that they became great heroes largely because of their political roles in extraordinary historical events.

This was not the case of Franklin. Though far removed from Franklin's time, Americans seldom failed to marvel at his intriguing personality. In addition to his significant contribution to American independence, Franklin's varied achievements in science, literature, and
public affairs gained the kind of international renown that few other
American heroes have matched. More than one hundred years after
his death, his champions declared that Franklin was America's Leonardo da Vinci.

Franklin has always been a folk hero and his profound legacies
survived in the hearts and memories of ordinary citizens, not in political campaign slogans, party platforms, or governmental institutions. His humble origins, belief in liberty and freedom, genuine benevolence, and universally acknowledged tolerance, all made him a
household name. His native humor and spontaneous wit amused
generations of men, women, and children. Though the 1920s and
1930s saw his frailties often exploited and his image sometimes vulgarized, people continued to believe that Franklin was one of the
most exceptional human beings that America has produced.

For two centuries people have shown interest in Franklin's life,
concentrating first on his character and then captivated by his personality. The combined forces of his character and personality

---

1. Hawthorne, *Passages from the French and Italian Note-Books* (Riverside ed.:
Boston, 1897), 28.

53. Dusk falls on Franklin's grave on a winter day when all seems quiet for the moment. (Photographs by the author; reproduced by Dan Moseley)

amazed modern Americans. They sometimes wondered how this one eighteenth-century printer could make such a permanent imprint on the nation. Throughout the post-World War II era they still debated about him. Americans realized that Franklin's tremendous impact on the nation's character was intermingled with numerous uncertainties about his own identity. This singular mix has occurred, not only because Benjamin Franklin was an exceedingly complex figure, or because his popular *Autobiography* obscured his real life, but also because Americans themselves and their changing social and cultural conditions have continuously shaped and reshaped their own perceptions of him.

Selected Bibliography

Cultural and Image Studies

Adair, Douglass, *Fame and the Founding Fathers: Essays by Douglass Adair*, ed. Trevor Colbourn (New York, 1974).

Bodnar, John, *Remaking America: Public Memory, Commemoration, and Patriotism in the Twentieth Century* (Princeton, 1992).

Boorstin, Daniel J., *The Image or What Happened to the American Dream* (New York, 1962).

_____, *The Americans: The National Experience* (Vintage Books ed.: New York, 1965).

_____, and Boorstin, Ruth F., *Hidden History* (New York, 1987).

Browne, Pat, *Heroines of Popular Culture* (Bowling Green, Ohio, 1987).

Browne, Ray B., et al., eds., *Heroes of Popular Culture* (Bowling Green, Ohio, 1972).

_____, and Fishwick, Marshall, eds., *Icons of America* (Bowling Green, Ohio, 1978).

Comini, Alessandra, *The Changing Image of Beethoven: A Study in Mythmaking* (New York, 1987).

Geyl, Pieter, *Napoleon: For and Against*, trans. Olive Renier (New Haven, 1949).

Hobsbawm, Eric, and Ranger, Terence, eds., *The Invention of Tradition* (Cambridge, England, 1983).

Kammen, Michael, *People of Paradox: An Inquiry Concerning the Origins of American Civilization* (Vintage Books ed.: New York, 1973).

_____, *A Season of Youth: The American Revolution and the Historical Imagination* (New York, 1978).

_____, *A Machine That Would Go of Itself: The Constitution in American Culture* (Vintage Books ed.: New York, 1987).

_____, *Mystic Chords of Memory: The Transformation of Tradition in American Culture* (New York, 1991).

Levine, Lawrence W., *Highbrow/Lowbrow: The Emergence of Cultural Hierarchy in America* (Cambridge, Mass., 1988).

Loveland, Anne C., *Emblem of Liberty: The Image of Lafayette in the American Mind* (Baton Rouge, La., 1971).

Lowenthal, David, *The Past Is a Foreign Country* (Cambridge, England, 1985).

Marling, Karal Ann, *George Washington Slept Here* (Cambridge, Mass., 1988).

_____, and Wetenhall, John, *Iwo Jima: Monuments, Memories, and the American Hero* (Cambridge, Mass., 1991).

Marx, Leo, *The Machine in the Garden: Technology and the Pastoral Ideal in America* (New York, 1964).

Middleton, David, and Edwards, Derek, eds., *Collective Remembering* (London, 1990).

Peterson, Merrill D., *The Jefferson Image in the American Mind* (Galaxy Book ed.: New York, 1962).

Schwartz, Barry, *George Washington: The Making of an American Symbol* (New York, 1987).

Silverman, Debora, *Selling Culture: Bloomingdale's, Diana Vreeland, and the New Aristocracy of Taste in Reagan's America* (New York, 1986).

Smith, Henry Nash, *Virgin Land: The American West as Symbol and Myth* (Cambridge, Mass., 1970).

Susman, Warren I., *Culture as History: The Transformation of American Society in the Twentieth Century* (New York, 1984).

Trachtenberg, Alan, *The Incorporation of America: Culture and Society in the Gilded Age* (New York, 1982).

Ward, John William, *Andrew Jackson: Symbol for an Age* (New York, 1955).

Wecter, Dixon, *The Hero in America: A Chronicle of Hero-Worship* (New York, 1941).

Williams, Raymond, *Culture and Society* (London, 1958).

_____, *Keywords: A Vocabulary of Culture and Society* (revised ed.: New York, 1985).

Wyllie, Irvin G., *The Self-Made Man in America: The Myth of Rags to Riches* (New Brunswick, N.J., 1954).

Zuckerman, Michael, *Almost Chosen People: Oblique Biographies in the American Grain* (Berkeley, 1993).

General Bibliography

B[ridgwater], D[orothy] W., "The Mason-Franklin Collection," *Yale University Library Gazette* 15 (July 1940): 16–19.

Buxbaum, Melvin H., *Benjamin Franklin, 1721–1983: A Reference Guide* (Boston, 1983–88), 2 vols.

Eddy, George Simpson, "A Ramble through the Mason-Franklin Collection," *Yale University Library Gazette* 10 (April 1936): 65–90.

Ford, Paul Leicester, *Franklin Bibliography: A List of Books Written by, or Relating to Benjamin Franklin* (Brooklyn, N.Y., 1889).

Ford, Worthington Chauncey, *List of the Benjamin Franklin Papers in the Library of Congress* (Washington, 1905).

"Franklin, Benjamin," *Dictionary Catalog of the Research Libraries of the New York Public Library, 1911–1971* (New York, 1979), 283: 130–98.

"Franklin, Benjamin," *Literary Writings in America: A Bibliography* (Millwood, N.Y., 1977), 3: 3604–32.

"Franklin, Benjamin," *The National Union Catalog: Pre-1956 Imprints* (London, 1971), 183: 100–181; *Supplement*, 726: 7–13.

Hays, I[saac] Minis, ed., *Calendar of the Papers of Benjamin Franklin in the Library of the American Philosophical Society* (Philadelphia, 1908), 5 vols.

Murphy, Gwendolen, *A Bibliography of English Character-Books, 1608–1700* (Oxford, 1925).

Roback, A[braham] A[aron], comp., *A Bibliography of Character and Personality* (Cambridge, Mass., 1927).

Swift, Lindsay, *Catalogue of Works Relating to Benjamin Franklin in the Boston Public Library* (Boston, 1883).

Franklin's Writings

Farrand, Max, ed., *Benjamin Franklin's Memoirs: Parallel Text Edition* (Berkeley, 1949).

Franklin, William Temple, ed., *Memoirs of the Life and Writings of Benjamin Franklin* (London, 1817–18), 3 vols.

Goodman, Nathan G., ed., *A Benjamin Franklin Reader* (New York, 1945).

Labaree, Leonard W., et al., eds., *The Papers of Benjamin Franklin* (New Haven, 1959–), 30 vols. to date.

_____, *The Autobiography of Benjamin Franklin* (New Haven, 1964).

Lemay, J. A. Leo, ed., *Benjamin Franklin: Writings* (Library of America ed.: New York, 1987).

_____, and Zall, P. M., eds., *The Autobiography of Benjamin Franklin: A Genetic Text* (Knoxville, [Tenn.], 1981).

Mott, Frank Luther, and Jorgenson, Chester E., eds., *Benjamin Franklin: Representative Selections* (New York, 1936).

Smyth, Albert H., ed., *The Writings of Benjamin Franklin* (New York, 1905–07), 10 vols.

Sparks, Jared, ed., *The Works of Benjamin Franklin* (Boston, 1836–40), 10 vols.

Books and Monographs

Abbott, Jacob, *Franklin, The Apprentice Boy* (New York, 1855).

Adams, Herbert B., *The Life and Writings of Jared Sparks* (Boston, 1893), 2 vols.

Aldridge, Alfred Owen, *Franklin and His French Contemporaries* ([New York], 1957).

_____, *Benjamin Franklin: Philosopher and Man* (Philadelphia, 1965).

_____, *Benjamin Franklin and Nature's God* (Durham, N.C., 1967).

Arnold, Howard Payson, *Historic Side-Lights* (New York, 1899).

Baida, Peter, *Poor Richard's Legacy: American Business Values from Benjamin Franklin to Michael Milken* (New York, 1990).

Bain, Alexander, *On the Study of Character, Including an Estimate of Phrenology* (London, 1861).

Barnum, P[hineas] T[aylor], *The Life of P. T. Barnum Written by Himself* (New York, 1855).

Bassett, John Spencer, *The Middle Group of American Historians* (New York, 1917).

Beard, George M., *American Nervousness* (New York, 1881).

Bercovitch, Sacvan, *The Puritan Origins of the American Self* (New Haven, 1975).

Bigelow, John, ed., *The Life of Benjamin Franklin; Written by Himself* (Philadelphia, 1874), 3 vols.

Bloom, Allan, *The Closing of the American Mind* (New York, 1987).

Boyce, Benjamin, *The Polemic Character, 1640–1661: A Chapter in English Literary History* (reprint 1969: Octagon Books, New York).

Breitwieser, Michael Robert, *Cotton Mather and Benjamin Franklin: The Price of Representative Personality* (New York, 1984).

Breen, T. H., *The Character of the Good Ruler: A Study of Puritan Political Ideas in New England, 1630–1730* (New Haven, 1970).

Brooks, Van Wyck, *America's Coming-of-Age* (New York, 1915).

Bruce, William Cabell, *Benjamin Franklin, Self-Revealed* (New York, 1917), 2 vols.

Buckingham, Joseph Tinker, comp., *Annals of the Massachusetts Charitable Mechanic Association* (Boston, 1853).

———, comp., *Supplement. Annals of the Massachusetts Charitable Mechanic Association, 1852 to 1860* (n.p., n. d.).

———, comp., *Annals of the Massachusetts Charitable Mechanic Association, 1795–1892* (Boston, 1892).

Bulfinch, Ellen Susan, ed., *The Life and Letters of Charles Bulfinch, Architect, With Other Family Papers* (Boston, 1896), 2 vols.

Bushman, Richard L., *From Puritan to Yankee: Character and the Social Order in Connecticut, 1690–1765* (Cambridge, Mass., 1967).

Call, Annie Payson, *Power through Repose* (Boston, 1892).

Carey, Lewis J., *Franklin's Economic Views* (Garden City, N.Y., 1928).

Carnegie, Dale, *How to Win Friends and Influence People* (New York, 1937).

Carr, William G., *The Oldest Delegate: Franklin in the Constitutional Convention* (Newark, Del., 1990).

Chinard, Gilbert, *Honest John Adams* (Boston, 1933).

Clapp, Margaret, *Forgotten First Citizen: John Bigelow* (New York, 1968).

Cohen, I. Bernard, ed., *Benjamin Franklin's Experiments; A New Edition of Franklin's Experiments and Observations on Electricity* (Cambridge, Mass., 1941).

———, ed., *Benjamin Franklin: His Contribution to the American Tradition* (Indianapolis, 1953).

———, *Franklin and Newton* (Philadelphia, 1956).

———, *Benjamin Franklin's Science* (Cambridge, Mass., 1990).

Conwell, Russell H., *Acres of Diamonds* (New York, 1915).

Corner, George W., ed., *The Autobiography of Benjamin Rush; His "Travels Through Life" together with His Commonplace Book for 1789–1813* ([Princeton], 1948).

Craven, Wayne, *Sculpture in America* (new and revised ed.: Newark, Del., 1984).

Crèvecoeur, J. Hector St. John, *Letters from an American Farmer* (1782; New York, 1968).

Cunliffe, Marcus, ed., *The Life of Washington by Mason L. Weems* (Cambridge, Mass., 1962).

Currey, Cecil B., *Road to Revolution: Benjamin Franklin in England, 1765–1775* (Garden City, N.Y., 1968).

———, *Code Number 72/Ben Franklin: Patriot or Spy* (Englewood Cliffs, N.J., 1972).

Curti, Merle, *The Growth of American Thought* (New York, 1943).

Dallek, Robert, *Ronald Reagan: The Politics of Symbolism* (Cambridge, Mass., 1984).

Dawson, Jan C., *The Unusable Past: America's Puritan Tradition, 1830 to 1930* (Chico, Calif., 1984).

Dearborn, Nathaniel, *Boston Notions; Being an Authentic and Concise Account of "That Village," From 1630 to 1847* (Boston, 1848).

Derby, J[ames] C[ephas], *Fifty Years among Authors, Books and Publishers* (New York, 1884).

Diamond, Sigmund, *The Reputation of the American Businessman* (Cambridge, Mass., 1955).

Drake, Samuel Adams, *Old Landmarks and Historical Personages of Boston* (Boston, 1873).

DuBois, Paul Z., *Paul Leicester Ford: An American Man of Letters, 1865–1902* (New York, 1977).

Du Ponceau, Peter Stephen, *An Historical Account of the Origin and Formation of the American Philosophical Society Held at Philadelphia for Promoting Useful Knowledge* (Philadelphia, 1914).

Eliot, Charles William, *Four American Leaders* (Boston, 1907).

Everett, Edward, *The Mount Vernon Papers* (New York, 1860).

Exman, Eugene, *The House of Harper* (New York, 1967).

Farrand, Max, *The Framing of the Constitution of the United States* (New Haven, 1913).

Faÿ, Bernard, *Franklin, The Apostle of Modern Times* (Boston, 1929).

———, *The Two Franklins: Fathers of American Democracy* (Boston, 1933).

Fiering, Norman, *Moral Philosophy at Seventeenth-Century Harvard: A Discipline in Transition* (Chapel Hill, N.C., 1981).

Fisher, Sydney George, *The True Benjamin Franklin* (Philadelphia, 1899).

Fleming, Thomas J., ed., *Benjamin Franklin: A Biography in His Own Words* (New York, 1972).

Follett, Frederick, *History of the Press of Western New-York* (Rochester, 1847).

Foner, Eric, *Free Soil, Free Labor, Free Man* (New York, 1970).

Ford, Paul Leicester, *The Many-Sided Franklin* (New York, 1899).

Fromm, Erich, *Man for Himself* (New York, 1947).

Frothingham, Paul Revere, *Edward Everett: Orator and Statesman* (Boston, 1925).

Goodrich, Samuel G., *The Life of Benjamin Franklin: Illustrated by Tales, Sketches, and Anecdotes* (New York, 1832).

———, *Recollections of a Lifetime* (New York, 1859), 2 vols.

Granger, Bruce Ingham, *Benjamin Franklin: An American Man of Letters* (Ithaca, N.Y., 1964).

Groves, Ernest R., *Personality and Social Adjustment* (New York, 1924).

Hamilton, Milton W., *The Country Printer, New York State, 1785–1830* (New York, 1936).

Haroutunian, Joseph, *Piety versus Moralism: The Passing of the England Theology* (New York, 1932).

Harris, Neil, *The Artist in American Society: The Formative Years, 1790–1860* (New York, 1966).

Herring, James, and Longacre, James Barton, eds., *The National Portrait Gallery of Distinguished Americans* (New York, 1834–39), 4 vols.

Hetherington, Hugh W., *Melville's Reviewers: British and American, 1846–1891* (Chapel Hill, N.C., 1961).

Higham, John, *History: Professional Scholarship in America* (Baltimore, 1983).

Hofstadter, Richard, *Social Darwinism in American Thought, 1860–1915* (Philadelphia, 1945).

Houghton, Walter E., *The Victorian Frame of Mind, 1830–1870* (New Haven, 1957).

Howard, Leon, *Herman Melville: A Biography* (Berkeley, 1951).

Jones, Thomas Firth, *A Pair of Lawn Sleeves: A Biography of William Smith (1727–1803)* (Philadelphia, 1972).

Kashatus, William C., III, *Historic Philadelphia: The City, Symbols & Patriots, 1681–1800* (Lanham, Md., 1992).

Kellock, Harold, *Parson Weems of the Cherry-Tree; Being a Short Account of the Eventful Life of the Reverend M. L. Weems* (New York, 1928).

Kirker, Harold, *The Architecture of Charles Bulfinch* (Cambridge, Mass., 1969).

Koch, G[ustav] Adolf, *Republican Religion: The American Revolution and the Cult of Reason* (New York, 1933).

Lee, Charles, *The Hidden Public: The Story of the Book-of-the-Month Club* (Garden City, N.Y., 1958).

Lemay, J. A. Leo, *Ebenezer Kinnersley: Franklin's Friend* (Philadelphia, 1964).

———, *The Canon of Benjamin Franklin, 1722–1776: New Attributions and Reconsiderations* (Newark, Del., 1986).

Leuchtenburg, William E., *The Perils of Prosperity, 1914–32* (Chicago, 1958).

Link, Henry C., *The Return to Religion* (New York, 1937).

Lopez, Claude-Anne, *Mon Cher Papa: Franklin and the Ladies of Paris* (1966; New Haven, 1990).

_____, and Herbert, Eugenia W., *The Private Franklin: The Man and His Family* (New York, 1975).

McMaster, John Bach, *Benjamin Franklin As a Man of Letters* (Boston, 1895).

Macpherson, C[rawford] B[rough], *The Political Theory of Possessive Individualism: Hobbes to Locke* (Oxford, 1962).

Mather, Cotton, *Magnalia Christi Americana* (1702; John Harvard Library ed.: Cambridge, Mass., 1977).

_____, *Bonifacius: An Essay upon the Good* (1710; John Harvard Library ed.: Cambridge, Mass., 1966).

Mathews, William, *Getting on in the World; or, Hints on Success in Life* (Chicago, 1873).

Matthiessen, F. O., *American Renaissance: Art and Expression in the Age of Emerson and Whitman* (New York, 1941).

Meade, Bishop, *Old Churches, Ministers and Families of Virginia* (Philadelphia, 1878), 2 vols.

Meyer, Donald, *The Positive Thinkers* (revised ed.: Middletown, Conn., 1988).

Miller, Perry, *The New England Mind: The Seventeenth Century* (1939; Cambridge, Mass., 1982).

_____, *The New England Mind: From Colony to Province* (1953; Cambridge, Mass., 1983).

Morais, Herbert M., *Deism in Eighteenth[-]Century America* (New York, 1960).

Morse, John T., Jr., *Benjamin Franklin* (Boston, 1898).

Mosier, Richard D., *Making the American Mind: Social and Moral Ideas in the McGuffey Readers* (New York, 1947).

Mott, Frank Luther, *A History of American Magazines* (Cambridge, Mass., 1957), vol. 1.

_____, *American Journalism, A History: 1690–1960* (3rd ed.: New York, 1962).

Myerson, Abraham, *The Foundations of Personality* (Boston, 1927).

Nye, Russel Blaine, *George Bancroft: Brahmin Rebel* (New York, 1944).

Oswald, John Clyde, *Benjamin Franklin in Oil and Bronze* (New York, 1926).

Parker, Wyman W., *Henry Stevens of Vermont: American Rare Book Dealer in London, 1845–1886* (Amsterdam, 1963).

Parrington, Vernon Louis, *Main Currents in American Thought: An*

Interpretation of American Literature from the Beginnings to 1920 (one volume ed.: New York, 1930).

Parton, James, *Life and Times of Benjamin Franklin* (New York, 1864), 2 vols.

Place, Charles A., *Charles Bulfinch: Architect and Citizen* (New York, 1968).

Platt, John, *Franklin's House: Historic Structures Report* (Washington, 1969).

Pocock, J. G. A., *The Machiavellian Moment: Florentine Political Thought and the Atlantic Republican Tradition* (Princeton, 1975).

Rabinowitz, Richard, *The Spiritual Self in Everyday Life: The Transformation of Personal Religious Experience in Nineteenth-Century New England* (Boston, 1989).

Randall, Willard Sterne, *A Little Revenge: Benjamin Franklin and His Son* (Boston, 1984).

Roback, A[braham] A[aron], *Personality: The Crux of Social Intercourse* (Cambridge, Mass., 1931).

———, *Personality* (Cambridge, Mass., 1950).

———, *The Psychology of Character; With a Survey of Personality in General* (3rd ed.: London, 1952).

Rockefeller, John D., *Random Reminiscences of Men and Events* (Garden City, N.Y., 1933).

Rodgers, Daniel T., *The Work Ethic in Industrial America, 1850–1920* (Phoenix ed.: Chicago, 1979).

Roselle, Daniel, *Samuel Griswold Goodrich, Creator of Peter Parley: A Study of His Life and Work* (Albany, N.Y., 1968).

Ross, David, Sir, trans., *The Nicomachean Ethics of Aristotle* (London, 1925).

Russell, Phillips, *Benjamin Franklin: The First Civilized American* (New York, 1926).

Sanderson, John, ed., *Biography of the Signers to the Declaration of Independence* (Philadelphia, 1822), vol. 2.

Schneider, Herbert W., *Adam Smith's Moral and Political Philosophy* (New York, 1948).

Sellers, Charles Coleman, *Benjamin Franklin in Portraiture* (New Haven, 1962).

Shaw, Peter, *The Character of John Adams* (Chapel Hill, N.C., 1976).

Silver, Rollo G., *The American Printer, 1787–1825* (Charlottesville, Va., 1967).

Silverman, Kenneth, *The Life and Times of Cotton Mather* (New York, 1985).

Skeel, Emily Ellsworth Ford, ed., *Mason Locke Weems: His Works and Ways* (New York, 1929), 3 vols.

Slater, John Herbert, *Engravings and Their Value: A Complete Guide to the Collection and Prices of All Classes of Prints* (6th ed.: New York, 1929).

Smiles, Samuel, *Character* (New York, 1876).

_____, *Self-Help; With Illustrations of Character, Conduct, and Perseverance* (revised ed.: New York, 1884).

Smith, Horace Wemyss, ed., *Life and Correspondence of the Rev. William Smith* (Philadelphia, 1880), 2 vols.

Smith, Jeffery A., *Franklin and Bache: Envisioning the Enlightened Republic* (New York, 1990).

Smyth, Albert H., *The Philadelphia Magazines and Their Contributors, 1741–1850* (Philadelphia, 1892).

Stauffer, David McNeely, *American Engravers upon Copper and Steel* (New York, 1964), 3 vols.

Steell, Willis, *Benjamin Franklin of Paris, 1776–1785* (New York, 1928).

Stevens, George A., *New York Typographical Union No. 6: Study of a Modern Trade Union and Its Predecessors* (Albany, 1913).

Stifler, James Madison, *The Religion of Benjamin Franklin* (New York, 1925).

_____, *"My Dear Girl," The Correspondence of Benjamin Franklin with Polly Stevenson, Georgiana and Catherine Shipley* (New York, 1927).

Storke, Elliot G., *History of Cayuga County, New York* (Syracuse, 1879).

Susman, Warren I., *Culture as History: The Transformation of American Society in the Twentieth Century* (New York, 1984).

Tagg, James, *Benjamin Franklin Bache and the Philadelphia Aurora* (Philadelphia, 1991).

Taft, Lorado, *The History of American Sculpture* (new ed.: New York, 1924).

Theophrastus, *The Characters of Theophrastus* (London, 1960).

Thomas, George F., *Christian Ethics and Moral Philosophy* (New York, 1955).

Thomas, Isaiah, *The History of Printing in America* (New York, 1970).

Thwing, Annie Haven, *The Crooked and Narrow Streets of the Town of Boston, 1630–1822* (Boston, 1930).

Tolles, Frederick B., *Meeting House and Counting House: The Quaker Merchants of Colonial Philadelphia, 1682–1763* (Chapel Hill, N.C., 1948).

Tocqueville, Alexis de, *Democracy in America* (Anchor Books ed.: Garden City, N.Y., 1969).

Tracy, George A., comp., *History of the Typographical Union* (Indianapolis, 1913).

Turner, James, *Without God, Without Creed: The Origins of Unbelief in America* (Baltimore, 1985).

Van Doren, Carl, *Benjamin Franklin* (New York, 1938).

Warren, Mercy (Otis), *History of the Rise, Progress and Termination of the American Revolution* (Boston, 1805), 3 vols.

Watson, Winslow C., ed., *Men and Times of the Revolution; or Memoirs of Elkanah Watson* (New York, 1856).

Weber, Max, *The Protestant Ethic and the Spirit of Capitalism* (Charles Scribner's Sons ed.: New York, 1958).

Weems, Mason Locke, *The Life of Benjamin Franklin* (Philadelphia, 1818).

Weld, Horatio Hastings, *Benjamin Franklin: His Autobiography* (New York, 1848).

[____? or Frost, John?], *Pictorial Life of Benjamin Franklin* (Philadelphia, 1846).

Whipple, Edwin P., *Character and Characteristic Men* (Boston, 1877).

White, Charles W., *Benjamin Franklin: A Study in Self-Mythology* (New York, 1987).

Williams, Gatenby [pseud.], *William Guggenheim* (New York, 1934).

Williams, William Carlos, *In the American Grain* (New York, 1933).

Wood, Gordon S., *The Creation of the American Republic, 1776–1787* (Norton Library ed.: New York, 1972).

____, *The Radicalism of the American Revolution* (Vintage Books ed.: New York, 1993).

Wright, Esmond, *Franklin of Philadelphia* (Cambridge, Mass., 1986).

Miscellaneous: Articles, Pamphlets, Speeches, Anthologies, and Records of Festivities

Abbott, Jacob, "Early and Private Life of Benjamin Franklin," *Harper's New Monthly Magazine* 4 (January 1852): 145–65; "Public Life of Benjamin Franklin," 4 (February 1852): 290–309.

Amacher, Richard E., ed., *Franklin's Wit and Folly: The Bagatelles* (New Brunswick, N.J., 1953).

[American Philosophical Society], *The Record of the Celebration of the Two Hundredth Anniversary of the Birth of Benjamin Franklin* (Philadelphia, 1906).

Anon., "Franklin's 'Our Lady of Auteuil,'" *Atlantic Monthly* 74 (December 1894): 858–60.

Annual Dinner of the Typothetae of New York (New York, 1884–96), 13 pieces.

Baker, Peter C., *Franklin; An Address Delivered before the New York Typographical Society, On Franklin's Birthday, January 17, 1865* (New York, 1865).

Barbour, Brian M., ed., *Benjamin Franklin: A Collection of Critical Essays* (Englewood Cliffs, N.J., 1979).

Barnum, P[hineas] T[aylor], *The Art of Money-Getting* (New York, 1882).

Bassett, John Spencer, ed., "Correspondence of George Bancroft and Jared Sparks, 1823–1832," *Smith College Studies in History* 2 (January 1917): 67–143.

Beard, Charles A., ed., *The Journal of William Maclay* (New York, 1927).

———, *Charles A. Beard Exposes Anti-Semitic Forgery about Benjamin Franklin* [New York, 1938].

Beck, James M., *The Youthful Franklin* (Philadelphia, 1914).

———, *The Memory of Benjamin Franklin* (New York, 1924).

———, *The Memory of Franklin* (Washington, 1932).

Becker, Carl L., *Benjamin Franklin: A Biographical Sketch* (Ithaca, N.Y., 1946).

Bier, Jesse, "Weberism, Franklin, and the Transcendental Style," *New England Quarterly* 43 (June 1970): 179–92.

Boston City Council, *The Railroad Jubilee; An Account of the Celebration Commemorative of the Opening of Railroad Communication between Boston and Canada, September 17th, 18th and 19th, 1851* (Boston, 1852).

Bowle's Moral Pictures; or Poor Richard Illustrated, Being Lessons for the Young and the Old (London, n.d.).

Branscombe, Arthur, *The Cradle of the Washingtons and the Home of the Franklins* (London, 1901).

Brinley, Francis, Jr., *An Address Delivered before the Franklin Debating Society in Chauncy Hall, January 17, 1830* (Boston, 1830).

Bruce, W. J., "The Death and Funeral of Franklin," *American Historical Record* 3 (1874): 13–16.

Brumbaugh, Thomas B., "The Art of Richard Greenough," *Old-Time New England* 53 (1963): 61–78.

Burdick, William, *An Oration on the Nature and Effects of the Art of Printing; Delivered in Franklin-Hall, July 5, 1802, Before the Boston Franklin Association* (Boston, 1802).

Bushman, Richard L., "On the Uses of Psychology: Conflict and Conciliation in Benjamin Franklin," *History and Theory: Studies in the Philosophy of History* 5 (1966): 225–40.

Carlyle, Thomas, "Characteristics," *Critical and Miscellaneous Essays* (New York, 1865), 296–310.

Carnegie, Andrew, *The Gospel of Wealth and Other Timely Essays* (Cambridge, Mass., 1962).

Carr, William G., *The Postage Stamp Life of Benjamin Franklin, 1706–1790* (Indianapolis, 1987).

Ceremonies Attending the Unveiling of the Statue of Benjamin Franklin, June 14, 1899 (Philadelphia, 1899).

[Channing, William Ellery], "Reflections on the Literary Delinquency of America," *North American Review* 2 (November 1815): 33–43.

Chernow, Barbara A., "Robert Morris: Genesee Land Speculator," *New York History* 58 (April 1977): 195–220.

Chinard, Gilbert, "The Apotheosis of Benjamin Franklin, Paris, 1790–1791," *Proceedings of the American Philosophical Society* 99 (December 1955): 440–73.

Clark, Jefferson, *Address Delivered at the Anniversary Celebration of the Franklin Typographical Society, July 17th, 1826* (Boston, 1826).

Cohen, I. Bernard, *Science and American Society in the First Century of the Republic* (Columbus, Ohio, 1961).

Collini, Stefan, "The Idea of 'Character' in Victorian Political Thought," *Transactions of the Royal Historical Society*, 5th ser., 35 (1985): 29–50.

Dedication of the Benjamin Franklin Memorial [Philadelphia, 1938].

[Dennie, Joseph], *Prospectus of a New Weekly Paper, Submitted to Men of Affluence, Men of Liberality, and Men of Letters* [Philadelphia, 1800].

Duane, Russell, *An Oration Delivered at the Unveiling of the Statue of Dr. Benjamin Franklin* (Philadelphia, 1894).

Ellis, Harold Milton, "Joseph Dennie and His Circle: A Study in American Literature from 1792 to 1812," *Studies in English* (University of Texas), 3 (July 1915): 9–285.

Emerson, Ralph Waldo, "Character," *Essays & Lectures* (Library of America ed.: New York, 1983), 493–509.

Evans, William B., "John Adams' Opinion of Benjamin Franklin," *Pennsylvania Magazine of History and Biography* 92 (April 1968): 220–38.

Everett, Edward, *An Address Delivered as the Introduction to the Franklin Lectures, in Boston, November 14, 1831* (Boston, 1832).

———, "The Character of Washington," *Orations and Speeches on Various Occasions* (Boston, 1879), 4: 3–51; "Franklin the Boston Boy," 4: 108–29.

Farrand, Max, *Self-Portraiture: The Autobiography*, reprint from *General Magazine and Historical Chronicle*, July 1940.

Firmin, Albert, *The Hall of Fame and Benjamin Franklin* ([New York] 1918).

First Exhibition of the Massachusetts Charitable Mechanic Association. At Faneuil and Quincy Halls, In the City of Boston, September 18, 1837 (Boston, 1837).

Fleet, Elizabeth, ed., "Madison's 'Detatched Memoranda,'" *William and Mary Quarterly*, 3rd ser., 3 (October 1946): 534–68.

"The Franklin Bicentenary," *Independent* 60 (January 1906): 69–108.

[Franklin Institute], *Meet Dr. Franklin* (Philadelphia, 1943).

Gilpin, Henry D., *The Character of Franklin; Address Delivered before the Franklin Institute of Pennsylvania, on the Evening of the Fourth of December, 1856* (Philadelphia, 1857).

Goldberg, Alfred, "School Histories of the Middle Period," in Eric F. Goldman, ed., *Historiography and Urbanization* (Baltimore, 1941), 171–88.

Griswold, A. Whitney, "Three Puritans on Prosperity," *New England Quarterly* 7 (September 1934): 475–93.

Harding, Walter, ed., *Thoreau: A Century of Criticism* (Dallas, 1954).

Hart, Charles Henry, ed., "Life Portraits of Great Americans: Benjamin Franklin," *McClure's Magazine* 8 (January 1897): 263–72.

Hetherington, Hugh W., *Melville's Reviewers: British and American, 1846–1891* (Chapel Hill, N.C., 1961).

Higham, John, "Hanging Together: Divergent Unities in American History," *Journal of American History* 61 (June 1974): 5–28.

Homes of American Statesmen: With Anecdotal, Personal, and Descriptive Sketches (Hartford, [Conn.] 1855).

Howe, Henry, "Benjamin Franklin," *Memoirs of the Most Eminent American Mechanics* (New York, 1841), 37–67.

Illustrated Magazine of the Eighth Exhibition under the Direction of the Massachusetts Charitable Mechanic Association at Faneuil and

Quincy Halls, Boston, September, 1856 (Boston), no. 4 (26 September 1856).

International Benjamin Franklin Society, *Benjamin Franklin Vindicated* (New York, [1938]).

Jewett, John L., *Franklin—His Genius, Life, and Character; An Oration Delivered before the N.Y. Typographical Society, on the Occasion of the Birthday of Franklin, at the Printers' Festival, Held January 17, 1849* (New York, 1849).

Jordan, Helen, and Jordan, Clarence, eds., *Benjamin Franklin's Unfinished Business* (Philadelphia, [1956/57?]).

Kennedy, Gail, ed., *Democracy and the Gospel of Wealth* (Boston, 1949).

_____, ed., *Pragmatism and American Culture* (Boston, 1950).

Kern, Alexander, "Emerson and Economics," *New England Quarterly* 13 (December 1940): 678–96.

Knowles, William J., *Features of Inauguration of the Franklin Statue in Boston, September 17th, 1856* (Boston, 1856).

Koopman, Harry Lyman, *Franklin's Claims to Greatness* ([Providence] 1923).

Lawrence, D. H., "Benjamin Franklin," *Studies in Classic American Literature* (Doubleday Anchor Books ed.: Garden City, N.Y., 1951), 19–31.

Leary, Lewis, "Joseph Dennie on Benjamin Franklin," *Pennsylvania Magazine of History and Biography* 72 (July 1948): 240–46.

Lemay, J. A. Leo, ed., *The Oldest Revolutionary: Essays on Benjamin Franklin* ([Philadelphia] 1976).

_____, ed., *Reappraising Benjamin Franklin: A Bicentennial Perspective* (Newark, Del., 1993).

Levin, David, ed., *The Puritan in the Enlightenment: Franklin and Edwards* (Chicago, 1963).

Lindberg, Stanley W., ed., *The Annotated McGuffey: Selections from the McGuffey Eclectic Readers, 1836–1920* (New York, 1976).

Medill, Joseph, *Benjamin Franklin: A Typical American* (Chicago, 1896).

Metropolitan Museum of Art, *Benjamin Franklin and His Circle: A Catalogue of an Exhibition* (New York, 1936).

Miles, Richard D., "The American Image of Benjamin Franklin," *American Quarterly* 9 (Summer 1957): 117–43.

Miller, Perry, "Jonathan Edwards to Emerson," *New England Quarterly* 13 (December 1940): 589–617.

Mitchell, Silas Weir, *Wear and Tear, or Hints for the Overworked* (5th ed.: Philadelphia, 1887).

M'Neile, Hugh, *A Lecture on the Life of Dr. Franklin* (Liverpool, [England] 1841).

Morgan, Edmund S., ed., *Puritan Political Ideas, 1558–1794* (Indianapolis, 1965).

Muscalus, John A., ed., *An Index of State Bank Notes That Illustrate Washington and Franklin* (Bridgeport, Penn., 1938).

Neill, Edward D., "The Ideal versus the Real Benjamin Franklin," *Macalester College Contributions*, 2nd ser., no. 4 (1892): 97–108.

Parker, Theodore, "Franklin," *Historic Americans* (Boston, 1870), 13–72.

[Pemberton, Thomas], "A Topographical and Historical Description of Boston, 1794," *Collections of the Massachusetts Historical Society* 3 (1794): 241–304.

Prelinger, Catherine M., "Benjamin Franklin and the American Prisoners of War in England during the American Revolution," *William and Mary Quarterly*, 3rd ser., 32 (April 1975): 261–94.

Proceedings at the Printers' Banquet, Held by the N. Y. Typographical Society, On the Occasion of Franklin's Birth-day, Jan. 17, 1850 (New York, 1850).

The Proceedings at the Printers' Festival, Held by the Franklin Typographical Society, At Hancock Hall, January 15, 1848 (Boston, 1848).

Proceedings of the Franklin Typographical Society at the Observance of the Semi-Centennial of Its Institution, January 17, 1874 (Boston, 1875).

The Record of the Celebration of the Two Hundredth Anniversary of the Birth of Benjamin Franklin, Under the Auspices of the American Philosophical Society (Philadelphia, 1906).

Record of the Proceedings and Ceremonies Pertaining to the Erection of the Franklin Statue in Printing-House Square (New York, 1872).

Reid, Ronald F., "Edward Everett: Rhetorician of Nationalism, 1824–1855," *Quarterly Journal of Speech* 42 (October 1956): 273–82.

Rischin, Moses, ed., *The American Gospel of Success* (Chicago, 1965).

Sainte-Beuve, Charles Augustin, "Benjamin Franklin," *Portraits of the Eighteenth Century, Historic and Literary* (New York, 1964), 1: 311–75.

Sanford, Charles L., ed., *Benjamin Franklin and the American Character* (Boston, 1955).

Schutz, John A., and Adair, Douglass, eds., *The Spur of Fame: Di-*

alogues of John Adams and Benjamin Rush, 1805–1813 (San Marino, Calif., 1966).

Scott, Donald M., "The Popular Lecture and the Creation of a Public in Mid-Nineteenth-Century America," *Journal of American History* 66 (March 1980): 791–809.

Shalhope, Robert E., "Republicanism and Early American Historiography," *William and Mary Quarterly*, 3rd ser., 39 (April 1982): 334–56.

[Shurtleff, Nathaniel Bradstreet, ed.], *Memorial of the Inauguration of the Statue of Franklin* (Boston, 1857).

Smith, William, *Eulogium on Benjamin Franklin* (London, 1792).

Smyth, J. Henry, Jr., ed., *The Amazing Benjamin Franklin* (New York, 1929).

[Sparks, Jared], "[Timothy] Pitkin's History of the United States," *North American Review* 30 (January 1830): 1–25.

[Stephens, Brad, ed.] *The Pictorial Life of Benjamin Franklin* (Philadelphia, 1923).

Stevens, Henry, *Stevens' Historical Collections* (London, 1881).

Stewart, Ethelbert, "A Documentary History of the Early Organizations of Printers," in U.S. Department of Commerce and Labor, *Bulletin of the Bureau of Labor* 11 (November 1905): 857–1033.

Sumner, Charles, "Monograph from an Old Note-Book," *Atlantic Monthly* 12 (November 1863): 648–62.

Towle, George Makepeace, "Franklin, The Boston Boy," in Justin Winsor, ed., *The Memorial History of Boston, Including Suffolk County, Massachusetts, 1630–1880* (Boston, 1881), 2: 269–96.

Trowbridge, John, "Benjamin Franklin and Electricity," *Nation* 82 (1 February 1906): 93–94.

Twain, Mark, "The Late Benjamin Franklin," *Galaxy* 10 (July 1870): 138–40.

Two Hundredth Anniversary of the Birth of Benjamin Franklin, 1706–1906 (Franklin, Mass., [1906]).

Tyler, John, Jr., *An Oration on the Life and Character of Benjamin Franklin, Delivered before the Franklin Society of William and Mary College, on the 17th January, 1840* (Norfolk, Va., 1840).

Ward, John William, "Who Was Benjamin Franklin?" *American Scholar* 32 (Autumn 1963): 541–53.

Washington, Booker T., *Character Building; Being Addresses Delivered on Sunday Evenings to the Students of Tuskegee Institute* (New York, 1903).

Webster, Charles K., "Some Early Applications from American Historians to Use the British Archives," *Journal of Modern History* 1 (September 1929): 416–19.

Weems, Mason Locke, comp., *The Immortal Mentor, or, Man's Unerring Guide to a Healthy, Wealthy, and Happy Life* (Carlisle, Penn., 1815).

Willson, Marcius, *A Critical Review of American Common School Histories* (New York, 1847).

Winthrop, Robert C., "Archimedes and Franklin," *Addresses and Speeches on Various Occasions* (Boston, 1852–86), 2: 102–39; "The Inauguration of the Statue of Franklin," 2: 258–91.

Witherspoon, John, *An Annotated Edition of Lectures on Moral Philosophy* (Newark, Del., 1982).

Wright, Esmond, comp., *Benjamin Franklin: A Profile* (New York, 1970).

Wright, Louis B., "Franklin's Legacy to the Gilded Age," *Virginia Quarterly Review* 22 (Spring 1946): 268–79.

Zall, P. M., ed., *Ben Franklin Laughing: Anecdotes from Original Sources by and about Benjamin Franklin* (Berkeley, 1980).

Dramas and Fiction

Alger, Horatio, *Ragged Dick* (Boston, 1868).

Banks, Polan, *The Gentleman from America* (New York, 1930).

Benton, Rita, *Franklin and Other Plays* (New York, 1924).

Brougham, John, "Franklin: A New and Original Historical Drama, in Five Acts," [Samuel] *French's Standard Drama*, no. 166 (New York, 1856), 2–28.

Bruce, William Cabell, *Imaginary Conversations with Franklin* (New York, 1933).

Feuchtwanger, Lion, *Proud Destiny: A Novel* (New York, 1947).

Fitzgerald, F. Scott, *The Great Gatsby* (1925; New York, 1953).

Green, Paul, "Franklin and the King: An Historical Drama," in Betty Smith, comp., *20 Prize-Winning Non-Royalty One Act Plays* (New York, 1943), 54–70.

Hawthorne, Nathaniel, "Benjamin Franklin," *Tales, Sketches, and Other Papers* (Riverside ed.: Boston, 1897), 189–202.

Mackay, Constance D'Arcy, "Benjamin Franklin, Journeyman," in Frederick Houk Law, comp., *Modern Plays: Short and Long* (New York, 1924), 84–96.

Mathieson, Theodore, *The Devil and Ben Franklin* (New York, 1961).

Melville, Herman, *His Fifty Years of Exile (Israel Potter)* (1856; New York, 1957).

Merington, Marguerite, *A Dish O'Tea Delayed: One-Act Play for High School Girls; Founded on a True Incident When the Republic U. S. A. Was Young* (New York, 1937).

Newton, Alfred Edward, *Mr. Strahan's Dinner Party* (San Francisco, 1930).

Pidgin, Charles Felton, *A Nation's Idol: A Romance of Franklin's Nine Years of Happiness at the Court of France* (Philadelphia, 1904).

Pohl, Frederick J., *Made in Paris: A Play of Humor and History* ([Brooklyn, N.Y.] 1921).

Potter, Israel R., *The Life and Remarkable Adventures of Israel R. Potter* (New York, 1962).

Schack, Rena, *Then and '39: An Imaginary Travelogue in Which Benjamin Franklin and His Two Grandsons Visit the New York of 1939 and the New York World's Fair* (New York, 1950).

Shipman, Louis Evan, *Ben Franklin: A Comedy in Four Acts* (Boston, 1933).

Stone, Peter, and Edwards, Sherman, *1776: A Musical Play* (New York, 1973).

Thackeray, William Makepeace, *The Virginians; A Tale of the Last Century* (New York, 1899).

Thoreau, Henry David, *Walden* (1856; Princeton, 1971).

Tooley, Howard, "Benjamin Franklin's Birthday—January 17," in his *Radio Guild Plays* (Minneapolis, 1941), 7–15.

Twain, Mark, and Warner, Charles Dudley, *The Gilded Age; A Tale of Today* (New York, 1964).

Wade, Mary Hazelton, *Benjamin Franklin: A Story and a Play* (Boston, 1914).

Zochert, Donald, *Murder in the Hellfire Club* (New York, 1978).

Unpublished Theses

Barnes, Jack C., "Benjamin Franklin and His Memoirs" (Ph.D., University of Maryland, 1954).

Bodzin, Eugene Saul, "The American Popular Image of Benjamin Franklin, 1790–1868" (Ph.D., University of Wisconsin, 1969).

Fiering, Norman Sanford, "Moral Philosophy in America, 1650 to 1750, and Its British Context" (Ph.D., Columbia University, 1969).

Johnson, Richard L., "Contemporary Trends in Franklin Studies" (M.A., Claremont Graduate School, 1967).

Kabelac, Karl Sanford, "Book Publishing in Auburn, New York: 1851–1876" (M.A., State University College at Oneonta, New York, 1969).

Kushen, Betty Sandra, "Benjamin Franklin and His Biographers: A Critical Study" (Ph.D., New York University, 1969).

Mariboe, William Herbert, "The Life of William Franklin, 1730(1)–1813, *Pro Rege et Patria*" (Ph.D., University of Pennsylvania, 1962).

Newcomb, Robert Howard, "The Sources of Benjamin Franklin's Sayings of Poor Richard" (Ph.D., University of Maryland, 1957).

Sappenfield, James Allen, "The Growth of the Benjamin Franklin Image: The Philadelphia Years" (Ph.D., Stanford University, 1966).

Tagg, James Douglas, "Benjamin Franklin Bache and the Philadelphia *Aurora*" (Ph.D., Wayne State University, 1973).

Smart, Karl Lyman, "A Man for All Ages: The Changing Image of Benjamin Franklin in Nineteenth-Century American Popular Literature" (Ph.D., University of Florida, 1989).

Van Scyoc, Leo L., "Benjamin Franklin's Reputation among the Literati, 1790–1860" (Ph.D., University of Kansas, 1958).

Werly, John McIntyre, "The Millenarian Right: William Dudley Pelley and the Silver Legion of America" (Ph.D., Syracuse University, 1972).

Index

Index